Gasworks to Gallery : The Story of Tate St Ives
First Published 1995

Text by Janet Axten
Designed by Colin Orchard
Typesetting & Computer Layout
by The Design Bureau, Truro

Published by Janet Axten and Colin Orchard
3 Fore Street, St Ives, Cornwall TR26 1AB

ISBN 0 9524770 0 9

British Library Cataloguing-in-Publication Data
A catalogue record for this book is
available from the British Library

Printed by Robin Beckwith Ltd, Brighton

Cover: Detail of 'Sculpture for
Tate Gallery St Ives' 1993 by Trevor Vance
(see page 170)
Photograph: Bob Berry

Inset: Tate Gallery St Ives
Photograph: Bob Berry

GASWORKS TO GALLERY

The Story Of Tate St Ives

Janet Axten

St Ives gasworks c.1938

Contents

Tate Gallery St Ives from the air showing
Porthmeor Beach at low tide in the
foreground, and the Harbour with
Smeatons Pier in the background.

Preface

For many years a gallery at St Ives had been suggested, but it was the Tate exhibition in London in 1985 of St Ives paintings, sculpture and ceramics which began to crystallise people's thoughts.

A number of people saw this potential project as a wonderful opportunity. Here was the chance to house the work of an internationally renowned school of artists in a building of exceptional design; and to show them in the context in which they were conceived. It was a unique opportunity.

Cornwall County Council led the way supported by Penwith District and St Ives Town councils, and this at a time when central government was clamping down on local government expenditure. A Steering Committee was set up, architects chosen, finance raised from the private and public sectors, and the gallery was constructed. None of this could have been achieved without the full-hearted support, energy, drive and enthusiasm of the people of St Ives itself.

The result has far exceeded all expectations - visitor figures have trebled original estimates, and the whole area has received a tremendous boost in educational, artistic and economic terms. It exemplifies the fact that 'quality pays' and to decision makers that investment in the arts is a good one. Janet Axten, one of the foremost members of the St Ives Tate Action Group has set out in fascinating detail the story behind the building of the Tate Gallery St Ives.

Richard Carew Pole
Chairman of Cornwall County Council
Tate Gallery St Ives Steering Group
1988-93

Introduction

At breakfast time one late November in 1989 there was a knock at my front door. The Chairman of the St Ives Chamber of Trade, Derek White, came to tell me that he had been asked to get a group together from the town to hear, at first hand, the County Council's plans for a new gallery proposed for St Ives that would contain work from the Tate Gallery's collection. He asked me if I could type and take shorthand? When I told him I could, he invited me to come to the meeting and take notes of what was said.

That is how I met the Chairman of the Steering Group, Richard Carew Pole, for the first time and became part of an enthusiastic group involved in raising funds for an exciting and unique project. Through both planning and construction stages, the gallery became a large part of our lives over the next three and a half years.

The moment Tate Gallery St Ives opened to the general public, in late June 1993, I knew instinctively that our efforts to bring the project to fruition would soon be a distant memory. And so it has proved. Visitors from all over the world have, not unexpectedly, been completely unaware of how the gallery has come about.

It is not generally known that the project, which has become such an outstanding success, developed as a local achievement; a testimony to the efforts of Richard Carew Pole. It is he who inspired the officers and councillors at Cornwall County Council, the residents of St Ives, and anyone with whom he came into contact, to back so unusual a scheme. And Michael Tooby, as the gallery's first Curator, picked up the unfinished project - an exciting design on a spectacular site - and added to it his own vision and personality.

Together everyone worked for a common end: to show the work of the St Ives artists from about 1930 to 1975 in the town in which it had been created, and in a building and at a location that demonstrated to a wide public how the local landscape had been the artists' inspiration.

Fine works of art and buildings, hopefully, live for centuries. But the ideas, efforts, joys, disappointments and hopes of the people actually assisting to make a major project come into existence are soon forgotten. Other responsibilities, other campaigns, other projects come along; some people retire or move away from an area. But within each remains a feeling of intense satisfaction for a good job done.

I make no apology for telling the story of Tate Gallery St Ives in depth. When I was researching this book, in the autumn of 1993 I visited the National Museum of Wales at Cardiff the day after Her Majesty the Queen had opened its £24 million extension. I wanted to see for myself the unusual circular gallery that the architect Eldred Evans had remembered so well when her father, the late Merlyn Evans, exhibited there many years earlier. The space was apparently in her mind when she and her husband, David Shalev, designed the Terraces of Gallery Two at Tate St Ives. After seeing the gallery in Cardiff, I asked at the shop for a book containing a brief history of the museum. 'I'm very sorry' said the assistant, 'We haven't anything about the building. After all we haven't been open for a hundred years yet!'

Why should we wait a century for a book to be written about an art gallery, when all the people involved in its creation are no longer alive and contemporary records are forgotten, yellowing in inaccessible vaults? There are volumes being published continuously about works of art and artists. Yet in St Ives people are constantly asking: 'Whose idea was the gallery in the first place? Were there any objections to it? Where did the money come from to build it? How long did it take to plan? How was the site chosen?'

It seems to me that the gallery has opened people's eyes. Those who have only come to see a building they have heard or read about, or perhaps seen on television, knowing nothing about the works of art inside, have found themselves introduced to an art movement of international significance that came about during and after the Second World War in a remote and lovely part of England. Those who have come especially to see the paintings, sculpture and ceramics, have been made strikingly aware of the gallery's unusual design and have felt an intense sense of place. The two are inextricably linked in St Ives.

This book tells the story of how the County Council and South West Arts, in an effort to boost cultural tourism in Cornwall, were able to respond to the Tate Gallery's policy to bring important works of art to the regions. They were later encouraged by a group of local people who, over several years, gave their enthusiastic backing to see that both challenges were met.

The story, taken from a very wide range of sources - Tate Gallery St Ives is probably one of the best documented projects - is dedicated to everyone who has helped to make the gallery a success. Most have lived or still live in Cornwall. While secretary of the local fund raising group I was privileged to become acquainted with many of them. They have all generously contributed to this book; allowing me to read their files, dredge deep in their memories (some going back sixty or seventy years), to watch unedited film of some of the events that took place in 1990 and early 1991, and to borrow both archival and contemporary photographs. I have acknowledged everyone's assistance at the end of the book, but I should particularly like to thank Colin Orchard, whose idea this originally was and who has been responsible for the book's design.

I should also like to remember the many people in St Ives who, known and unknown, in earlier decades, hoped for a gallery to house a permanent collection of St Ives art locally. They are no less important to the overall story. Organisations, businesses, charities and government departments, have their names engraved on plaques for all to read, but individuals are usually forgotten. It is they who, living in communities or working in organisations of which they are intensely proud, make things happen, or not happen.

It is my personal wish that all who enter Tate St Ives can sense something of its creation. By learning a little of the way everyone co-operated to bring the project to fruition, visitors will hopefully return to their own communities and think: 'Having seen what has been achieved in St Ives, we can work together to bring about something of lasting value for ourselves.'

Janet Axten

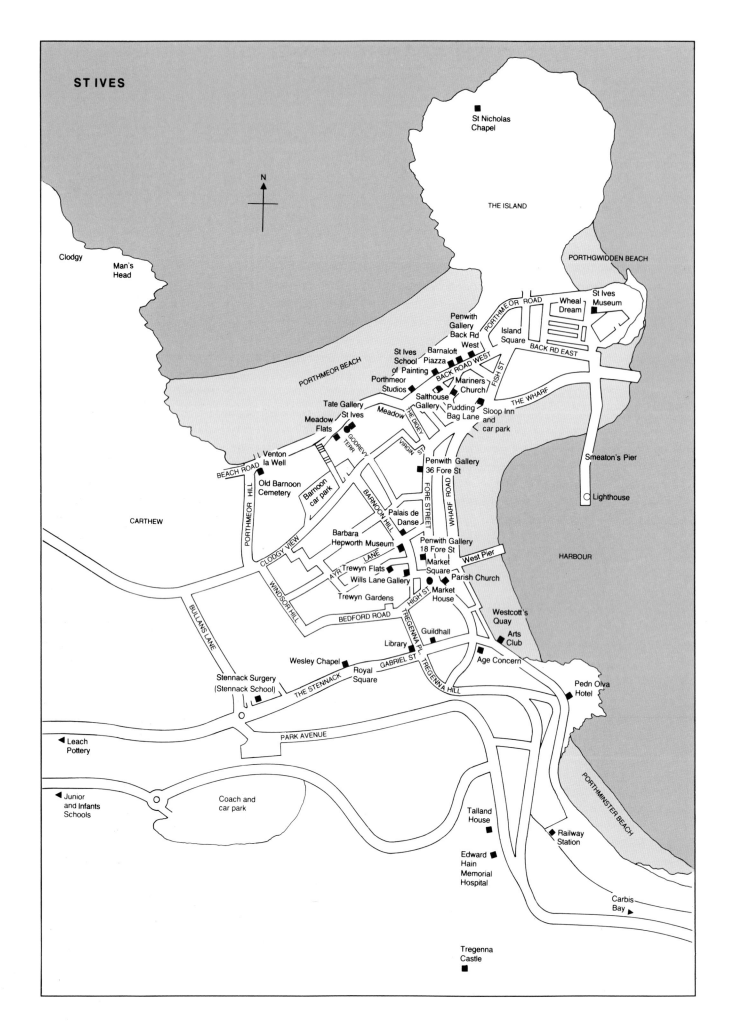

ST IVES

Clodgy

Man's Head

THE ISLAND

St Nicholas Chapel

N

PORTHGWIDDEN BEACH

PORTHMEOR BEACH

St Ives Museum

PORTHMEOR ROAD

Wheal Dream

Penwith Gallery Back Rd West

Island Square

BACK RD EAST

St Ives School of Painting

Barnaloft Piazza

BACK ROAD WEST

FISH ST

THE WHARF

Porthmeor Studios

Mariners Church

Tate Gallery St Ives

Salthouse Gallery

Meadow

THE DIGEY

Pudding Bag Lane

Sloop Inn and car park

Meadow Flats

GODREVY TERR

Smeaton's Pier

VIRGIN ST

Venton la Well

Penwith Gallery 36 Fore St

BEACH ROAD

Lighthouse

PORTHMEOR HILL

Old Barnoon Cemetery

Barnoon car park

BARNOON HILL

FORE STREET

WHARF ROAD

CARTHEW

Palais de Danse

Barbara Hepworth Museum

CLODGY VIEW

LANE

Penwith Gallery 18 Fore St

HARBOUR

AYR

Trewyn Flats

Market Square

West Pier

WINDSOR HILL

Wills Lane Gallery

Trewyn Gardens

HIGH ST

Parish Church

Market House

Westcott's Quay

BULLANS LANE

BEDFORD ROAD

TREGENNA PL.

Arts Club

Library

Guildhall

TREGENNA HILL

Age Concern

Wesley Chapel

GABRIEL ST

Pedn Olva Hotel

Stennack Surgery (Stennack School)

THE STENNACK

Royal Square

Leach Pottery

PARK AVENUE

PORTHMINSTER BEACH

Junior and Infants Schools

Coach and car park

Talland House

Railway Station

Edward Hain Memorial Hospital

Carbis Bay

Tregenna Castle

1   Early Ideas For A Gallery

On a gloriously sunny but windy morning on Wednesday 23 June 1993, His Royal Highness the Prince of Wales, Duke of Cornwall, unveiled a plaque in the Loggia of Tate Gallery St Ives. This act was the climax to an hour long tour of the building.

Earlier that day the Prince had arrived at the outskirts of the town by helicopter. A car had swiftly brought him into St Ives, down steeply sloping Porthmeor Hill. A spectacular sight greeted him as he made his way into Beach Road. He was confronted by the dramatic sandy bay of Porthmeor Beach with its dazzlingly blue sea on his left, while ahead loomed The Island, its small granite chapel perched on top of a green hillside. On the Prince's right a gleaming white building, with curved facade, nestled into the hillside - the new Tate Gallery.

Waiting for the Prince and Lord Falmouth, Lord Lieutenant of Cornwall, in the Loggia was the High Sheriff of Cornwall and representatives of some of the groups who had brought Tate Gallery St Ives to fruition: the County Council, the Tate Gallery, Penwith District Council and St Ives Town Council. The small reception committee was kept waiting, however. Before ascending the gallery's sand-coloured steps, the Prince stopped to talk to the waiting crowd that had come to greet him.

Prominent among these excited onlookers were the occupants of Meadow Flats, the buildings that flanked the new gallery. Their elderly residents, having endured discomfort, noise and dust during two years' building work, had been given ringside seats from where they were introduced personally to the Prince. With him they proudly viewed the dramatic building that now filled the sad, derelict space that had been their immediate neighbour for so many years.

Neither these elderly residents, nor the majority of guests and onlookers who witnessed the Prince's visit, both from inside and outside the gallery, were aware that the occasion they were celebrating was, in fact, the culmination of many local attempts over the previous seventy-five years, to provide a permanent art gallery for St Ives.

With patience, it is relatively easy to follow the thread of these attempts, because St Ives is privileged to have had a succession of weekly newspapers that have taken a special interest in the artistic life of the town. On 1 October 1910 Martin Cock, a Cornishman who had moved to St Ives in his teens, founded *The St Ives Times*, a successor to the journal *The St Ives Weekly Summary, Visitors' List and Advertiser*, owned by James Uren White (which continued publication until 1918). In 1957 *The St Ives Times* [1] merged with a local rival *The Western Echo* (founded in 1899), to form *The St Ives Times & Echo*, a broadsheet that is still read by local residents and subscribers around the world.

Glancing through issues produced in the first two and a half months of *The St Ives Times'* existence, certain news items can be seen, with hindsight, to have a relevance to the story of Tate Gallery St Ives:

'A link with an older St Ives has been broken' because an ancient carpenter's shop was demolished on Barnoon Hill to make way for what was to become the Palais de Danse (this would be bought by Barbara Hepworth in the early 1960s for making her largest sculptures);

The stokers at the Corporation-owned gasworks, the site on which Tate Gallery

1 In 1951 *The St Ives Times* was bought from the then owner, James Lanham, by the St Ives Printing and Publishing Co. of which J R Carver (who had previously worked on the *Birmingham Mail* and *Coventry Evening Telegraph*) was the proprietor.

1 H R H The Prince of Wales, Duke of Cornwall, in the Loggia of Tate Gallery St Ives after he had unveiled the plaque to commemorate the opening of the gallery on 23 June 1993.

2 Councillor John Hain, Mayor of St Ives between November 1918 and November 1919, who first proposed that St Ives should house a permanent collection of works from its 'Art Colony'.

3 St Ives Arts Club is still housed in the town's last remaining timbered building at Westcotts Quay, overlooking the Harbour. It is now a popular venue for the dramatic arts. In 1991 the Club hosted a number of events that raised funds for Tate Gallery St Ives.

4 The front page of the Supplement to *The Royal Cornwall Gazette and Cornwall County News* dated 11 June 1919, showing an engraving of the New County Museum and Art Gallery in Truro. The article accompanying the illustration gives a detailed description of the expanded museum, and an account of the visit of the Prince of Wales (later King Edward VIII) who opened the new building.

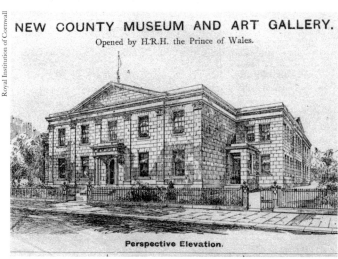

NEW COUNTY MUSEUM AND ART GALLERY.
Opened by H.R.H. the Prince of Wales.

Perspective Elevation.

St Ives would be built, were given an increase in wages of one half penny an hour to bring their pay up to twenty-seven shillings and sixpence a week for a seventy-eight hour week;

At the 1910 Mayoral Banquet, the Mayor toasted 'the St Ives Art Colony' to whom the town owed 'a debt of gratitude...for what they had done to advertise the town'.

By 1910 St Ives had been a recognised art colony for exactly twenty years. The Arts Club, founded in 1890, had acted as the focal point not only for resident and visiting artists, but also for musicians and writers. Located on the top floor of an old fish cellar at Westcotts Quay, overlooking the Harbour and buffeted by winter storms, the Grade II listed building, constructed sometime between 1858 and 1882, is the only surviving timber clad building in the town.

As generations of artists arrived in St Ives to live and work permanently or temporarily, suggestions were regularly made that the town should have its own public gallery. None of these ideas came to fruition, but they throw light onto the artistic and social development of the town.

The importance of the early artists, many of whom had taken over old sail lofts for their studios, was recognised by some (but not all) of those who presided over the town's civic affairs. It was at a gathering of such a group that, in 1919, the first serious idea for a public gallery was put forward. At a Mayoral banquet the retiring Mayor, Captain John Hain, welcomed back to St Ives those who had 'served us faithfully during the war'. In order to honour them, as well as to find a way of remembering those who had not returned from the trenches, he proposed 'the foundation of an art gallery, where works by local Artists should be represented'. He considered such a memorial 'a worthy record of the St Ives Art Colony'.

To have put this idea into practice would, however, have been highly unusual; most towns and villages across the country were already making plans to erect conventional war memorials in honour of their dead.

It is likely that this suggestion was not plucked out of thin air. The Mayor, in fact, had been one of six hundred guests attending the official gala opening of the Royal Cornwall Museum at its new premises on River Street in Truro, by HRH the Prince of Wales, on 11 June 1919. The occasion must have made a lasting impression on him.

The Museum had first been established in 1818, expanding on its first site in Union Place throughout the nineteenth century. [2] When plans were made to transfer to its present location, it was proposed that the new building should, for the first time, contain an art gallery, and an area measuring 67 by 25 feet was created for this purpose. A contemporary account in the *Royal Cornwall Gazette* pointed out that 'one of the aims of the Institution is to form a permanent collection of paintings representative of the Cornish schools'. [3] In the first of many coincidences surrounding the story of Tate Gallery St Ives, John Stengelhofen noted in *The County Museum Past, Present and Future*, that for the official opening in 1919, 'the art gallery had a loan exhibition from the Tate Gallery, which was hung by our Council member Stanhope Forbes with the assistance of Mr H Scott Tuke'. [4]

Perhaps Captain John Hain hoped that what had been achieved in Truro was worth attempting in St Ives. The Mayor's staunchest supporter was R Borlase Smart, a Devon artist born in 1881, who had studied early in the century with Julius Olsson RA, one of the founder members of the St Ives Arts Club. Smart had moved permanently to the town in 1919 after serving in the Army on the Western Front.

Smart would be remembered for encouraging the emerging avant-garde painters and sculptors, during and after the Second World War, to exhibit with the

2 Union Place is where Marks & Spencer currently stands.

3 Although the Museum does have a permanent collection, few 'modern' works were purchased over the years from the St Ives artists.

4 *The Royal Cornwall Gazette* reported that the Director of the Tate Gallery, Mr C Aitken, was not able to be present at the opening ceremony of the Royal Cornwall Museum.

St Ives School of Painting Archive

1 Borlase Smart in his studio 'Ocean Wave', close to the St Ives Arts Club near the Harbour, in the 1930s. Smart welcomed visitors of all ages to his studio for, in 1929, he wrote to *The St Ives Times* that on Show Day, before the St Ives artists sent their paintings to the Royal Academy by train: 'I had scores of young children in my studio...unaccompanied by any grown up, and I found their behaviour all that could be desired.'

2 The town's war memorial consisted of a celtic cross designed, without fee, by Mr G Tarland Goosey of St Ives and erected in November 1922. At a later date a garden was planted around the memorial. After the Second World War the names of those who had died in action between 1939 and 1945 were added.

3 Sir Edward Hain (1851-1917) had a distinguished career. Mayor of St Ives on six occasions between 1894 and 1899, a county councillor for fifteen years and a Member of Parliament between 1900 and 1906, as a Liberal Unionist, Hain was also made High Sheriff of Cornwall in 1912, the year he received his knighthood for services to British shipping.

Colin Orchard

St Ives Society of Artists, and also for fostering the work of the younger artists. He played an important part in the civic life of the town. In the 1920s he became a member of the St Ives Town Council, and was to remain a prolific letter writer on numerous topics until he died in 1947.

In 1919 Smart immediately welcomed the retiring Mayor's suggestion for a gallery, and pointed out in *The St Ives Times* that the idea:

would no doubt find favour with the inhabitants of the old town, and it is the old town that after all has provided subjects for some of the greatest pictures of modern art... A suitable site in every way (being central) would be the enclosed ground, bottom of High Street. The running expenses of such an institution would be easily paid for by a small charge of admission.

There were also letters of dissent to this proposal, of course. Townspeople were particularly concerned about where the money would come from to pay for construction of a gallery. The idea was soon forgotten. The only positive outcome of the Mayor's suggestion was that the piece of land suggested by Borlase Smart as being suitable for a gallery *did* become the site for a conventional war memorial for St Ives. However, the Town Council's plans took so long to come to fruition that it was not until 2 November 1922 that a distinctive celtic cross designed by Mr G Tarland Goosey of St Ives, was unveiled next to the fifteenth century Parish Church by Lady Hain, who had bequeathed the site to the town.[5]

Lady Hain was the widow of Sir Edward Hain, owner of Treloyhan Manor, on the outskirts of the town. (This building would feature again in the search for an art gallery.) Sir Edward had for several years been a most distinguished resident. Mayor of St Ives on no less than six occasions, he was created the first Freeman of the Borough, and knighted in 1910. As far as his business interests were concerned he was the fourth and last member of a shipping family, but by far the most entrepreneurial and successful.[6] The Memorial Cottage Hospital at the entrance to St Ives, which was opened by Sir Edward's widow in April 1920, acts as a permanent reminder of his achievements.

The next suggestion for an art gallery, the newspaper records, was penned by an unknown hand. On 10 April 1925 someone calling himself 'M A Honest' wrote a critical article entitled 'On a Public Hall'. He thinly disguised the object of his grievance:

In a certain town (it shall be nameless) there is a very fine public hall, which in the opinion of many people is, as things are at present, wasted to a great extent, as it is but occasionally used for dance, concerts or amateur theatricals... One suggestion, I am told, is that the hall in question might be used as a picture gallery.

The walls of the hall apparently were covered with 'magnificent and florid decorations'. 'But', said MA Honest sarcastically, 'it is possible that some of the productions of the more modern school...might survive the ordeal...'. The subject of this letter was the large space on the first floor of Number 18 Fore Street, close to the Castle Inn, with a back door onto the road leading up to Barnoon Hill.

Coincidentally, twenty-four years later, in 1949, that property, which had become a sale room, [7] did become a gallery. The forty Members and ten Associate Members of the newly-formed Penwith Society of Arts in Cornwall made use of the room's large size for its first permanent space. Paintings, sculpture, ceramics, jewellery, metalwork, furniture and calligraphy were regularly exhibited there. The Society rented the property, which was above Hodder's grocery shop, from Mr Tom Trevorrow, at a rent of thirty-five shillings a week.[8] The gallery, with its high ceiling and windows overlooking Fore Street, was rapidly painted white by members of the Society in time for their first exhibition in the summer of 1949. The 'florid decoration' was a thing of the past.

5 Construction of the war memorial was financed solely by public subscription, an appeal being organised by the Mayor. The sum of 886 pounds and 18 shillings was finally raised by that November day, but it was still not quite the total amount required. Sadly, one of the names included on the memorial was Lady Hain's son, Edward, who had been killed in Gallipoli in 1915.

6 In 1878 the young Edward Hain had persuaded his father to modernise his small shipping company by making the conversion from sail to steam. The resulting Hain Steamship Company expanded rapidly, and numbered twenty-three vessels by 1917, the year of Sir Edward's death. The fleet, although sold to the Peninsula & Oriental Steam Navigation Company in that year, maintained its own identity until as recently as 1972, through its practice of giving each ship a Cornish name. (There is a Hain Room at the St Ives Museum.)

7 Wilhelmina Barns-Graham recalls that the Public Hall was used to camouflage fishing nets during the Second World War. She worked there with other women in the town because she: 'wanted to get to know the local people'. She remembers that the women earned between eight pence and two shillings and sixpence an hour, depending on their experience.

8 The St Ives Labour Club rented the upstairs room, which was reached by a back entrance.

1 This photograph of the Porthmeor Galleries, home of the St Ives Society of Artists, appeared at the top of their headed notepaper. It shows the space after a second gallery was added in 1932. The arched doorway, which connects the two rooms, can still be seen today. The nearer gallery (Number 5 - which was taken over by Borlase Smart after the St Ives Society moved to the Mariner's Church in 1945) became Ben Nicholson's studio in 1950, and he passed it on to Patrick Heron after Nicholson left St Ives for Switzerland in 1958.

2 Treloyhan Manor was built for Sir Edward Hain in 1892 by Silvanus Trevail, this photograph was taken when it was used as a hotel. On several occasions Borlase Smart suggested that the Manor would be a perfect location to house the works of the St Ives artists.

2

The Fore Street space had never been of interest to the Penwith Society's predecessor, the St Ives Society of Artists. Formed in January 1927, its members chose as *their* first permanent exhibition space one of the wooden Porthmeor studios on Back Road West. Thought to have been built around 1850, and part of a vast group of sail lofts extending along the eastern end of Porthmeor Beach, most of the studios had large north-facing windows looking out onto the beach itself. The gallery, originally part of an enormous studio used by the painter Julius Olsson, RA, was opened to the public in June 1928 - admission six pence - by Julius Olsson himself.

Five years later an adjacent studio was acquired by the Society to enlarge its hanging space. The report of its opening in *The St Ives Times* on 25 November 1932, observed:

Let me start by claiming that easily the best picture is the view from the great window of the new gallery. Even the most conceited and swollen-headed artists...would scarcely dare to argue that anything he (or she) has ever put on canvas can rival the view of Porthmeor, the Atlantic, the Island and Carthew, as viewed from the gallery window on a day when sunlight and shadow are alternating.[9]

The year the St Ives Society moved into its first Porthmeor Studio, a rather fanciful idea for a public gallery was put forward in *The St Ives Times* by 'WB'. The anonymous letter-writer suggested that the land at Carthew, adjacent to Man's Head at the western end of Porthmeor Beach, be planted with pines, mountain ash, orange trees and 'sweet briars'.

If our Cornish fairy tales ever come true and the aeroplanes from Southern Europe bring visitors for Cornwall's tonic breezes...they will be so overwhelmed with our summer splendour that they will invite us all back for winter to Egypt and the Riviera. In fact the golden age will have returned.

WB went on to suggest that this 'golden age' might be hastened if St Ives acquired Treloyhan, the home of the late Sir Edward Hain, and now on the market. Such a property could be used as 'pleasure grounds with a picture gallery for a permanent collection of works of all the famous artists, a library reading room with books by Cornish and visiting writers, and the loveliest swimming pool in the west'. The editor of *The St Ives Times* for once, must have felt that this idea was going too far, for he appended a comment to his readers: 'We do not necessarily agree with the views of our correspondent.'

Treloyhan, in fact, was bought that year by a private syndicate of local residents. It was reported that the group hoped to develop and transform it into a 'miniature Torquay' with 'delightful crescents on the sea front' between St Ives and Carbis Bay. Mercifully nothing came of these 'improvements', but the house itself, Treloyhan Manor, which had been built for Sir Edward Hain in 1892 and designed by Mr Silvanus Trevail[10] was enlarged and became a hotel.

The idea for a public gallery was next raised by a Katharine Thompson, who lived in Wheal Ayr, at the top of Porthmeor Hill (an area of St Ives which was, incidentally, selected to be one of the alternative sites for the Tate Gallery). She wrote in April 1937:

Is St Ives to offer only a temporary 'apartment' and not a permanent Home to her Cornish artists who have loved her and worked here? Think of it. If only we had a Whistler and many others of world fame. Are we to let other cities and towns have the honour when it is possible to acquire them now for the place that has been the home of their inspiration?

There appears to have been no response to this appeal, not even from the editor of the newspaper. But it may be that the storm clouds beginning to gather over Europe meant that projects of this kind were unlikely to be occupying people's minds.

9 The sentences describing the view out of the gallery window might well have been written by a journalist standing in Gallery Two of Tate Gallery St Ives just over sixty years later.

10 Silvanus Trevail was the Cornish architect who in 1878 designed the St Ives Board School on The Stennack. (See Chapter 6 - Saving the Stennack School.)

Colin Orchard

1

The St Ives Times & Echo Archive

2

1 A recent photograph of the Mariner's Church, home of the St Ives Society of Artists from 1945. In front of the gallery is Norway Square, a small garden designed and created in the late 1970s. To the right, the building with the chimney houses the Salthouse Gallery.

2 Councillor W J Sullivan, Mayor of St Ives between November 1944 and November 1945. At his election speech he suggested St Ives should have its own museum and art gallery, although he made it plain that this was not an idea he had previously discussed with the Town Council.

Before the War, one more possible venue for a gallery was put forward. The Town Council, for many years housed in the old Market Hall, was acutely short of space and looking for a new site for its offices. At the end of 1937 the Council acquired 'The Retreat', St Ives' last remaining Georgian building on Street-an-Pol.[11] The Mayor hoped that part of the historic property might be preserved as a museum and art gallery.[12] However pressure from other sources to make use of the site, for what appeared to be more practical purposes, was so strong that a Public Inquiry was convened to hear all the evidence. Late in 1938 the recommendation was made that the old building be demolished. Within the year 'The Guildhall', containing a large concert hall, and with accommodation for the Mayor, Council and offices, was built in its place at a cost of £20,500.

The Second World War brought artists to St Ives with totally different sensibilities, the international importance of whose work would finally bring the idea of a permanent gallery to fruition. As their impact was yet to be felt locally, it was with the older generation of artists still in mind that another Mayor, Councillor W J Sullivan, raised the subject of an art gallery yet again. With post-war reconstruction already under discussion at Council meetings, Councillor Sullivan announced at his Mayoral Speech in November 1944:

There are many more things I want for St Ives. I want to see it in proud possession of its own art gallery and museum...

A week later, at the Mayor's Lunch, Borlase Smart, now Secretary of the St Ives Society of Artists, responded eagerly to this latest initiative. He pointed out that Treloyhan Manor was again on the market at an asking price of £23,000.[13] He observed that the property was 'an obvious site for such a museum as, in addition to having suitable buildings, there was a large space which could be used as a public park.' He believed the house and grounds could be acquired by public subscription, rather than out of the rates. With similar sentiments to those of the earlier mayor in 1919, it was again hoped that the project might be a war memorial, this time to those who had died in the Second World War.

There was a certain amount of support for this idea, and debate on the subject continued for several weeks. A variety of responses was published in the newspaper. One 'Exile' believed it was perfectly within the realms of possibility that the money could be raised, but he did not favour 'talk', he wanted 'decisive action'. Others, however, felt that the money should go towards housing both the homeless and those returning from the war. Then there was the question of running costs, which, it was believed, might total as much as £1,000 a year.

The Mayor admitted that he had not been thinking of using Treloyhan Manor as a gallery. He was considering the deconsecrated Mariner's Church in Norway Square in the heart of the town and close to the Harbour. But he was unaware that already others had their eye on this building. In August 1945 it became the second and current home of the St Ives Society of Artists. The Society had felt, for some years, that they had outgrown their gallery at the Porthmeor Studios, and had been looking for more suitable premises. The imposing and spacious church, consecrated as recently as 1905, had been empty for some time. With the help of Borlase Smart the building, with its large crypt, was converted by the artists themselves into a fine gallery which, they hoped, would become 'a Community Arts Centre for artists...and a constructive force in the life of St Ives'.

The Mayor then suggested another possible location for a public gallery: the top floor of the Public Library situated at the busy corner of Tregenna Place and Gabriel Street. The library had been one of nearly seventy public institutions in Cornwall and elsewhere in the south of England (including the Whitechapel Art Gallery in London's East End) founded by the nineteenth century Cornish-born

11 'The Retreat' was owned by the businessman James Lanham. Every Saturday afternoon he hosted gatherings of local artists and writers.

12 The idea for using part of 'The Retreat' for a Museum and Art Gallery was supported by the St Ives Society of Artists, the St Ives Arts Club and the Old Cornwall Society.

13 Treloyhan Manor was used during the Second World War to temporarily house pupils of the Downs School from Seaford in Sussex.

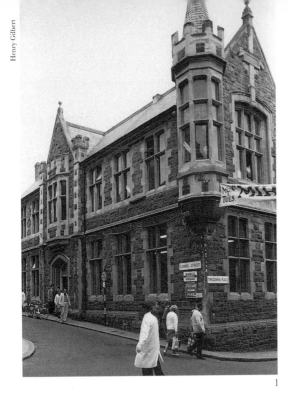

1

1 The Public Library (built in 1896) at the corner of Gabriel Street and Tregenna Place, photographed in the 1960s, when the upper floor still contained the Museum, as the notices in the windows indicate. It had been hoped that the Museum (which moved to its present location at Wheal Dream in May 1969) might house a collection of the works of the St Ives artists.

2 The painter Marjorie Mostyn sitting at a desk in the Mariner's Church, collecting donations for the Borlase Smart Memorial Fund in 1948, in order to acquire the nearby Porthmeor Studios for the perpetual use of the artists in the town. Behind her is an exhibition of paintings by members of the St Ives Society of Artists.

3 Porthmeor Square and the Porthmeor Studios, taken in the late 1940s. In front of the wall is a pig bin used for collecting the local swill which was taken to Hellesveor, at the top of the Stennack, by James Bros. to feed the pigs. On the far right is the house which was regularly painted by Alfred Wallis, who lived only a few doors away from the Porthmeor Studios.

2

3

newspaper proprietor and philanthropist, J Passmore Edwards. Known originally as The Free Library, the building opened in April 1897.[14]

Six years after the Mayor's suggestion, in June 1951, the top floor of the library, previously the Food Office, was converted into a Museum and run by the St Ives Old Cornwall Society. The facility grew in importance; townspeople bequeathing to it many items of interest over the following years. At the time of the Museum's opening, one wall was set aside for the display of works of art, and it was hoped that the space might be extended 'to include a special section devoted to a municipal art gallery'. This suggestion never materialised, however, and in 1968, when the library found that it was required under the new Library Act to provide more space to the general public, the Museum was transferred to a much larger and permanent location, a building previously occupied by the Seaman's Mission at Wheal Dream, between the Harbour and Porthgwidden Beach. It opened in May 1969.[15]

To return to the Mayor's suggestion: as the war was still not over, the Councillors decided not to burden the ratepayers with a gallery project. A Mr F G Ling of Carbis Bay summed up the general feeling on the subject when he wrote to *The St Ives Times* on 26 December 1944:

Such an unnecessary, extravagant and costly venture should be nipped in the bud as speedily as possible...If [this clique] desire to run it and foot the bill of £23,000...let them get on with it.

The project was shelved.

Borlase Smart died in 1947, his longstanding dream unrealised. The artists lost a great supporter and the town lost a man of diverse ideas. His name has not been forgotten, however. At the time of his death, the number of studios in the town had dwindled from one hundred to thirty-eight. The studios at Porthmeor, owned by the artist Moffatt Lindner, were therefore purchased in the name of the Borlase Smart Memorial Trust in 1948 for sole use of artists in perpetuity. They were acquired by the local artists who raised a proportion of the £6,000 purchase price themselves. The remainder came from an interest free loan of £4,500 from the Arts Council of Great Britain. Three Trustees were appointed to administer the twelve studios as well as the adjacent premises that had been occupied by the St Ives School of Painting since 1938: the Director of the Tate Gallery, the Director of Visual Arts at the Arts Council, and a local representative - the first of whom was Gerald Cock, of James Lanham the estate agents, who was appointed managing agent.[16]

When the acquisition of the Porthmeor Studios took place, the Deputy Mayor was reported to have said:

Many of us were sceptical of this ambitious memorial scheme achieving success, but enthusiasm and faith in the ideals of Borlase Smart had [sic] attained the goal.

Meanwhile Treloyhan Manor was acquired in 1947 by the Wesley Guild as a guesthouse 'principally for youths who are able to spend holidays at reasonable terms and to enjoy the fellowship of fellow members'. It has been used by the Guild ever since.

The idea for a gallery to house a permanent collection of works was now taken up by the new generation of St Ives artists who, throughout the 1940s and 50s, were increasingly making their presence felt, both locally and internationally.

14 One of the Public Library's earliest benefactors was Sir Leslie Stephen, father of Virginia Woolf. When, on the death of his wife, he finally sold his summer residence Talland House, in 1895, adjacent to the building that would become the Edward Hain Memorial Hospital, Sir Leslie gave part of his collection of books to the town.

15 The Seaman's Mission, which was in a poor state of repair, was bought by the Borough Council for £19,000 and converted into the town's Museum by Henry Gilbert of the Borough Surveyor's Department.

16 The estate agency was part of a general merchant business originally founded by James Lanham in 1869 and located in the High Street. Eighteen years later Lanham was to open the town's first private art gallery above his shop.

Wilhelmina Barns-Graham

1 A rare photograph of a corner of the interior of the first Penwith Gallery at 18 Fore Street. It shows part of an exhibition of the Penwith Society of Arts in 1952. Above the table is a painting by Wilhelmina Barns-Graham, below which are two Bernard Leach pots. Other works on the wall are by Denis Mitchell, David Haughton and Terry Frost.

2 A contemporary photograph of the site of the first Fore Street Gallery rented to the Penwith Society of Arts. It was located in spacious rooms above the Castle Inn.

1

Colin Orchard

2

2 The Ill-Fated Permanent Collection

From 1949 onwards the avant-garde artists in St Ives became known to a growing international public. Over the next few years they searched for the kind of exhibiting space they hoped would complement the work they were now creating. More importantly, by the 1970s, the artists themselves were planning to put together a permanent collection of the paintings, sculpture and ceramics of past and current members of the Penwith Society of Arts. Unfortunately, the hard working organisers were soon to learn that, without outside financial help, it was impossible to manage such a complex and expensive project on a long-term basis.

Radical artistic change came to the town soon after Borlase Smart's death in 1947. Following the formation of the 'Crypt Group' of 'advanced' artists who, for four years had shown their work in the lower gallery of the Mariner's Church, the famous split between the 'traditionalists' and the 'moderns' of the St Ives Society of Artists took place. Wilhelmina Barns-Graham remembers that there were meetings at Peter Lanyon's house where the negative treatment of the avant-garde artists was discussed, but it was on 8 February 1949, at a meeting at the Castle Inn in Fore Street, that 'The Penwith Society of Arts in Cornwall' officially came into being, founded as a tribute to Borlase Smart. As already recounted, its members took over the spacious Public Hall in Fore Street for their first exhibiting space.

Two years later there might have been a serious opportunity to assemble a public collection of works of art for the town. To celebrate the Festival of Britain in 1951, leading members of both the St Ives Society of Artists and the Penwith Society of Arts presented the town with paintings, sculpture and pots.[1] Councillor James W Daniel, Chairman of the town's Festival of Britain Committee, said that he hoped the works would 'form the nucleus of a collection which would provide a permanent and representative record of the achievements of artists who had worked in this beautiful town.' Although some of the works are displayed in the Public Library to this day, nothing was done to extend the collection.

The artist who now had his views and achievements regularly reported in *The St Ives Times* throughout much of the 1950s, was Ben Nicholson. The first artist to apply to the Borlase Smart Memorial Trust for a Porthmeor Studio, Nicholson said in 1957:

St Ives is perhaps the most important art centre in Britain after London. This was a fact that was not generally realised in St Ives... An art centre that was world famous would attract a steady flow of visitors in all seasons [as well as] artists, art students, art dealers and collectors.

The same year, the Penwith Society of Arts feared that the lease on their gallery at 18 Fore Street was unlikely to be renewed. The Arts Council, which was providing a small grant, said that no more money would be forthcoming unless a proper lease was negotiated. David Brown in his 'Chronology' in the Tate Gallery's exhibition catalogue *St Ives 1939-64* detailed what happened next:

Hepworth proposes that Society should move from 18 Fore Street, where premises on first floor, to 36 Fore Street, premises on the ground floor, with a shop front. (The premises were owned by the Chairman of the Penwith Society, Bruce Taylor, and were only half the area of 18 Fore Street, the rent was higher at No. 36...In the end the move was made but resentment and adverse criticism resulted when Hepworth took over 18 Fore Street herself...)

1 Barbara Hepworth, Wilhelmina-Barns Graham and Bernard Leach were among the 'modern' artists who gave their work to the town.

1

1 An early view of the Penwith Gallery after it had moved to Back Road West, shortly after the sculpture court had been created in 1964 (seen at the far end of the gallery with a Barbara Hepworth sculpture visible, next to a screen hiding the main entrance). The fine gallery appears very spacious (although this effect is heightened by use of a wide-angle lens). Ceramics were shown alongside paintings and sculpture.

2 The small room created at one end of the Penwith Gallery. The photograph was taken shortly before the sculpture court was made in 1964, at which date small windows were inserted into the wall on the left-hand side. This gallery is now used almost exclusively for ceramics and prints.

2

The new gallery had been Armour's antique shop. Above, but separate from the Society's premises, were studios and workshops for use by both resident and visiting artists. The Penwith Society's first summer exhibition held in the new space, which contained canvases of up to six feet, was opened by the Society's President, Sir Herbert Read. He remarked:

The Penwith is a centre of new painting: and new painting the world over...is revelling in an altogether new sense of scale.[2]

The next year, in 1958, the art critic Dr J P Hodin opened the Society's Summer Show. In his address he suggested:

The local authorities and the artists might co-operate in providing a permanent art centre at St Ives...The Cornwall County Council and St Ives Town Council should create a public fund to help the arts in St Ives.

The Society did not remain in its cramped location for very long. In 1959 the owner of the building, Bruce Taylor, left St Ives for health reasons and sold the property. The Society's lease came to an end two years later. Members felt that now was the time to find a permanent home. During their search they looked at a number of possible locations: a building in Street-an-Pol, opposite The Guildhall, and then the Palais de Danse across the road from Barbara Hepworth's Trewyn Studio. (At a price of £9,000, they considered the latter too expensive.)

The next possibility was the site of the redundant gasworks on Porthmeor Beach, ultimately the home of Tate Gallery St Ives. A small item in *The St Ives Times & Echo* of April 29, 1960 reported:

St Ives Town Council have declined a request from the Penwith Society of Arts asking them to consider providing an art gallery as part of the development of the Gasworks site at Porthmeor [3] ...The Council confirmed a recommendation from the Housing Committee that the Society should be informed that as the Gasworks site was purchased for housing purposes, it was not possible to consider their proposal.

Under the Chairmanship of the architect and part-time sculptor Roger Leigh, the Society finally found an old pilchard-packing factory with net and sail lofts above, which included 'St Peter's Loft', the school of painting founded in 1955 by Peter Lanyon, Terry Frost and William Redgrave. The complex, in Back Road West, next to the new Barnaloft housing development, belonged to the builder Mr William Thomas. The Society acquired the property for £4,300 with the aid of a grant from the Gulbenkian Foundation. Announcing this grant, the Foundation said that the Penwith Society was:

a nursery of the avant-garde in painting and sculpture, it has produced more artists of standing and more impact on the art world than any other society in the country.

St Ives Borough Council made a loan of £1,500 towards the cost of refurbishment, and members of the Society assisted in the fundraising by organising a number of events, including an Arts Ball and a 'Hop' at the Palais de Danse.

The large space, containing a number of fine granite pillars, (with a door onto Porthmeor Road, originally used for bringing in works of art) was turned into a spacious gallery, sixty-five feet long, by the members themselves. It was opened by Sir Herbert Read in September 1961, who observed that he thought the gallery to be 'one of the most beautiful places for the exhibition of art I have ever seen'.

Before too long the Penwith Society discovered that it needed to appoint someone who could deal with the many administrative tasks that surfaced now that it owned rather than leased its premises. The fabric of the building, too, was in need of a facelift. In 1964 the members made a decision to appoint a non-artist as Chairman for the first time. Proposed by Barbara Hepworth and seconded by

2 Sir Herbert Read's comments about the internationalism of St Ives was proving to be true, for Patrick Heron recalls five or six New York art dealers visiting St Ives at this time, especially to see the work of the Penwith Society. They were Martha Jackson, Bertha Schaefer, Eleanor Ward (the Stable Gallery) and the Saidenbergs.

3 Two rooms on the top floor of a development of homes for elderly people were proposed for the Society's use on the gasworks site.

Henry Gilbert

1 Barbara Hepworth and Bernard Leach being escorted into the Council Chamber at The Guildhall by the Mayor, Councillor Edward Jory (on Barbara Hepworth's right), where they received the Freedom of the Borough of St Ives in September 1968.

2 The ballroom of The Guildhall was temporarily converted into an exhibition space by Henry Gilbert in September 1968, to coincide with the presentation of the Freedom of the Borough of St Ives to Barbara Hepworth and Bernard Leach. The corner of the room shown here contains work by Hepworth; sculpture displayed on brick plinths, and drawings attached to false walls covered in white silk.

3 John Crowther was Chairman of the Penwith Society between 1964 and 1966. During those years he was responsible for refurbishing and improving the Penwith Gallery, as well as giving it a more professional image.

4 The interior of the Public Library as it appeared at the time Barbara Hepworth and Bernard Leach received the Freedom of the Borough of St Ives. The Library had recently been redesigned and refurbished by Henry Gilbert. The display case, in the foreground, housed a special exhibition of books and catalogues about Hepworth, Leach and Nicholson.

Henry Gilbert

Juncker-Jensen, Copenhagen

Henry Gilbert

Alexander Mackenzie the Truro-based architect John Crowther took on the responsibility for the next two years.[4] Crowther agreed, and his legacy was to give to the Penwith a more professional image. He designed its letterhead, produced smart exhibition catalogues and ensured that the work of the Society was properly publicised.

With the Chairman's support and enthusiasm the gallery was smartened up. John Crowther recalls:

I raised sufficient donations from contractors and sub-contractors to pay for the removal of the wall between the main gallery and the outside area to form a hard landscaped sculpture court. The court was used for the display of major works of sculpture and has since become overgrown. The adjacent store room was converted to a second gallery and the main gallery walls which had recently been flushed were provided with heaters at high level and improved lighting. The floor was sealed and painted. A new separately screened storage space was provided to the rear. The members of the committee decided at that time not to paint the granite columns white. [5]

Henry Gilbert, who designed the sculpture gallery, also designed a new entrance which in fact was never built.

1968 was also the year that the arts in St Ives won local official recognition. Ben Nicholson, Barbara Hepworth and Bernard Leach were invited to accept the honourary Freedom of the Borough of St Ives, the only people to be so honoured since Sir Edward Hain in 1911. Ben Nicholson, however, declined, but he sent an etching which hangs in the Public Library to this day.

The 'Freedom of the Borough' was conferred in September 1968 at a unique ceremony in The Guildhall. The Mayor, Councillor Edward Jory, presented Barbara Hepworth and Bernard Leach each with a 'casket', a beautiful purpose-built wooden box made by Robin Nance and decorated in silver by Breon O'Casey, inside which was a scroll. Speakers at the formal occasion expressed the hope that it 'would lead to a greater appreciation and understanding by the town of the artists in their midst'. A special exhibition of the works of Ben Nicholson, Barbara Hepworth and Bernard Leach was organised by Henry Gilbert, who transformed the Concert Hall of The Guildhall into a splendid showing area by covering the multi-coloured walls in white linen. Norman Reid, Director of the Tate Gallery since 1964, opened the exhibition.

To coincide with these events, an exhibition was also mounted at the Public Library and an outdoor sculpture exhibition was held in the gardens surrounding the Parish Church.

Then in April 1969, Marjorie Parr, who already had a large gallery on the Kings Road in Chelsea showing painting, sculpture, pottery and eighteenth century glass, opened a gallery in St Ives on the site of the Cottage Antique Shop in Wills Lane. *The St Ives Times & Echo* warmly welcomed this fine addition to the local arts scene, and reported:

it is the only private gallery of modern art of its size and scope in West Cornwall and probably the only one west of Plymouth.

The idea of a permanent collection, however, was never far from the Penwith Society's mind. As early as the spring of 1964 Bernard Leach, a senior and venerated member of the Society, had remarked that it:

had got to think in terms of a permanent gallery. [The Society wanted] the support of people outside Cornwall, and to see the gallery becoming something which that part of England could be proud of.

In 1971, under the Chairmanship of Marcus Brumwell, a Director of the Design Research Unit in London, and for many years a friend of Ben Nicholson, Barbara

4 The members of the Penwith Society of Arts had recently made the acquaintance of the Truro architect John Crowther, who, although originally unfamiliar with their work, had been introduced to Alexander Mackenzie, a member of the Society, when Crowther was seeking advice on hanging modern art on the walls of his office. During the period of his Chairmanship, John Crowther recommended the placing of a number of major art works in the south west by members of the Penwith Society; for example at County Hall, Truro, and the University of Exeter.

5 The columns of the gallery were painted white in the late 1970's. Also, later, the main gallery space was divided to provide screening and a reception counter.

3

2

1 Construction of the extension to the Penwith Gallery, which was opened in 1976. Previously used as a fish cellar and later as an area to park cars, the ground was lowered to achieve the required ceiling height. To the right is the space that was to become the gallery; to the left, at the higher level, is the area that was to become an internal courtyard, around which, at the upper level, were added artists' studios and a print workshop.

2 The finished extension to the Penwith Gallery, taken from a similar vantage point as the photograph above. The new gallery housed the Penwith Society's permanent collection of paintings, sculpture and ceramics, loaned from the artists themselves. In 1980 owing to the cancellation of the Art's Council grant, which helped to fund the running of the gallery, the collection was dismantled, much to the anger of the members of the Penwith Society.

3 The sculpture court, paved with granite, designed for the Penwith Gallery by Henry Gilbert. Sliding doors led from the gallery into the court. The windows in the rear wall light the Penwith's small gallery, illustrated on page 24.

Hepworth and Henry Moore, and a collector of modern art, the Society acquired the property adjoining the Penwith Gallery for £28,000. This latest purchase was made possible with the combined assistance of Barbara Hepworth and the Gulbenkian Foundation, as well as the Department of the Environment, the Arts Council, the Crafts Advisory Committee, the English Tourist Board and others. One of the sponsors was James Holman, a local businessman.[6]

The new property consisted of a large open space (which had been used as a coal cellar, and then later for car parking), another pilchard packing factory, a terrace of six cottages, some of which were unmodernised, and outbuildings.[7]

It was under the Presidency of Sir Norman Reid, who was invited by the Penwith Society of Arts to succeed Sir Herbert Read on the latter's death in 1968, that the complex was converted into a second large gallery with studios and print workshop above. The substantial project was undertaken by the Redruth builder, Leonard Williams, to designs by Henry Gilbert, at a cost of around £12,000. Because part of the gallery space was located underneath the cottages, a satisfactory ceiling height was achieved only by lowering the ground of the site by five feet. Along one side of the new gallery, which was ninety feet long by thirty feet wide, a series of alcoves with rubbed-finished Delabole slate were created, and the ceiling was supported by granite columns similar to those in the main gallery.

Here finally was a space suitable to house a 'permanent collection' of paintings, sculpture and pottery. The large number of exhibits gathered together, consisting of both outright gifts and loans - short and long term - represented some of the best avant-garde work made in the town since 1920.[8] A separate charitable company was formed to manage this venture - Penwith Galleries Limited - under the Chairmanship of Marcus Brumwell.

Such was the influence of Dame Barbara Hepworth that a glittering array of sponsors was lined up to support the scheme. They included Benjamin Britten, The Rt. Hon. Baroness Lee of Asheridge[9] Henry Moore, Peter Pears, Sir Michael Tippett, Sir Hugh Willatt, Secretary General of the Arts Council of Great Britain and Mr and Mrs James Holman. The building complex was selected by HM Secretary of State for the Environment for inclusion in the statutory list of buildings of special architectural interest.

The new gallery was opened by Sir Norman Reid, on 10 April 1976, the same day that he opened the Barbara Hepworth Museum in St Ives. As he said in his opening speech, he 'did not know of any other town in England that could claim to have opened two galleries in the same day'. Now visitors to the town felt that they were able to see a collection of the avant-garde art that had made the area famous.

Some time after Barbara Hepworth's death in 1975 the Society faced a crisis. Without the sculptor's support, encouragement and access to her influential friends, curating the permanent collection was bringing the Penwith into financial difficulties. In 1977 the tiny grant that the Arts Council annually made towards paying the interest on the gallery's loans, and which was so vital for its continued operation, was suddenly withdrawn. Penwith Galleries Limited still had a debt of about £55,000 as a result of high interest rates that refused to fall. It was feared that the bank would foreclose and the permanent collection be dispersed.

A publicity campaign was put into operation. A major article appeared in *The Guardian*. Members of the Arts Council's Finance Committee (most of whom had never been to Cornwall before, let alone St Ives) were invited to visit both the Barbara Hepworth Museum and the Penwith Gallery. There had been a certain amount of hostility by the members of the Arts Council to St Ives, and the Society was very proud to be able to show them the gallery and its collection.[10] It must have made an impression because, on the way back to London, the Committee decided to give a considerable grant to the Penwith over the next two years, which allowed a very varied exhibition programme to be put into effect.

6 The Founder and Chairman of the Friends of St Ives, James Holman, planned and financed the restoration of St Nicholas' Chapel, on The Island, with the assistance of Henry Gilbert in 1971, in the form we see it today.

7 The Vice Chairman of the Penwith Society, Douglas Portway, prophesied in a letter to *The St Ives Times & Echo* of 14 January, 1972: '...The proposed collection will celebrate [the artists'] unique achievement, and add a new dimension to the prestige of St Ives as well as enormously increasing the large number of visitors, who come here in and out of season primarily because this is one of the most important centres of artistic activity in the country...'

8 1920 was the year Bernard Leach arrived in St Ives with his Japanese friend Shoji Hamada to set up a pottery. The workshops at the Upper Stennack are open to this day.

9 The Rt. Hon. Baroness Lee of Asheridge, in 1969, as Miss Jennie Lee, Parliamentary Under-Secretary of State at the Department of Education with special reference to the arts, had previously visited the Penwith Gallery.

10 There was never to be much support from the Arts Council for St Ives at the end of the 1970s. Patrick Heron, who was appointed Member of the Council's Art Panel for three years beginning 1 January 1975 recalls two specific instances of its inactivity. In the Autumn of 1975 he recommended that the exposed and vulnerable roofs of the historic Porthmeor studios be replaced at a cost of £20,000. And in March 1977 he suggested that the Hayward Gallery in London use their entire exhibition space to mount a major show 'St Ives and the Penwith: 1921-1979'. (Letter from Patrick Heron to Robin Campbell, Art Director, The Arts Council of Great Britain, 16 March 1977.) Neither of these ideas was taken up; in fact after Patrick Heron's term of office came to an end they were both abandoned.

Henry Gilbert

1 The Penwith Gallery as it appeared around 1976 in its Back Road West location, looking away from the entrance. Its pillars and beams were left unpainted until the late 1970s. This exhibition, with its sparse hang, made use of temporary screening.

2 A photograph of the Penwith Gallery taken from a similar vantage point, in the late 1970s, by which time the granite pillars had been painted white, and new walls had been created along the back of the room to hide the planks of wood.

3 Marcus Brumwell, Chairman of the Penwith Society of Arts between 1969 and 1976, photographed by Dr Roger Slack on the occasion of the Chairman's seventieth birthday party at the Penwith Gallery in 1971. In his buttonhole is a large bouquet of violets.

St Ives School of Painting Archive

Dr Roger Slack

But then, in 1980, this grant, too, was greatly reduced. The Arts Council felt that the Penwith should return to being a society rather than operating as a company with a curatorial role. It was not, in any event, the Council's responsibility to finance permanent exhibitions.

Alan Groves, Chief Architect with Cornwall County Council, by now was Chairman of Penwith Galleries. He had been recommended for the position by his friend and neighbour Marcus Brumwell due, he believes, to his business background. The new Chairman came to the position knowing of the Society's financial difficulties. After discussions with the bank, Alan Groves reluctantly conceded that the permanent collection would have to be taken down - and this is what happened in February 1980. The works were suddenly returned to their owners. There was no way that sufficient money could be found to employ a curator, provide the necessary heating and lighting, and, most importantly, pay for insurance and security.

Sadly, no other organisation came to the gallery's aid. It was infuriating for the members of the Penwith Society that, at the same time that their funding was withdrawn, substantial grants were given to the Newlyn Gallery on the south coast by the Arts Council in London.[11]

The Society continued to show the work of its members through changing exhibitions, but it was quite clear that in order for a collection of St Ives art to be *permanently* housed, both short and long term financing was critically important. Good will and enthusiasm were not sufficient.

Tom Cross, Principal of Falmouth School of Art, and by late 1981 Chairman of Penwith Galleries, realised what was necessary to seriously start and maintain a permanent collection in St Ives. Approaches to national institutions for help and assistance were a possible answer, one of which might be the Tate Gallery, he believed. He was aware that the Tate held a large number of paintings and sculpture by Penwith Society artists. He knew, too, that only a small proportion of these were normally exhibited at Millbank, because of a severe shortage of space. Tom Cross thought that, with the right organisation, there might be a chance to display them in a context which could show the important artistic events that had taken place in the area from 1939 to about 1970.

It would be another five years before anyone would take up this idea however, but within four, a much wider public was able to see for themselves many of the St Ives works at the Tate Gallery in London. This major exhibition, had come about only after many years of planning.

11 A full account of the events surrounding the dispersal of the permanent collection at the Penwith Gallery is detailed in an article entitled 'Writing is on the wall for gallery' by Jean Campbell in The *Western Morning News* of 1 February 1980.

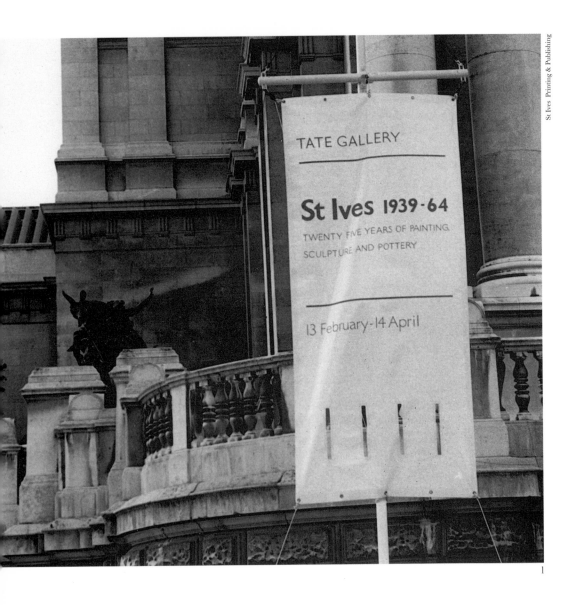

St Ives Printing & Publishing

TATE GALLERY

St Ives 1939·64

TWENTY FIVE YEARS OF PAINTING.
SCULPTURE AND POTTERY

13 February-14 April

1

1 A banner outside the front entrance to the Tate Gallery in London advertises the exhibition 'St Ives 1939-64 - Twenty five years of painting, sculpture and pottery', which was held between 13 February and 14 April 1985. For many people this was the first time they had been able to see the full range of artistic wealth by the St Ives artists, as a result of which they started to enquire whether it was possible to see such a collection in St Ives itself.

2 David Lewis, who lived in the West Penwith between 1947 and 1955 before moving to Leeds and then Pittsburgh, Pennsylvania, helped on two occasions to mount a show of St Ives paintings in the United States. He is pictured here in his Pittsburgh office, where he practices as an architect.

David Lewis

2

3   St Ives Exhibition At The Tate Gallery - 1985

A major event stimulated people's interest and awareness in St Ives and its artists: the exhibition 'St Ives 1939-64 - Twenty five years of painting, sculpture and pottery' held at the Tate Gallery in London between 13 February and 14 April 1985. As Alan Bowness, the Tate Gallery's Director, pointed out in his Foreword to the copious and detailed catalogue that accompanied the exhibition: 'There has never been a survey of St Ives art, and so far little serious preparatory research has been done.'

However, the next paragraph hints at what might have been organised:

The exhibition was first proposed to the museum at Pittsburgh by the architect David Lewis. The Director of the Carnegie Institute, Jack Lane, approached the Tate, and we had planned to do the exhibition together.

The full story of this attempt is an interesting one.

David Lewis was no stranger to St Ives. In 'A Personal Memoir 1947-55' he contributed to the exhibition catalogue, Lewis recalled the kaleidoscope of events that took place while he lived in the area, and recounted his own involvement with them. As a young aspiring writer he, like many others, was drawn to the western tip of Britain, leaving London for Cornwall in 1947. Living on the wild north coast beyond St Ives, he soon made the acquaintance of some of the avant-garde artists: first Peter Lanyon and John Wells, then Ben Nicholson and Barbara Hepworth.

In the summer of 1949 David Lewis married the painter Wilhelmina Barns-Graham. A year later he assisted Barbara Hepworth to catalogue her sculptures and drawings for the first time. From 1951 to 1954 he was Curator of the Penwith Society at its first Fore Street gallery.

David Lewis left St Ives in 1956 when his marriage broke up. He then changed career, moving north to study architecture at the Leeds College of Art[1]. From there he crossed the Atlantic. Settling in Pittsburgh, he started up his own architectural practice, Urban Design Associates, in 1964. Continuing to teach, he came into contact with both the Carnegie Institute of Technology in Pittsburgh (where he was Andrew Mellon Professor of Architecture & Urban Design at the Carnegie-Mellon University from 1963 to 1967) and Yale, where he lectured from 1968 to 1974.

Meanwhile Lewis had kept in touch with his St Ives friends. During a visit to England in 1976 he and the painter Patrick Heron discussed the fact that there now seemed to be little public interest in St Ives artists. More than a decade earlier their work had been included regularly in major touring shows around the world, many organised by the British Council. Now it was hardly ever seen, especially in the United States.[2] For some years, attention had focussed on a younger generation of painters and sculptors based in London, despite the fact that the St Ives artists were continuing to produce major new work.

On David Lewis' return to Pittsburgh, concerned by what he had learned, he took the matter up with Leon Arkus, the Director of the Museum of Art at the Carnegie Institute in Pittsburgh, who immediately showed enthusiasm for helping to rectify the situation. Together they made initial plans to exhibit the work of some of the St Ives painters, who had been given the epithet the British 'Middle Generation' by the art dealer Leslie Waddington; a term also known in the United States. The venue they selected was the newly built Scaife wing of the Museum of Art at the Carnegie Institute in Pittsburgh, close to both the Carnegie-Mellon

1 The St. Ives painter, Terry Frost, was already in Leeds. In 1954 he had been awarded a Gregory Fellowship in Painting for two years at Leeds University. During this time Frost took part in Harry Thubron's 'legendary' classes at the Leeds College of Art. (See 'The Leeds Connection' by Ronnie Duncan, pp.62-66 of *Terry Frost*, Scolar Press, 1994, which includes a personal narrative by David Lewis in which he describes Terry Frost's classes that he attended while studying architecture at the College of Art.)

2 David Lewis was pleased, however, to learn that Patrick Heron was shortly to have an exhibition of large paintings at the University of Texas at Austin Art Museum.

University and the University of Pittsburgh.

Pittsburgh was an interesting choice for such an exhibition. The home of the acclaimed four-yearly 'Pittsburgh International', it had given its first prize for painting to Ben Nicholson in 1952. And Peter Lanyon too had connections with that city. One of his paintings had been acquired by the Carnegie Institute in 1958.

After a discussion as to whose work should be exhibited, given the amount of space available, four painters were finally proposed by Arkus: Peter Lanyon and Roger Hilton, who were no longer alive, and Patrick Heron and William Scott. The planned retrospective accompanied by a substantial catalogue, was to consist of around one hundred and fifty works from the mid-fifties onwards and take place at the end of 1978. Later Toronto and Dallas were contacted with a view to the exhibition touring to those cities, and Lewis hoped that there would be a major English venue included.[3]

Patrick Heron, encouraged this scheme throughout from the London end. He had discussions with two dealers: Waddingtons who represented Heron and Hilton and Gimpel Fils who represented Scott and Lanyon. And when David Lewis mentioned the exhibition to his friend Alan Bowness, he found him to be enthusiastic. Bowness put forward the suggestion that assistance might be given by the British Council upon whose Board he was a member.

Despite Lewis' efforts to move the project along, the exhibition was complex to organise. He was attempting, in his own time, to make the detailed arrangements, while gallery Directors worried about costs and administrative problems such as crating the works of art. Decisions had to be made as to who should eventually be responsible for selecting the works and writing the catalogue. Although Lewis was beginning to get support from the Smithsonian Institute Travelling Exhibitions Service (SITES - an organisation set up to put shows together for museums) funding had to be found from the museums themselves. An official English organisation was urgently required for SITES to communicate with, and the natural choice was the British Council. However, if it was to be involved in this transatlantic project, it was likely that the council would also expect to play a large planning role in the show.

By early 1978, despite hard work and optimism by the artists and their families, the British Embassy in Washington made it known to David Lewis that the British Council was unlikely to find the required funds. Shortly afterwards this was confirmed by the British Council themselves when they formally declined to take on the assembly and shipping of works. The exhibition had to be abandoned.

The next chapter opened two years later. David Lewis had not given up the idea of showing the work of St Ives artists in the United States. In July 1980 he was invited to exhibit his personal collection of mainly English works at the Carnegie Institute.[4] The Museum of Art at the Institute now had a new Director, John Lane, following the retirement of Leon Arkus through ill health. Lewis thought that now might be the time to revive his idea of a 'Middle Generation' exhibition. John Lane, who had come from the Brooklyn Museum, was impressed by the work in David Lewis' show. He and his colleague, Gene Baro[5], met with Lewis and they discussed the idea of an exhibition of St Ives artists. Baro, however, was not interested in a four-man show. He preferred to present a general survey of British painting and sculpture of the 1950-1965 period that included work of non-St Ives artists.

Despite Baro's reservations, John Lane was supportive of a St Ives show, and the idea of a larger exhibition began to take shape. Lewis, now freed from being responsible for its organisation, hoped to play a peripheral role in the project.

John Lane and Gene Baro arrived in London to talk to Alan Bowness, who was now Director of the Tate Gallery. They discussed the possibility of a collaboration.

3 Patrick Heron hoped that the exhibition he had proposed to the Arts Council on 16 March 1977, 'St Ives and the Penwith: 1921-1979' at the Hayward Gallery, could coincide with the four man touring exhibition, thereby forestalling 'American accusations of British neglect of the British.' (See note 9, Chapter 2.)

4 Artists in the show at Gallery D, Museum of Art, Carnegie Institute, Pittsburgh, included Ben Nicholson, Barbara Hepworth, Victor Pasmore, Terry Frost, Wilhelmina Barns-Graham, Bryan Wynter, John Wells, Patrick Heron and Roger Hilton.

5 Gene Baro had known Alan Bowness when Baro was Cultural Attaché at the US Embassy in London.

Prior to his Tate appointment, when still at the Courtauld Institute, Bowness had, in 1979, organised a large Post Impressionism exhibition at the Royal Academy. Interested now in putting on major shows at the Tate, he recalls that:

We [were] happy to consider a St Ives retrospective, because this is something we at the Tate (especially David Brown and myself) had already talked about.

The proposal put forward was for an exhibition of St Ives art, possibly organised by the Tate Gallery with US assistance, to be held in late 1984/early 1985, and whose time-span was to be 1939-1964. There were to be about one hundred and twenty-five works on show from a large number of painters, sculptors and potters; a scholarly catalogue was to be produced, and David Lewis planned to write an introductory essay and assist with archive research by taping oral histories of many of the artists concerned, in conjunction with the Tate Gallery's Archive.

Alan Bowness was initially cautious about taking on the responsibility himself, partly because of his very close connections, through marriage, with the Nicholson/Hepworth family, and partly because of his duties as Director of the Tate Gallery. At this early date, therefore, he appointed David Brown, Assistant Keeper in the Modern Collection at the Tate Gallery since 1974, to plan the exhibition from the London end. Brown had met a number of the St Ives artists, and he was, in particular, a good friend of Roger Hilton, whom he had known since 1961. In 1977 he had been asked to assist in the preparation of a catalogue for the exhibition 'Cornwall 1945 - 1955' at the New Art Centre in London, for which he also wrote the introduction: a brief history of painting in Cornwall which included the work of both St Ives and Newlyn artists. He prepared a general chronology of events, starting as early as 1811.

By the end of 1981 plans were taking shape. A meeting at the Tate Gallery with the Americans, David Lewis, David Brown and other Tate staff, including Michael Compton and Ruth Rattenbury, set the agenda. It was planned for the exhibition to start at Pittsburgh and then travel to the Yale Centre for British Art in New Haven, Connecticut.[6] From there it was hoped that the exhibition might tour to a third gallery, perhaps in Canada, ending in London at the Tate Gallery in the summer of 1985. Being a joint US/UK venture, indemnity for the works would be sought from both governments. Other costs would also be shared.

With this outline agreed, another meeting took place, which Alan Bowness, Iain Bain (from Tate Gallery Publications) and Sarah Fox Pitt attended. The Director outlined his more detailed plans. He proposed that the exhibition should be arranged chronologically and divided into six sections, the selection of artists being discussed by all. The catalogue would be published by the Tate Gallery and would contain historical essays by David Lewis and Gene Baro, as well as a detailed chronology and biographies of the artists prepared by David Brown. (At that time David Lewis was planning to write a book on his return to the Penwith landscape after twenty-five years absence, which would contain the extensive tape recordings of the artists that he was undertaking with Sarah Fox Pitt from the Tate's Archive department.)

Then, as on the first attempt, problems began to surface. By the summer of 1982 a fourth venue had still not been found. At the same time Alan Bowness felt that the exhibition should start at the Tate Gallery instead of in America. He remembers that:

The decision to have the show in London first was a practical one, made on conservation grounds - so that condition could be checked and necessary work done on works of art and frames before shipping anything across the Atlantic.

Because the suggested London dates conflicted with the Tate Gallery's Francis Bacon retrospective, he also proposed to bring the St Ives exhibition forward to the

6 The Yale Centre for British Art in New Haven, Connecticut, is a major building by the American architect Louis Kahn which had been donated to Yale University by Paul Mellon to house Mellon's bequest of eighteenth and nineteenth century British Art. It includes galleries for invited exhibitions of all periods including the twentieth century.

1

1 Professor Alan Bowness photographed in the garden of the Barbara Hepworth Museum on the occasion of its opening by Sir Norman Reid on 10 April 1976. At that time Alan Bowness was a Trustee of the Barbara Hepworth estate and a lecturer at the Courtauld Institute in London.

2 David Brown, with beard, at the centre of a group holding a debate at the Penwith Gallery in the late 1970s. Leaning forwards, to his right, is George Melly; to his left, in the glasses, is the painter Patrick Hughes.

3 The cover of the catalogue for the exhibition 'St Ives 1939-64 - Twenty five years of painting, sculpture and pottery'. The illustration is 'This is Sain Fishery That use to be' by Alfred Wallis.

2

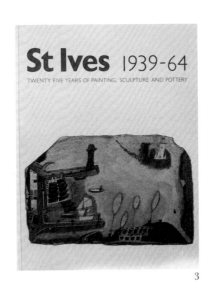

St Ives 1939-64
TWENTY FIVE YEARS OF PAINTING, SCULPTURE AND POTTERY

3

4

4 Part of the archive display at the entrance to 'St Ives 1939-64'. To the right are photographs of Peter Lanyon; to the left photographs of Ben Nicholson. The central section shows: (top left to right) Wilhelmina Barns-Graham, David Haughton, Paul Feiler, Adrian Ryan; (middle) Peter Potworowski, Kate Nicholson, Alexander Mackenzie; (bottom) John Wells, Patrick Hayman, Simon Nicholson and Alan Lowndes.

spring of 1985.

David Lewis, meanwhile, found he was unable to write an independent book because of other commitments. Then Gene Baro died. The change of dates in London did not fit in with the British Art Centre's long-term exhibition schedule, and that institution dropped out, reducing the amount of US finance available. Other financial backing from the US side, too, was cancelled because no company could be found to sponsor a show in only one US location. Reluctantly, John Lane decided that the Carnegie Institute would also have to cancel because it could not raise the large costs involved alone.

A new exhibition was now organised for a single showing at the Tate Gallery. By the autumn of 1983 detailed plans were well underway for what would become 'St Ives 1939-64 - Twenty five years of painting, sculpture and pottery', selected by David Brown. Brown had very firm views as to whose work he would like to see included in the exhibition. His final list contained forty-nine painters and sculptors and eighteen potters; an exhibition of far wider scope than that previously envisaged, and with a greater timespan than the years in the exhibitions title indicated. Early painters who had worked in a more traditional style, and whom David Brown considered to be forerunners of the later artists, were represented, as was craft work. He asked Dr Oliver Watson, Assistant Keeper in the Department of Ceramics at the Victoria & Albert Museum, to curate that part of the show dealing with ceramics, and write an introduction to the Leach Pottery in the catalogue.

Alan Bowness played a major part in choosing the works and arranging each room's displays. Sarah Fox Pitt organised the large archival display at the entrance to the exhibition, which was to create a great deal of public interest. The publication was put together by David Brown with substantial input from his assistant Ann Jones. David Lewis in the end did play a part: he contributed a 'Personal Memoir, 1947-55', based on his tape recordings of the artists themselves. Also included in the catalogue were a number of moving poems by W S Graham on the deaths of some of his painter friends.

For the chronology, David Brown spent many hours in St Ives poring over back numbers of the *St Ives Times*, together with minutes of the meetings of the Penwith Society of Arts. As a result he created a very detailed account of the events taking place in the town over those critical years. For the first time, the friendships, achievements, jealousies and conflicts of the artists were publicly revealed.

The exhibition proved a success. It was seen by over 38,000 visitors between 13 February and 14 April. A series of films was shown in the gallery during the period. A posthumous film on Ben Nicholson was described in the exhibition literature as being about 'England's most significant modern artist'. Other contemporary films were shown on Barbara Hepworth, Terry Frost, Naum Gabo, Alfred Wallis, Bernard Leach, Michael Cardew and David Leach, as well as the Leach Pottery itself.

Newlyn Gallery organised a special 'Art Train' from Penzance to Paddington one day in March. The inclusive ticket covered entry not only to the Tate Gallery. The Cornish visitors could choose to see one of three other important exhibitions showing concurrently in the capital: Renoir at the Hayward; Munch at the Barbican or Chagall at the Royal Academy.[7] At the Tate exhibition itself, the catalogue, of which 3,000 were printed, sold for £8.50.[8] Also available was a printed silk scarf designed by Patrick Heron and printed by Alexander MacIntyre, titled 'St Ives 1948'.

Three other exhibitions were simultaneously held in London to complement the Tate show: 'Five St Ives Artists' at the New Art Centre; 'The St Ives Tradition' at

7 Visitors to the exhibition from St Ives recall how proud they felt when they arrived in London and saw the words 'St Ives' prominently displayed in Paddington station and on the side of buses.

8 The continuing popularity of the catalogue led to it becoming a rare collector's item within a few years, with prices reaching as high as £100.

2

1

3

1 Tom Cross during the filming of 'Painting the Warmth of the Sun' in 1984 seen interviewing, off camera, Monica Wynter at the Carne, Zennor, the house Bryan Wynter lived in from late 1945 until he and Monica moved to St Buryan in 1964.

2 Filming 'Painting the Warmth of the Sun' on a hot August day in 1984, in the grounds of the Tregenna Castle Hotel, St Ives, by Television South West. Pictured at the table (each of which housed a microphone to pick up conversations) are: Monica Wynter (back to camera), Denis Mitchell (left), Jane O'Malley (facing) and Jane Mitchell (right).

3 A contemporary photograph of Kerris Vean (built in 1875) one of the buildings on Woodlane belonging to Falmouth School of Art and Design (now Falmouth College of Art). The School started as a private venture in 1902, was taken over by the Local Authority in 1938 and moved to Kerris Vean in 1950. The four storey building had studios for painting, printmaking, graphics, textiles and dress-design and, in the basement, ceramics. The School has expanded greatly in the intervening years. Tom Cross, who wrote *Painting the Warmth of the Sun*, was its Principal between 1976 and 1989.

Montpelier Studio and 'Cornwall 1925-1975 - a sense of place...a sense of light' at Michael Parkin Fine Art. As a result, a number of the artists, whose work had not been seen for some time, suddenly became known to a much wider public. There was also a new awareness of the significant historical events that had taken place since 1939 in what, for most people, seemed a very remote part of England.

The exhibitions generated fifteen major reviews in the national press, which were mostly very complimentary. Terance Mullaly in the *Daily Telegraph* of 16 February wrote:

The achievements of St Ives should be trumpeted from the roof tops...here is a perfect exhibition for the Tate. This is a moment when clear headedness about our national collections and what they can achieve is needed.

John Russell Taylor in an unsigned article in *The Times* on 19 February wrote:

...it seems to me that any tendency to pigeonhole St Ives art as a lot of agreeable, merely decorative pieces from talented minor artists must be flatly contradicted by the experience of the work itself, at the Tate and elsewhere.

The notable exception to these views was the article written for *The Guardian* by Waldemar Januszcak on 26 February. His complaint was that:

...the exhibition is a dull disappointment. It suffers from chronic overcrowdings.

But readers possibly felt that his views somehow missed the point, for he wrote, a few lines on:

Indeed the pots of Bernard Leach himself are unnecessary barnacles attached to the hull of the smooth, hard, modernism which Nicholson, Hepworth and Gabo launched from here.

David Brown received a letter from Tom Cross dated 28 February 1985. He wrote:

...I think at last the true merit of this national school of painting can be fully recognised. My most particular congratulations on the catalogue and the archival material which has greatly helped the understanding of this period.

Tom Cross had reason to be pleased with the Tate's exhibition. The book that David Lewis was to have written had been abandoned, but another, quite coincidentally, was to take its place, and Cross was its author.

Tom Cross was Principal of Falmouth School of Art, the only art college in Cornwall. Its reputation was such that it attracted a wide range of well known artists to tutor the students on a part-time basis. A succession of annual 'Delia Heron Memorial Lectures' had brought such eminent speakers to the School as Leslie Waddington and Richard Rogers in the early 1980s.

Cross' first involvement with St Ives artists went back to 1962 when, as Assistant Director for Wales of the Arts Council, he had created the exhibition 'British Art and the Modern Movement, 1930-1940' at the National Museum of Wales in Cardiff. The large number of works shown were grouped into various art movements.[9] Cross personally selected the works from the artists themselves or their families. Many came from their personal collections and had never been shown before. At the same time he met significant collectors of St Ives works, such as Margaret Gardiner. The introduction to the catalogue was written by Cross' colleague, Alan Bowness (who was then a lecturer at the Courtauld Institute in London, and who had become acquainted with Cross through the Arts Council Art Department). Herbert Read, the distinguished critic, long-time friend of Ben Nicholson and Barbara Hepworth, and Chairman of the Penwith Society of Arts, opened the exhibition.

9 The art movements included 'Seven & Five', Post Cubism, Abstract Art and Surrealism.

Fourteen years later Cross moved to Cornwall to take up his appointment at Falmouth. He knew some of the artists living in St Ives personally, and the idea gradually formed in his mind that he would like to write a book about them. The year before he arrived Barbara Hepworth, Bryan Wynter and Roger Hilton had died, and Cross says that Terry Frost was among a number of artists who thought that, with the demise of these three prominent figures, St Ives was now finished, artistically. Cross realised, of course, that many artists were still living and working in the area, and would have clear recollections of earlier events. He reasoned that now was the time to make a record of what had occurred. Following in the footsteps of David Lewis and Sarah Fox Pitt, he began to make tape recordings of artists such as John Wells, Denis Mitchell, Patrick Heron and Wilhelmina Barns-Graham. Then he started to assemble the personal memoirs into a book.

Because of his college commitments, progress was slow. But in 1983, while he was taking a year's sabbatical in the United States, as a part-time teacher and visiting artist at Charleston College, University of South Carolina, he received a call from his Cornish-based publisher, Alison Hodge, asking for his book to be completed in three months' time![10] So *Painting the Warmth of the Sun* was written, published and launched without fanfare in a very short time. It reached the bookshops in October 1984, a few months before the St Ives exhibition opened at the Tate Gallery, and became an important complement to the show.

The illustrations for the book came about as a result of collaborating with the newly formed regional television company Television South West. When TSW applied for its franchise, it set up a number of advisory committees, one of which covered the arts. Tom Cross was asked to be a member. Each committee put forward projects to be included in the overall franchise bid. Cross suggested a film of his proposed book, and the idea was taken up. During the summer of 1983 a film crew, with Kevin Crooks as the producer, and assisted by Jonathan Harvey, TSW's art advisor, shot many hours of film of St Ives' artists and collectors, while 'off camera', Tom Cross conducted most of the interviews. Filming began with a party on the lawn of the Tregenna Castle Hotel for as many of the artists, their spouses and close friends as could be brought together, about two hundred in all. It was a very hot August day. Tom Cross remembers great friendships being resumed immediately, as well as old arguments and rivalries re-appearing.

The resulting three-hour film was narrated by Tim Pigott-Smith, who had become well known through his appearance in 'The Jewel in the Crown', TV's adaptation of Paul Scott's Colonial Indian epic. The programme was screened in three hour-long episodes, on Channel 4, in the early evenings of Easter Sunday, Monday and Tuesday 7, 8 and 9 April, 1985. It was, however, first shown at the Tate Gallery on 26, 28 and 29 March.[11]

Tom Cross came upon the unusual and apt title for his book and the film from a letter the painter John Wells had written to his friend Sven Berlin in 1948. Wells was describing to the sculptor his reasons for painting.

The morning air and the sea's blue light with points of diamond, and the gorse in-candescent beyond the trees; countless rocks ragged or round and of every colour; birds resting or flying, and the sense of a multitude of creatures living out their minute lives... But who can paint the warmth of the sun; the journey of a beetle across a rock?...All this is part of one's life and I want desperately to express it; not just what I see, but what I feel about it.

Not surprisingly, many of the visitors to the exhibitions at the Tate Gallery and elsewhere, readers of the book and viewers of the film, were to ask: 'But where can we see the works of these artists in St Ives?'

It was not quite true to say that there was no opportunity to see any of the work in St Ives, of course. The Barbara Hepworth Museum had been an important port of call for modern art lovers, from all over the world, since it opened in 1976.

10 Alison Hodge, who started publishing under her own imprint in 1979, has outlined her involvement with Tom Cross's book *Painting the Warmth of the Sun*. 'Tom Cross first approached me in early 1983. He had seen one of the earlier publications *Cornwall, Drawings and Photographs* by Peter Lanyon and Andrew Lanyon, and liked the production. He asked if I would be interested in doing a book on the St Ives artists. I had such a book in mind, so it was a happy meeting...'. (Letter to the author 29 November 1994)

11 The film 'Painting the Warmth of the Sun' was the most ambitious and lengthy arts programme ever made by TSW.

4 The Tate Gallery's First Outpost : The Barbara Hepworth Museum

There was one artist whose work had been easily accessible to the public, in St Ives, for a number of years before the Tate Gallery's exhibition in 1985. That artist was Barbara Hepworth. In April 1976 the 'Barbara Hepworth Museum', comprising the sculptor's studio and garden, opened to the public as a private museum funded by the artist's family. From this small beginning, St Ives would become the Tate Gallery's first outpost.

Barbara Hepworth acquired Trewyn Studio, with its secluded walled garden, in September 1949. She tells how she had always wondered what was on the other side of the high wall that rises up from Back Street and Barnoon Hill. The studio had originally been part of a large estate known as Trewyn, located higher up the hill on a site at which, in the eighteenth century, John Wesley had preached. A Georgian property originally built by Mr James Halse, a local solicitor, mine adventurer and politician, the grand house must have been a prominent landmark, surrounded as it was by fields and orchards. The mansion's first name was Halse's Court. In 1878 it became Brunswick House, because it stood at the top of what was then called Brunswick Place, later known as Richmond Place. At the end of the nineteenth century the house was acquired by the Trewhella family who gave it the name 'Trewyn' meaning 'the fair place' or 'the place of innocence'.

Mr William Trewhella made many alterations to the main property. Buildings at the foot of Barnoon Hill, perhaps an old stable block, were demolished in 1908, and he was able to incorporate the additional land into his garden. He then constructed a large retaining wall to prevent his newly acquired land from slipping down the hill. It is believed that in about 1910 he built a small house at the lower end of the garden for his children's use. It was this property that was to become Barbara Hepworth's house and studio.

For at least fifty years the estate remained in the ownership of the Trewhella family. After the Second World War, however, it came up for sale. St Ives Town Council considered compulsorily purchasing the main house and much of its extensive grounds, to make a large public car park on the site of the gardens. There were various uses proposed for the house itself, including a maternity home, a telephone exchange or even a museum and art gallery with a public open space in front. However, so many objections were made to the car parking scheme that a public inquiry was held. Early in 1948 the Inspector announced that he had refused the Council's application.

A decision was finally reached that benefitted everyone in the town. Soon after the Queen's Coronation in June 1953, a beautiful quiet public garden was opened. It had two entrances: one on Richmond Place and the other at the bottom of Bedford Road. A decade later St Ives' first housing scheme for elderly people was built on the derelict allotments that occupied the upper part of the land. Designed by Henry Gilbert, the complex contained sixteen flats.

The main house was purchased in 1957 by Professor Cosmo Rodevald of the University of Manchester. He suggested that his friend, John Milne, one of Barbara Hepworth's early assistants, might like to make use of it. The entire property, other than the self-contained flat whose entrance is in Ayr Lane, was handed over to Milne just over ten years later.

Barbara Hepworth purchased the small house in Barnoon Hill at an auction at the Palais de Danse (across the road from the property) on 16 September 1949.[1]

1 W H Lane & Sons auctioned Trewyn and the Studio at the Palais de Danse on 16 September 1949 in two lots. Lot 2 was described as a 'Stone-built studio, premises and garden (of particular interest to artists and others) 30ft 3in x 21ft 9in, having store and two w.c.'s underneath, with two separate entrances. Attractive front Rose Garden with lean-to Greenhouse and store.'

1

1 The completed block of sixteen flats for elderly people on the upper section of Trewyn Gardens, designed by Henry Gilbert, was officially opened in December 1964. The scheme was made possible through a bequest by Alderman William Craze, who was Mayor of St Ives in 1929, 1930 and 1934.

2 The building that once housed Captain Short's Navigation School and then became a carpenter's shop, seen from Ayr Lane. It was demolished in 1910 to make way for the Palais de Danse. The railings of the house next door (also demolished) can clearly be seen.

3 The Palais de Danse looking down Barnoon Hill towards the Parish Church, with its rusting sign and side entrance, in the early 1920s.

2

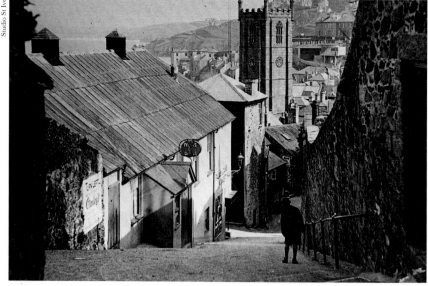

3

Brian Smith, who later became Curator of the Museum, remembers that its upper storey contained a billiard table. Alan Bowness recalls that 'the downstairs was a store with hooks on the ceiling, probably for hanging bacon and game etc.' The secluded land and workshops behind the house made the property very desirable for use as a sculptor's studio.

Sir Anthony Lousada, a former Chairman of the Tate Trustees, later recalled how Barbara Hepworth came to buy the property:

Encouraged by her old friend Marcus Brumwell, she went to the auction with a friend who was to bid for her. The friend asked what the bid was to be and she told him she would stop him when it got beyond her figure. The first bid was far beyond her figure and, apparently, she went pale green and fainted. So the bidding went on and she got the studio.

Before she moved into St Ives, Barbara Hepworth had worked in the front room of the house she and Ben Nicholson had rented in Carbis Bay, Chy an Kerris, since July 1942. According to Alan Bowness, when making her carvings, she used a shed in the garden. But space was limited, and Hepworth's growing reputation, which led to her being chosen to represent Great Britain at the Venice Biennale in 1950, meant that she needed more space to make much larger works. Trewyn Studio, with its pure white walls and sunlit rooms, served the sculptor's needs admirably, and there was now space for her to take on a succession of assistants, the first being Denis Mitchell, who had joined her when she still lived at Chy an Kerris.[2]

In 1951 Hepworth and Nicholson were divorced and Hepworth made Trewyn Studio her permanent home. Shortly afterwards, concerned at where their triplets would stay during school and later, college holidays, a small cottage on the other side of Barnoon Hill was purchased for their use. Barbara Hepworth lived and slept in the downstairs part of her house at this time, and used the upstairs as an indoor studio. The garden was planned, rebuilt and planted with the help of her great friend, the composer Priaulx Rainier. It was extended in 1968 when John Milne sold her a piece of land at the bottom of his garden, together with a small out-building, which had formerly been his studio, and which became known as 'the greenhouse'. The garden contained a number of sculptures.

In 1956 Barbara Hepworth began to work in bronze. Her son-in-law recalls:

this required a separate studio from the carving workshop (she also liked to separate stone and wood carving studios if she could). She began to work on a larger scale, and she began to get public commissions.

In order to cope with this increased workload she looked around for additional space.[3] In 1957 she took over the rental of the premises at 18 Fore Street, recently vacated by the Penwith Society of Arts, which conveniently had a back door close to her studio.

But even this additional space was eventually too small for Barbara Hepworth's needs. She was now creating works at least fifteen feet in height, one of which was to commemorate the achievements of her friend, the United Nations' late Director General, Dag Hammerskjold. She began to look for an appropriate studio where she could undertake this important and personal commission.[4]

By coincidence, across the road from Trewyn Studio stood the Palais de Danse, a building constructed before the First World War on the site of the old Navigation School, next to which had stood a large house with railings around it.

The Palais still brings back nostalgic memories to older St Ives residents. Many recall its dance hall with 'the best sprung maple floor in the south-west of England'. On Saturday nights young men, and women in their best taffeta dresses, would travel into the town from as far away as Penzance, to dance the night away to the

2 Barbara Hepworth's friend, the painter Misomé Piele, described the atmosphere of the new studio just before the works were sent to Italy, in *The St Ives Times* on 17 February 1950: 'The visit was paid about eleven o'clock at night, and the moonlight shone on a huge tarpauline-covered sculpture looming up in the garden. Inside and upstairs on the bare boards stood a number of carvings in wood and stone, reposeful, remote, yet seeming to spring to life from the roots in the floor.'

3 By the time Barbara Hepworth was working in bronze she was sleeping in her upstairs studio. This room continued to be her bedroom, sitting room and office.

4 The sculpture Barbara Hepworth made in memory of Dag Hammerskjold, 'Single Form', was placed outside the United Nations Secretariat Building in New York. It was unveiled in July 1964.

1

1 The top of Fore Street, near the Parish Church, in 1920 showing advertisements for the Mary Pickford film 'Suds' currently showing at the Barnoon Cinema (Palais de Danse) around the corner.

2 The interior of the Palais de Danse after it had been acquired by Barbara Hepworth in 1961. Behind the sculptor is the small stage; to the left is the door she had constructed to load her sculptures onto waiting lorries; to the right a glass door leads to an area that once contained the bar. The sprung maple floor 'the best dance floor in the west' can clearly be seen.

3 William Cecil Drage, the tenor who took over the Palais de Danse in 1925 and modernised it especially to accommodate concerts. Drage was also Manager of the Scala Cinema in High Street, and the Royal Cinema when it opened in Royal Square in 1939. The photograph shows the impresario when he was elected Mayor of St Ives in November 1941.

2

3

music of 'Jimmy Rickard's New Band'. And during the War, the girls' partners were not only the British Commandos stationed locally, but young American soldiers from the 29th Division billeted in hotels and guest houses in the area, and waiting to take their part in the D-Day landings. It was a poignant time, the great majority of the young Americans would never return from France.

But residents of the town, now in their late eighties, also remember the building as St Ives' second cinema, the Scala in the High Street being the first. Such was the popularity of this novel entertainment in the early part of the century, that the silent films at both venues, accompanied by the obligatory piano, changed twice a week. Mr Roland Hill was the first manager of what was originally called the Barnoon Cinema. Jane Mitchell remembers him standing at the entrance to the building, which was then half way up the hill, with pennies in his hands. He personally collected the money from the children who, on Saturdays in 1922, paid two and a half pence to occupy the long wooden benches near the screen. An advertisement at the beginning of that year in *The St Ives Times* proudly proclaimed: 'In the interests of public health this theatre is disinfected daily with Jeyes Fluid'. Joseph Plummer, who was hired to operate the projector in 1920, remembers that the electricity for the equipment was powered by a town gas engine.

Neither of the town's cinemas appears to have been run very efficiently. In May 1925, both establishments were taken over by an impresario and, by all accounts, fine tenor, Cecil Drage, who began to organise orchestral concerts at the Palais. These appear to have been very well attended, perhaps because he made good use of the advertising facilities in *The St Ives Times*.[5]

As well as holding regular concerts and dances in peace and war (Borlase Smart compèred a Vaudeville in aid of the Local Ambulance Division in March 1940) the Palais became a venue for public meetings; political gatherings being particularly popular.[6]

In the winter months during the 1930s, the Conservative Club made arrangements with Mr Drage to use the Palais for meetings, pantomimes and dances. In 1934 the group had two full-sized billiards tables installed upstairs. The meeting place, run by Borlase Smart, was called 'The Constitution Club' because the Conservatives wished to encourage a greater use of its facilities. Joseph Plummer became the Club's caretaker.

For a while the Palais' popularity waned. By 1939 it no longer showed films, as in the July of that year 'St Ives New Super Cinema', the Royal, opened in Royal Square, not far from the Public Library. There was competition, too, from the newly built 'Guildhall' in Street-an-Pol which, from 1939, provided a large luxurious space for dancing.[7] Both venues, however, were popular places of entertainment during the War, but afterwards, there was little call for the two amenities.[8] In the early 1950s, under its new manager Mr Garfield Daniel, who also owned the Scala and the Royal cinemas and was the tenant of Porthminster Beach,[9] the Palais was modernised and its facilities improved. For a while dancing became a popular pastime again.

Despite this modernisation, however, the Palais ceased to be viable as a dance hall, probably due to the growth of television. During the 1950s the ballroom was used by both Lanhams in St Ives and Lanes in Penzance for auctioning properties. Dancing still occasionally took place there nevertheless and, in 1960, the Penwith Society of Arts hired the space for an 'Artists' Hop' to raise money for their new premises on Back Road West.

At the beginning of the 1960s, Barbara Hepworth made it known that she was afraid she would have to leave St Ives if she could not find a suitable place for her newest large sculptures. The Palais across the street suited her purposes perfectly.

5 Cecil Drage took over from the Palais' second owner, Mr. G. Ramsey. By the spring of 1926, he had completely renovated the building, providing a balcony at one end and excellent amenities for visiting musicians. Later Mr Drage became a local councillor and then in 1941-42 had the honour of becoming the first Mayor of the Borough who had been born outside the area. He died in California in 1972 at the age of 81.

6 Some of the public meetings held at the Palais included a rally in 1936 of the 'Blackshirts'. In 1946 the United Nations Association hosted a discussion on the subject 'The United Nations and our peace'. (Barbara Hepworth made a large sculpture for the UN in the Palais - see Note (4).) And in 1959 the St Ives Group of the Campaign for Nuclear Disarmament hosted a talk entitled: 'What would happen if an H-Bomb fell on Devon?'

7 The Palais, unexpectedly, became a ballet school in the early years of the War. According to Wendy Guthrie, the renowned dancer and teacher, Phyllis Bedells, in an attempt to find a beautiful, safe and quiet haven from the London blitz, moved to St Ives with her students. She installed full length mirrors and barres around the walls of the Palais, and her students practised for six hours a day, seven days a week for the next three of four years.

8 The Palais later had an advantage over The Guildhall when it obtained a drinks licence.

9 Ownership of all these amenities meant that Mr Garfield Daniel could make a living whether summer holidays were wet or fine!

1

1 The upper floor of the Barbara
Hepworth Museum looking out into the
secluded garden. Just visible through the
window on the left is the Parish Church.

3

2 The semi-tropical garden of the Barbara
Hepworth Museum, showing a number of
the sculptor's larger works.

3 Sir Norman Reid on the occasion of the
opening of the Barbara Hepworth Museum
in April 1976. On that day Sir Norman,
who was not only a Trustee of the Barbara
Hepworth Estate, but also Director of the
Tate Gallery, opened the Penwith Gallery's
extension on Back Road West.

2

By now Mr Garfield Daniel was anxious to dispose of his property, and so the sculptor's suggestion to acquire it came at an opportune time.

After purchasing the building in 1961, Barbara Hepworth retained the interior fittings: the sprung floor, balcony and projection room, small stage, bar, kitchen and cloakrooms. She painted the walls white and later enlarged the door onto Barnoon Hill so that her biggest sculptures could be loaded straight onto waiting lorries for delivery to various parts of the country, or perhaps the world. It is likely that the traffic would have been held up for some considerable time while such operations were taking place. Alan Bowness remembers that she 'had a good relationship with the police in St Ives, who were very understanding.'

Other rooms, and a yard at the side of the Palais, were used by Barbara Hepworth and her assistants for storage and packing, and there was ample space to park her car. A 'studio warming party' was held in April 1961. From then on a growing number of influential and interested clients travelled considerable distances to see the growing collection of Hepworth's work in their very spacious surroundings.

Barbara Hepworth was created a DBE in 1965 and received the Freedom of St Ives in 1968, together with Bernard Leach. She began to plan for the future. A press release and information sheet issued by the executors of her estate on 22 March 1976, said that in her will she had asked her executors to consider 'the practicality of establishing a permanent exhibition of some of my works in Trewyn Studio and its garden.' She envisaged 'small sculptures, carvings and drawings...on the first floor...my working studio being shown as closely as possible as it has been in my lifetime...and a few large works...in the garden.' Her son-in-law had suggested that the family should try to turn the studio into 'a little museum' which could be set up and then given to the Tate Gallery.

Barbara Hepworth died tragically on 20 May 1975, at the age of 72, in a fire at her studio. Very soon afterwards arrangements were made to put her wishes into effect.

Two of the executors of Dame Barbara's estate had close links with the Tate Gallery. Sir Norman Reid had been its Director since 1964, and was a regular visitor to St Ives in his additional capacities as a Trustee of the Porthmeor Studios and President of the Penwith Society of Arts. Sir Anthony Lousada was a former Chairman of the Trustees of the Tate Gallery and Dame Barbara's legal adviser. The other two Trustees were David Jenkins of Touche Ross, Chartered Accountants, who had been Dame Barbara's financial adviser, and Alan Bowness, the sculptor's son-in-law through marriage to Sarah, one of the Nicholson/Hepworth triplets.[10] Immediately after the sculptor's death, Alan Bowness began the work that would transform the damaged house and its contents into a small museum.

On 15 January 1976, Sir Norman Reid told the Tate Gallery's Trustees of Dame Barbara's wishes. He informed them that the studio contained at least twelve works, and the garden contained fifteen bronzes and three or four stone carvings. He must have already hoped that the studio and garden might be taken over by the Tate Gallery, as the Department of the Environment had already looked at the property with a view to itself becoming responsible for the buildings.[11] However, it was calculated that to be properly administered, the museum would need a staff of four. The Tate Trustees were enthusiastic about the idea in principle, but were cautious about putting the idea into practice. Although willing to take over responsibility for the works of art, they felt that, without extra funding from the Department of Education and Science, they were not in a position to provide the money to pay for staffing. They were also not happy about binding future Trustees to keep the museum open in perpetuity.

In the event, the DES declined to come up with the additional funds required,

10 Alan Bowness had met Sarah Nicholson in 1956, when he had come to see Barbara Hepworth in his capacity as Arts Officer for the South West region of the Arts Council. Based in London he made regular visits to the area. He had known St Ives as a child, however, visiting the town in 1934 and later in 1948. At the same time as Alan Bowness married Sarah, in July 1957, he left the Arts Council for a lectureship at the Courtauld Institute. The couple made regular holiday visits to St Ives, shortly buying a property there.

11 In the 1970s no national museum looked after its own buildings, neither was it the practice to have outstations.

1

2

3

1 One of Barbara Hepworth's workshops, preserved as it was on the day of her death in 1975. The overalls of her assistants hang on the door.

2 A recent photograph of the Palais de Danse looking towards the main entrance. (Compare with the photograph on page 42.) The wall of the Barbara Hepworth Museum is on the right.

3 A recent photograph of the Palais de Danse looking down Barnoon Hill towards the Parish Church. (Compare with the photograph on page 42.)

4 Exterior of the Barbara Hepworth Museum looking down Barnoon Hill.

5 The Barbara Hepworth Museum was formally handed over to the Tate Gallery on 3 October 1980. Sir John Nott (MP for St Ives - far left) accepted the Museum on behalf of the nation from Sir Anthony Lousada, one of the Trustees of the Hepworth Estate. Next to him stands Lord Hutchinson, Chairman of the Tate Gallery Trustees and Alan Bowness (by that date, Director of the Tate Gallery), Roy Ray and Linden Holman.

4

5

and the family decided to open the house and garden to the public at their own expense until they felt it was properly established.

The opening ceremony took place on the afternoon of 10 April 1976. A report in *The St Ives Times & Echo* of 16 April said:

Months of careful preparation have produced one of the most beautiful and evocative museums of its kind in Britain...The opening ceremony was in the garden which perfect spring weather made it look at its best...Sir Norman Reid said: 'In spite of [the] complete lack of government support we have gone ahead in the belief that attendances at Barbara Hepworth's Museum will demonstrate more vividly than any other argument what a valuable addition it is to the amenities of this part of England. I speak as an interested party in more ways than one because the intention was that the works here should form part of the national collection at the Tate and, in fact, the works were chosen specifically to complement the splendid collection we already have of Dame Barbara's work in London. The arrangements which we envisaged would have enabled loans and exchanges to take place between St Ives and London greatly to the benefit of both, but particularly, I think to St Ives. We hope that if we raise the question of Government support again in a year or two's time we may get a rather warmer response.'

The executors' idea was to try to 'reconstruct something of the feeling Trewyn Studio had in the 1950s'. Alan Bowness himself planned and created the museum, with approval from Sir Norman Reid. Work was chosen that complemented that already owned by the Tate Gallery. Alan Bowness remembers:

We chose a representative group of work from what was left in the Estate, with particular attention to a wide chronological span from early work to late, and to a good range of different materials.

The upstairs room, which had become Dame Barbara's sitting room and bedroom later in her life, contained some of her furniture, together with wood and stone carvings. Alan Bowness again recalls:

The upstairs room and all its contents were blackened by fire and I wanted to make it the plain white space that it had been in the 1950s when I first visited Barbara.

A door led directly into the garden, which had been planted with red and white roses, white tulips and blue cineraria. The garden contained a number of bronzes as well as a few large stone carvings.

The workshops were left in the same condition as on the day she had died, with unfinished works, tools, and her assistants' overalls hanging on their pegs. Everything looked as though, at any moment, she might walk through the door and pick up where she had left off. However, to give the public a sense of the personality of the museum's owner, downstairs the kitchen and bathroom were taken out and five showcases were installed, inside which letters, photographs and memorabilia were carefully displayed to give the visitor a chronological account of Dame Barbara's life, work and ideas without verbal explanation.[12]

Brian Smith was appointed, under Alan Bowness' Directorship, to take over the running of the museum. Brian Smith had for some time lived in St Ives and began to work for Dame Barbara at the time of her Tate Gallery Retrospective exhibition in 1968. When the sculptor's secretary, Miss Moir, retired in 1974, he took over responsibility for her correspondence.

The other three staff also kept their jobs: George Wilkinson, Jackie Watson and the odd-job man Jim Peters. The museum opened its doors to the general public charging '50p (25p for children, students and OAP's)'. It became a quiet haven devoted to the achievements of one person, amidst the bustle of a busy seaside town and was an immediate success. In its first twelve months, it received over 14,000 visitors.

12 The showcases in the downstairs room were borrowed from the Arts Council.

Alan Bowness sought the support of the local community. He wrote a letter to *The St Ives Times & Echo* on April 9, 1976:

...Mr Brian Smith, the curator, would be happy to hear from anyone who could give an hour or two each week to invigilate in the museum, especially during the summer months... Mr Smith would be pleased to give you a free tour of the museum, if you call in at a time when he's not too busy.

Sir Norman Reid would not let the matter of ownership rest, however, and he actively sought support for the Museum to come under the Tate Gallery's control as soon as finances permitted. Alan Bowness reported, perhaps optimistically, that running costs were around £18,000 a year, and that income from entrance charges amounted to around £10,000 a year, for he recalls now that the figures were probably more in the region of £20,000 and £6,000 - £8,000 respectively. The relatively small shortfall was not forthcoming from any government source, although Sir Norman did receive a luke-warm response from the Department of Education and Science in November of 1978:

We would have no policy objection to the Tate's taking [the Barbara Hepworth Museum] as an outstation - indeed there would be a lot to be said for it as helping to demonstrate the Government's concern to promote the arts in the regions - if the resources could be found... I realise that to acquire such a valuable collection is an attractive proposition and I think one should try to find the necessary resources, if not in 1979/80, then in a subsequent year.

At the same time Alan Bowness, who without success was looking for other organisations who might like to take on the running of the Museum (such as the National Trust), now set out clearly the terms under which any transfer would have to be made: that it remain substantially the same in presentation and appearance; that the collection could not be moved to London; and that Brian Smith be retained as Curator, directly responsible to the Director.

1979 brought a change of government and a new Minister for the Arts, Norman St John Stevas. Sir Norman Reid lost no time in putting forward his plans. He wrote to the Minister on 18 May of that year, ending his letter:

It occurred to me that a positive decision in this matter [giving the Tate Gallery an extra £18,000] coming at the beginning of your ministry, would be a splendid augury for a whole new attitude to the arts on the part of the government.

Alas, St John Stevas had nothing to offer either.

By the summer of 1979 matters had come to a head. Sir Norman Reid was conscious of the fact that his term of office at the Tate Gallery was coming to an end, and that Alan Bowness had been appointed to succeed him from 1 January 1980. Sir Norman was anxious to use his dual role as Director and executor of Dame Barbara's estate to greatest advantage in the time left to him. Suddenly a timely offer of financial assistance from a Tate Trustee in a personal capacity, amounting to £8,000 for the first year's operation, gave him the impetus he needed to push ahead with plans. In fact, due to a number of reasons, this financial help was never to materialise, but it acted as a catalyst to the Trustees, some of whom were probably still less than convinced that the Tate Gallery should open a small outstation three hundred miles from London.

Sir Norman Reid believed that it was now time to 'take a leap in the dark'. He felt confident enough to write to his fellow executor, Sir Anthony Lousada, late in 1979, that the Trustees:

would like to take up the offer made some time ago by the Trustees of the Dame Barbara Hepworth Museum to present the house and gardens at Trewyn and some of the sculptures they contain as a gift to the nation...We have had a word with the DoE who have expressed their willingness to accept responsibility for the building and the garden...[13]

13 When the plans to transfer the Museum to the Tate Gallery were made public, because of Alan Bowness' impending appointment, there were accusations of nepotism in the national press. Sir Norman Reid handled this with great diplomacy.

Arrangements were slower to put into practice than had been hoped. The Museum was not finally handed over to the Tate Gallery until 3 October 1980, almost a year after Sir Norman's retirement.

In the garden, where the transfer ceremony took place, the Government was represented by the Member of Parliament for St Ives, The Rt. Hon. John Nott. The Trustees of the Estate were represented by Sir Anthony Lousada, Sir Norman Reid, and Alan Bowness in his dual role.

The St Ives Times & Echo of October 10 began its report by announcing that:

A St Ives museum was given national status on Friday afternoon last week...Accepting the gift of the museum, Mr Nott said its future was now assured as a permanent national artistic presence in St Ives. It would be an integral part of the Tate Gallery - its first establishment outside London.

The report continued with the speech of the then current Chairman of the Tate Trustees, Lord Hutchinson. He pointed out that the remarkable museum would be the first outstation of the Tate. Lord Bullock, his predecessor, had spoken of the possibility of a Tate in the North. 'Here is the reality of a Tate in the South West', he announced, and he hoped the occasion marked the beginning of a close and lasting relationship between the Tate at Millbank and St Ives.[14]

Over the next few years Alan Bowness remembers visitors to the Barbara Hepworth Museum asking: 'We have loved seeing the sculptures, but where can we see St Ives painting - especially Ben Nicholson?'

With the success of the new Museum and the Tate Gallery's 'St Ives' exhibition in 1985, there was now, more than ever, a reason for showing a wider range of work in the area in which it had been created. The possibility of making this a reality came one year after the London show, and from rather unexpected sources.

14 Alan Bowness recalls that it was on the occasion when the Barbara Hepworth Museum was handed over to the Tate Gallery that the first public announcement was made about the plans for what would become Tate Gallery Liverpool. (See Chapter 18 - Links with Millbank, Liverpool, Kettle's Yard and Orkney).

1 Martin Rewcastle, Director of South West Arts from 1984 to 1990. It was he who approached Cornwall County Council in the summer of 1986 with the proposition that if the County Council could find a suitable building, Alan Bowness had promised that the Tate Gallery would loan its collection of St Ives paintings and sculpture for local display.

2 Councillor Doris Ansari was Chairman of the County's Policy Committee when the idea was put forward for a gallery. She believed that such an amenity would greatly improve the economy of the area.

Martin Rewcastle

1

3 Councillor John Hurst was Chairman of the County's Library and Arts Committee when he heard about the idea of a gallery for the area. He believed that cultural tourism was vital for improving the number of holiday makers to west Cornwall.

4 Cornwall County Council moved to its present prominent location, with rural views, in 1966. Designed by the County Architect's Department, it replaced Old County Hall in Station Road, Truro, where it had been since 14 August 1912.

Cornwall County Council

2

Leighton Gibbins ARPS

Cornwall County Council

3

4

52

5 Plans For A Public Gallery : May 1986 - May 1988

While both curators and makers of art searched for ways of bringing the works of the St Ives artists to a wider audience, there were different, yet parallel activities taking place in the South West. In the summer of 1986 the idea that the arts might be used as a significant cultural resource to improve the flagging economy of the area was put forward. Over the next two years these endeavours became more focussed, and by the summer of 1988 a permanent gallery in St Ives became a serious possibility.

In 1984 a report was prepared by South West Arts entitled *A Survey of the Arts in the South West*. This important consultative document outlined the availability of the visual arts, music, craft, poetry, and dance, county by county. It also detailed the way each local authority currently financially supported its artistic communities.

The Survey was initiated by the recently appointed Director of South West Arts, Martin Rewcastle. Rewcastle came to Cornwall after having been Education and Community Officer, and then Development Director at the Whitechapel Art Gallery in London. Under the directorship of Nicholas Serota since 1976, the Whitechapel was the first gallery in the independent system to employ an Education Officer.

Martin Rewcastle took up his new position shortly after Luke Ritner had been appointed Director of the Arts Council in London. Probably best known for *The Glory of the Garden*, Luke Ritner outlined in that document his future plans for the arts:

[a desire to create] a fairer balance of funding between London and the provinces; greater access outside London to metropolitan standards...and to a new sense of partnership among the organisations concerned with the arts, and especially between the Council itself and the Regional Arts Associations of which the Council sees new and enhanced functions.

Martin Rewcastle wanted to prove to the Arts Council that the South West was already giving serious thought to these matters. *The Survey of the Arts in the South West* was the result. Mostly written by Diana Johnson, Martin Rewcastle personally put together the section on the visual arts.

One of the Survey's findings was that:

Apart from the Isle of Wight, in 1983/4 Cornwall had the lowest local authority expenditure on cultural facilities in the country.

Moreover, Cornwall had no county policy for the arts, neither did it possess an Arts Officer. The Survey continued:

Although traditionally Cornwall has attracted artists, writers, craftworkers - and its tourist reputation partly rests on this - actual facilities for the arts are very scarce.

When the visual arts were looked at in particular, Rewcastle wrote:

There is a terrible irony that - apart from the Hepworth Museum now run by the Tate Gallery - there is nowhere in Cornwall to celebrate its extraordinary legacy.

The twentieth century, he observed, had produced two Cornish 'schools' of painting - Newlyn on the south coast, St Ives on the north.

Such a museum [that showed these works] could be a popular tourist asset, reinforcing the historic importance of the west of England as a force in the visual arts.

The new Director of South West Arts was no stranger to West Cornwall's artistic heritage. In the 1970s he had worked for the influential arts magazine *Studio International*; he had been a good friend of David Brown who had curated the 'St Ives' exhibition at the Tate Gallery in 1985; and he had been aware of the influence of Herbert Read, both as a writer and educator, and remembered that he had been Chairman of the Penwith Society of Arts in its early years. Most importantly, Rewcastle, like Tom Cross, knew that there were works of art from St Ives in the Tate Gallery's collection that had been acquired over a number of years, especially during the time of Sir Norman Reid's directorship. Rarely shown, they were held in the various stores owned by the Tate Gallery. In 1989, Simon Parker gave a graphic account of the way the Tate Gallery's works were kept at Millbank. In an article for the *Western Morning News* of 29 September, he wrote:

Descending the long staircase to the Tate's storage vaults beneath the great gallery's Pimlico premises is something like entering a mortuary to identify the body of a friend...heavy grey metal screens...stand in rows reaching 20 ft. to the ceiling. And there, against each uncomfortable steel mesh, lie anything between five and a dozen paintings. Moments of inspiration and intense passion inelegantly lying in state in their last resting place...Despite its record of taking the art to the people, just one in five of the Tate's total canvases are on show at any one time in the exhibitions in London and at the Tate of the North in Liverpool.

The 1984 Survey from South West Arts was widely circulated. At Cornwall County Council it arrived at the office of the Deputy County Planning Officer, Ian Martin, whose brief included tourism and economic development. Instead of dismissing its criticisms of the county Ian Martin immediately discussed the report's findings with Martin Rewcastle. They agreed to jointly commission a study that would look closely at every aspect of the arts in Cornwall.

Prepared by Ronald Perry, Patricia Noble and Susan Howe from Cornwall College in Redruth, and published in 1985, this second influential report had as its title *The Economic Influence of the Arts and Crafts in Cornwall*. The report noted:

When politicians and planners have, in the past, produced local policies to increase jobs they have ignored the economic potential of the artistic sector. Small businesses in the arts and crafts, unlike big corporations are environmentally acceptable, even desirable, they do not use much energy...and are high value-added.

Over a number of years, Cornwall's tourism had steadily declined. This was of concern to the County Council, and was the reason why the Planning Department, particularly, took such an interest in the findings of the report.

Recent surveys showed that the number of visitors coming to the far west of England for their traditional fortnight's holiday was in decline; it was becoming cheaper to travel to destinations like Spain, which could also guarantee the sun. The increasing popularity of the motor car over rail made visitors more mobile and less likely to stay in one place if the weather was fickle. Between 1978 and 1983, Ronald Perry's report confirmed that peak holiday demand in the popular coastal resorts fell by 8%.

At the same time there was a decline in the agricultural industry. During the 1970s farms were amalgamated and mechanised requiring a smaller labour force. Cornwall's small industrial base, too, was receding. Traditional industrial areas such as Camborne and Redruth were shrinking, and the tin mining industry, once such an important part of the county's economy, had nearly ceased to exist. The report concluded:

What Cornwall needs...is not more visitors but bigger spenders. Its unique arts and crafts ambiance could be channelled towards the higher-value-added visitor.

The authors, at the same time, singled out the fact that exhibitions of works by both the Newlyn and St Ives artists were very well attended by non-Cornish and overseas visitors, whether held in Cornwall or London.

The findings of *The Economic Influence of the Arts and Crafts in Cornwall* was discussed on 22 May 1986 at County Hall with, amongst others, Ian Martin, Martin Rewcastle and Councillor John Hurst, then Chairman of the Libraries and Arts Committee. Martin Rewcastle now brought the strands together from both surveys and suggested that one way of achieving their aims might be to approach the Tate Gallery with a view to their exhibiting the Cornish works they owned in the county.

Rewcastle wasted no time journeying to London to put his ideas to Alan Bowness. The two men talked for about an hour. Bowness confirmed the fact that a large number of works had to be in store at the Tate. He said that he would be very willing to recommend to the Tate Trustees that appropriate works be lent to a suitable art museum, should one be built. He also confessed that he was concerned about the future of the Hepworth Museum. Its isolation from London and the comparatively small number of people it could attract, because of its size, made it relatively expensive to run as an outstation. There was, however, no possible way that the Tate Gallery might involve itself in funding any further venture in Cornwall. At that time particularly, the energies of the Trustees were directed towards the setting up of Tate Gallery Liverpool, due to open in 1988. But Bowness recognised that the Barbara Hepworth Museum might take on a greater importance if it could be seen in a wider artistic context.

Rewcastle returned to the County Council on 25 June 1986, only one month after his original meeting, and put forward a proposition to a number of councillors and officers. He said that if a suitable building could be found, preferably in St Ives, the Tate Gallery's Trustees would be prepared to loan the works that had been created in the area and which were not readily available to the general public. The building was not to cost the Tate Gallery anything. However, the County Council would have to ensure that it complied with the correct security and invigilation regulations in order that the works could be insured under national indemnity requirements; that is, by the government.[1]

Ian Martin has estimated that only one project in ten, proposed to local authorities, makes it to completion. Why then should this proposal succeed when many other, less complex and expensive projects, have fallen by the wayside? Linden Holman who, with her late husband James Holman (the founder of Holman Bros. of Camborne), had lived in St Ives for many years, has said that Bernard Leach once remarked: 'You need a good idea and a good man'. The plan for a gallery had a great deal to commend it. However, the enthusiasm and confidence of the people who saw the project through its gestation period was vital if the gallery was to become a formal County Council project, under the kind of leadership that Bernard Leach might have had in mind.

Martin Rewcastle and Alan Bowness were the first prime movers, but without strong early support from the County Council the gallery would never have got past the first few hurdles. Amongst its officers Ian Martin was the right person to take up the proposal. He had joined the County Council in 1982, after being Assistant County Planning Officer for Clwyd County Council in North Wales. Part of that job was to take tourism up-market. When in the mid-70s a piece of derelict land became available in the small market town of Ruthin, it was decided to develop a craft centre there. Ian Martin was the officer responsible for its design and set it up. With funding from Europe, the Welsh Office, the Wales Tourist Board and local sources, he staffed the centre, set up the craft units, coffee shop and car park, and then, for nearly two years, managed it.

1 Insuring works of art under national indemnity requirements was vital. It would remove the insurance burden from the County Council.

When Ian Martin moved to Cornwall, tourism was not part of the Planning Department's remit. Because of his background, however, that function was transferred from the office of the Chief Executive to Planning in 1986. He was therefore particularly responsive to Martin Rewcastle's proposal. Both men realised that for the project to get off the ground and win approval from the county councillors, the gallery must be designated a tourism rather than an arts project. An important gallery of this kind would increase cultural tourism in Cornwall and would thus be of significant economic benefit to the area.[2]

Those who attended that June meeting were made even more aware of West Cornwall's declining industry; the impending closure of Geevor tin mine at Pendeen, which employed three hundred men, had become a well publicised tragedy, both in terms of the loss of jobs in the St Just area, and the loss of pride for those associated with a unique way of life. A potent link with a tradition stretching back to the sixteenth century was shortly to go for ever.

From the moment Ian Martin took up the idea of a gallery he was able to 'sell' it to his colleagues. As luck would have it, two enthusiastic councillors, John Hurst and Doris Ansari, were in influential positions to personally support the project, as well as to persuade other councillors to do the same over the months ahead.

John Hurst was first elected to the County Council in 1981, and became a member of the new small Liberal Democrat group in a council that still operated with a large number of Independents. From the beginning, his interest in music and the visual arts, coupled with his experience as a Lecturer of English at Exeter University, made him particularly conscious of the County Council's under-developed commitment to the arts. The Liberal Democrats, as party policy, encouraged a greater involvement in this area.[3]

In the 1985 election, the Liberal Democrats increased their numbers at County Hall to about thirty-one and, in fact, found themselves in the position of being the largest single group in the Council. Arrangements were made with the next largest group, the Independents, to share the Chairs and Vice Chairs of each of the Committees. John Hurst himself became the first Chairman of the newly formed Libraries and Arts Committee, and he also became Deputy Leader of the Liberal Democrats.

Hurst was asked to join the South West Arts Management Committee, the Chairman of which was Martin Rewcastle. In this capacity he assisted in formulating South West Arts policy. As a result of these changed circumstances, the Libraries and Arts Committee steadily raised the County Council's annual expenditure on grant aid for the arts from a low of £18,000 in 1985. Just as importantly, the County began to develop an arts strategy.

John Hurst's policital colleague, Doris Ansari, had been a member of Truro City Council since 1971. A life-long Liberal, she was elected onto Carrick District Council at the time of government reorganisation in 1974, and then in 1983 joined the County Council as a Liberal Democrat. For a short time she represented Truro in all three capacities.

Doris Ansari's major interest and strength, in her public life, had always been the economic development possibilities for Cornwall. These she continually pursued, believing them to be inextricably linked with tourism. And in spite of having no background in the visual arts, she believed that their development was as important as creating factory premises or manufacturing a product.

Appointed Chairman of the County Council's Planning and Employment Committee in 1984, Doris Ansari assisted in maintaining strong links with Europe, becoming a member of both the Council for Peripheral Maritime Regions and the Assembly of European Regions. She was in regular contact, too, with the European Commissioners in Brussels.

2 There were others looking at the same problem. An article on the front page of *The St Ives Times & Echo* dated 28 November, 1986 reported that Dr Alan Williams, an Exeter University don, who with his colleague Dr Gareth Shaw had been researching the economics of Cornish tourism for the English Tourist Board and the Development Commission, had concluded that 'The County needs major and permanent tourist attractions - such as a national fine arts collection in St Ives'.

3 Not long after John Hurst joined the County Council it was agreed to add responsibility for the Arts to the work of the Libraries Committee.

At the June meeting, which was attended, amongst others, by Ian Martin, St Ives Councillor Oakley Eddy and the Arts and Libraries Officer, John Farmer, the suggestion was made that an empty building in St Ives, which currently belonged to the County Council, might possibly convert into a gallery: the former primary school on The Stennack.

Financing was also discussed. Martin Rewcastle explained that South West Arts would be unable to assist with this because it had no budget for capital projects. However there was a small fund which could pay for feasibility studies. An alternative source of funding, it was pointed out, might be Europe.

On 18 August Martin Rewcastle, Alan Bowness, Patrick Heron and John Halkes, then Director of Newlyn Orion Gallery, visited the Stennack School. It had been empty for about two years, and the building was not in very good condition.[4] The consensus was that, although the school was not ideal for use as a gallery, the rooms were serviceable without major architectural modifications, and it had good car parking facilities.

South West Arts commissioned the architectural firm of Colquhoun and Miller to estimate roughly how much it would cost to convert the old school into a gallery. Martin Rewcastle chose Colquhoun and Miller because he had known one of the practice's partners, John Miller, from his days at the Whitechapel. John Miller, in his turn, knew Cornwall well, as did his wife Su. As the daughter of Marcus and Renée Brumwell,[5] she had spent her childhood at Feock, near Truro. The couple also had connections with the Tate Gallery and they were on friendly terms with Alan Bowness.

After John and Su Miller's visit to the school they prepared a brief report which estimated that it would cost around £1.2 million to convert - £975,000 for building work and £156,000 for fees, plus VAT. As far as Ian Martin and his colleagues were concerned this comparatively low figure put a conversion into the realms of possibility, and was certainly less expensive than constructing a new building.

In September 1986 Alan Bowness formally put the idea to the Tate Gallery Trustees. He pointed out to them that 'without a promise of Tate support, it was unlikely that the County Council would pursue the scheme'. Happily the Trustees 'warmly endorsed' the proposal that a loan of works should be forthcoming. But they made it clear that they did not want the project to be called 'The Tate of the West' despite the fact that the gallery at Liverpool (a Tate-inspired project) had been known, for a number of years, as 'The Tate in the North'.

Cornwall County Council had been actively attempting to sell the school that summer in order to capitalise on its now redundant property. Despite its value as a possible art gallery, the decision was taken not to take it off the market,[6] and in the autumn of 1986 the school was sold.

The proposition was not consigned to the waste-paper basket, however. Such was the enthusiasm of Martin Rewcastle and Ian Martin for the idea of an art gallery in principle, that they kept the embryo project alive throughout the next eighteen months. Regular meetings were held by those who were interested in pursuing the scheme, particularly the Chairmen of the Planning and Employment, Arts and Libraries and Tourism Committees, but Doris Ansari recalls that 'no-one knew what to do with the animal; we could not get our minds around how to progress it to get something sold to the Council'.

There was enthusiasm from other quarters. John Moore, the Chief Executive of Penwith District Council, the local authority covering the St Ives and Penzance area, took a particular interest in the project. And on 16 April 1987, Alan Bowness during one of his regular visits to Cornwall spoke to a number of officers and councillors at an informal lunch meeting at County Hall. John Hurst believes that this was a significant occasion. It suddenly gave the project a greater credibility in

4 Martin Rewcastle remembers the Stennack School being full of very aggressive seagulls who had become used to bringing up their young in peace, and who dive-bombed any unwelcome visitors.

5 Marcus Brumwell had been Chairman of the Penwith Society of Arts in the 1970s (See Chapter 2).

6 In the summer of 1988 the idea of having a gallery was, of course, only a general idea, discussed by a relatively small number of people. It was clear that it would take some time for funds to be allocated for conversion purposes; so to publicly hold on to the school, and miss a lucrative sale, might have been an embarrassment for the County.

the eyes of many of the senior people in the Council. On the Tate Gallery Director's part, Alan Bowness remembers that he felt: 'I was able to leave the Tate in September 1988 feeling confident about the future in St Ives'.

Despite this confidence, Ian Martin was concerned, not without reason, that with the Tate Gallery Director's term of office coming to an end during 1988, it was vital to keep the momentum going. Alan Bowness' successor, as yet unknown, might have no interest at all in taking on a commitment in Cornwall. More decisive action needed to be taken, therefore, if the scheme was to be pursued.

The way forward was to set up a working party within the County Council to look into the project further, and investigate financing, but no action was immediately taken to do this.[7]

In the wider political arena, there was some cause for optimism. The latest Conservative Party manifesto had announced that the nation should make its treasures available throughout the country. With this in mind, Martin Rewcastle organised for the then Arts Minister, Richard Luce, to meet County Council officers and councillors and talk about government indemnity. The Minister showed great interest in the project, and saw that Cornwall was one area of the country where an attempt was being made to put its manifesto into practice. At the same time, Ian Martin was aware that here was a project which could be funded jointly by both the public and private sectors, another policy being pursued at the time by the Conservative Party.

In 1988 the project developed an impetus. Martin Rewcastle was taking a number of initiatives. He identified several national figures who had homes or interests in the St Ives area and who, he believed, might be favourable to the idea of a gallery and give it high profile support. And on learning that the Tate Gallery's Director-designate was to be Nicholas Serota, his previous boss at the Whitechapel, Rewcastle immediately alerted him to the project and got his 'wholehearted support'.

The Assistant County Treasurer, Jo Jacques, for his part, prepared a report for the Budget Working Party, 'A Proposal for capital allocation to assist in the funding of a major art gallery and tourist attraction in Cornwall'. The report even at this early date anticipated that the project would create seven full-time and forty indirect jobs.

At this crucial moment the Stennack School appeared on the scene a second time. Its owner had not been able to use the building for any of the purposes he had been considering, such as studios or residential units. His many business commitments made plans difficult to put into effect. He heard that there was a possibility of turning the school into an art gallery and, believing this to be a good idea, decided to put the building back on the market, hopefully, for the County Council to re-acquire.

This action brought the idea for a gallery into the public arena for the first time. *The St Ives Times & Echo* announced on 22 April 1988: 'Tate of the West for St Ives is suggested...the Stennack School...has been identified as a possible site.'

Meanwhile, as a result of the earlier discussions between the Planning, Tourism and Libraries and Arts Committees, and with the possible availability of a building which might allow the project to go onto the next stage, the County's Policy Committee, under the Chairmanship of David Roberts, a leading member of the Independent Group, met to discuss the issue in depth. It welcomed the project and agreed that now was the time to appoint a working party to look into its feasibility, ascertain prospects of financial assistance from the private sector and examine the financial implications for the County Council.[8]

Martin Rewcastle was well pleased by this sudden progress. In less than two

7 In September 1987 a local group consisting of consultants, planners, architects and Newlyn Orion Gallery, independently put forward feasibility study proposals for Cornwall County Council 'To investigate and develop proposals for a major art gallery in the County to accommodate paintings and sculptures of Cornish artists.' No mention was made of St. Ives. The group hoped to undertake a four to six month study at a cost of £19,800 + VAT. As there was no budget for such a project, no further action was taken.

8 It was vital for the Policy Committee to formally welcome the scheme. One of its roles was, through the deliberations of its sub-committees, to give instructions to other committees to provide funds for particular initiatives.

years from his original meeting at County Hall, he was able to write to Patrick Heron: 'I have not seen this level of commitment from the county before and am extremely encouraged.'

The South West Arts Director's optimism would have been even greater if he had known more about the councillor who had been invited by Julian Williams, Chairman of the County Council, to lead the working group. This was Richard Carew Pole. But Ian Martin knew the significance of the appointment. Much later he would recall that, up until that moment the gallery project had been speculative, with Richard Carew Pole's appointment he believed 'there was now serious intent'.

But how was it that the Stennack School which, by all accounts, should have been demolished in 1986, was still standing and available for possible use as an art gallery?

The Stennack School (the Old Board
School) designed by Silvanus Trevail and
opened in 1881. This photograph was
taken between 1890 and 1894. The slime
pits of the Wheal Trenwith Mine are on the
lower slopes of the land to the right.

6　Saving The Stennack School

It was the people of St Ives, and they alone, who ensured that in the summer of 1986 the redundant school at the corner of The Stennack and Bullans Lane, on one of the main approach roads to the town from Zennor, St Just and Lands End, was still standing. As the school plays such an important early role in the story of the gallery, and will reappear before the end, this chapter looks at its history and shows why it engendered so much local affection.

For much of the nineteenth century a general education was an expensive privilege. The revolutionary Education Act of 1870 enforced the principle that, for the first time, every child under the age of ten should be able to attend school on a full-time basis. From that date locally elected Boards across the country were empowered to establish schools, partly financed through the local rates. In the case of St Ives, in 1878 a piece of land was purchased for the purpose for £700.

The proposed school was situated on ground that was then on the outskirts of the town, in the valley of the Stennack River, that had previously been used by a local farmer for growing vegetables. On the steep slope the other side of the small roadway, in front of the school, was an old copper mine. From 1908 until the beginning of the First World War, Wheal Trenwith, as the area was known, became virtually the only mine in the country to yield quantities of fine pitchblende. From this ore, pure radium was produced and exported to hospitals and physicians around the world.[1]

The new school was a handsome and imposing building, being one of thirty-five educational establishments in Cornwall designed by the county's distinguished Victorian architect, Silvanus Trevail of Par (who had been the architect for Treloyhan Manor). In 1878 the plans of the school were chosen by the architectural profession to be shown in the Exhibition of British Architecture at the Paris Exposition, and afterwards at exhibitions held in Melbourne and then Sydney. Such was the quality of design, a replica - still standing - was built in Queensland, Australia.

Constructed by Messrs Williams, Daniel and Troy at a cost of £4,450, the large school held nearly nine hundred young pupils.[2] It was made of fine cut local granite and had a delabole slate roof with decorative inlaid band courses. Its outstanding feature was the tower above the main entrance, originally carrying a pyramid-shaped spire, whose bell daily summoned the children to school.

The 'old Board School', as it was originally named, opened, apparently without ceremony, on 17 January 1881. Because fees of two-pence a week for infants and three-pence for older children were levied, in the early years many poor families could not afford to send their offspring there.[3]

The Stennack School went on to celebrate its centenary.[4] But, long before, the building was found to be inadequate for the town's needs. Secondary pupils moved out to a new building on the outskirts of St Ives at the Belyars in June 1940. Then a new Infants School, designed by Alan Groves, the County Architect,[5] opened at the Burrows in September 1966. It had panoramic views of the Harbour and bay. Constructed in steel sections it was partially sunk into the hillside to afford protection from the prevailing winds.

With the old school unsuitable for modern children's requirements, a replacement Junior School was planned to be built above the Infants School. It was generally understood that when the new building was finally completed, the old

1 Stanley Cock has written in his book *St Ives Museum* that Marie Curie visited Trenwith Mine, and the children of the Board School were taken by their head teacher up the hill to meet her. There is apparently no record of her actually making use of the pitchblende from St Ives.

2 The Stennack School was, in fact, three separate schools under one roof; infants, boys and girls each had their own headteacher.

3 Education was not freely available to all elementary school children until 1891.

4 In 1940, during the Second World War, the Stennack School was used as a reception centre for war evacuees who arrived by train from different parts of the country.

5 The new Infants School was Alan Groves' first project for the County Council, (which had now taken over responsibility for state education).

1

1 The interior of the St Ives Board School, with its distinctive windows and timber beams. Pictured is the school's first Headmaster, Mr Thomas A Kay, who took the photograph. The date on the blackboard is 23 January 1902, and the Headmaster has been preparing for a Geography lesson.

2 A close-up of the Stennack School from the side facing Bullans Lane. The distinctive delabole slate roof with decorated inlaid band courses can clearly be seen.

2

Board School would no longer be needed by the County. In the early 1980s, therefore, the County Council began to investigate ways for disposing of it.

The local police authority, under the control of the County had, for about ten years, been seeking new accommodation. Its offices in Wills Lane, in the centre of St Ives, were thought to be sub-standard. At the same time the fire station, since 1948 housed in a small building on the other side of the road from the Stennack School, was also now inadequate. A new and larger site was under investigation by the Fire Committee of the County Council. Without the local residents' knowledge, plans were being set in motion for these two utilities to share a single site.

On 25 November 1983, when the school was still in use, an insignificant notice appeared in *The St Ives Times & Echo*. It announced:

Cornwall County Council Application for Planning Permission (Fire and Public Protection Committee). Resolution to seek deemed consent for construction of fire station, Old County Primary School, The Stennack, St Ives.

By coincidence, one of the teachers at the Stennack School, Lu Simmons, was visiting Penwith District Council's offices in Penzance to check up on a planning application; something, she recalls, she never normally did. While looking down the list for the application she was seeking, she came upon a notice about the school. Not being a resident of St Ives, Lu Simmons was unaware of the entry in the local paper and, asking to see details, she was horrified to see the plans placed in front of her. The beautiful old school, it was clear, was to be demolished, and replaced by two modern facilities, one housing the fire service and the other the police force.

She immediately contacted a fellow teacher, Nan Todd, who lived in St Ives. Between them they decided to take immediate action. Lu Simmons wrote an angry letter to *The St Ives Times & Echo*, and pleaded: 'Please may I urge your readers to unite to try and prevent this happening - sign one of the many petitions around town...'. She had struck a chord; in the space of a month her petition was signed by over 2,000 people, many of whom had themselves attended the school.

A 'Save the Stennack School Building Group' was formed which, in the next few months, maintained pressure to make sure of the building's continued existence. Members of the group, led by Lu Simmons and Nan Todd, organised weekly letters to the newspaper. These acted as much needed morale-boosters because some Penwith Councillors were using the same medium to express their exasperation at the efforts of the protesters. George Washington Cocks, a Newlyn councillor on the District Council, as well as being a County Councillor, was particularly scathing. He wrote that the people of St Ives 'needed their heads examined'; the problem with them was that: 'They were always asking for more like Oliver Twist'. Next he tried to cause dissension in the town by suggesting that 'the intelligent section of St Ives...are all in favour of the decision...' That only angered the townspeople more.

A fund was opened to meet the rising costs of fighting the building's preservation. The Victorian Society offered valuable support. The Town Council was persuaded that it would be a bad idea to demolish the school; it was far better, the argument went, to use it for the benefit of the town. The idea of a community centre was put forward as being a more appropriate amenity.

The County Councillors were suprised by the outcry. In March 1984 the County's Planning Committee organised a public meeting in the town's Wesley Chapel, chaired by Councillor Richard Carew Pole, and attended by his colleague, Councillor Doris Ansari.[6] There an architect's impression was displayed of the new complex, which *The St Ives Times & Echo* described, a few days later, as 'a prisoner of war camp with its gun tower'.

6 Both Richard Carew Pole and Doris Ansari would shortly play a vital role in bringing Tate Gallery St Ives to fruition.

Doris Ansari remembers the occasion as one of the most stormy public meetings she had ever attended. A great deal of money had been spent on constructing the new Junior School, and the County Council wished to invest the proceeds of the sale of their old building for educational facilities elsewhere in Cornwall. She recalls that she arrived feeling rather cross. However, after seeing the school for herself she and Richard Carew Pole understood the passion it aroused in the townspeople. By the time the councillors left St Ives that day they felt very strongly that the school should not be demolished.

However, there were now *two* problems for the County Council to solve. It could not just hand over the building to the town, as it was necessary for the Education Department to recoup some of the money it had spent on its new building. Secondly, if the school was to remain standing, another site would have to be found for the fire and police services. Only two locations locally appeared to be large enough for both buildings to be constructed side by side: the Stennack School site and the Ayr playing field close by, and currently used by the school.

On the other hand, if the fire and police stations were separated, there were a number of possible sites for the fire station including the Paleman Best charity land higher up The Stennack. This was a piece of land containing a field and fine pine trees which had been bequeathed to the Borough in 1950 'for the enjoyment of the townspeople generally'. Currently the Town Council was unable to afford the high cost of maintaining this area. It had become an eyesore and an embarrassment. (It would later be identified as a possible site for the new gallery.)

The Devon and Cornwall Police Authority began looking for an alternative site. They earmarked the playing field at Wheal Ayr. When the townspeople heard about this they were again outraged. Cornwall County Council had, for many years, recognised the field as being a public open space and, as an overflow car park in the summer holidays, it provided much needed revenue for the town. A petition was organised to save the field.[7] The proposal was eventually dropped once the councillors refused to give planning permission for a change of use. (The site of the Ayr playing field, coincidentally, was also selected for Tate Gallery St Ives.)

Help, however, became available from a number of sources for the group saving the school. On 21 May 1984 a meeting was convened at the Penwith Gallery with the Regional Advisory Officer of the National Federation of Community Organisations, and attended by Joe Poynton, a local architect. This was a great boost to the protesters because they were shown how people-power *had* succeeded in other places. It also helped guide the Group through the planning maze. The session led to a survey being undertaken in the town; nearly nine hundred people responded to questions asking how they might use the Stennack School if it was made available for community purposes? The results were very encouraging. A large proportion said that they would use a community/leisure centre or youth club if it was provided.

Joe Poynton was at that time Chairman of the Cornwall branch of the RIBA and a member of the National Community Architecture Group. Established in 1982, this Group was funded equally by the RIBA and DoE, and empowered to finance feasibility studies for community projects. The architect was soon able to announce that a grant of £750 had been awarded to the Preservation Group to carry out a feasibility study on the school's possible conversion into a community centre. Joe Poynton was asked to undertake this study on the Preservation Group's behalf. News of the grant coincidentally arrived in St Ives the day before the fate of the school was debated by the County's Planning Committee at County Hall in Truro. At that session the councillors agreed not to demolish the school immediately, but look into the matter further.

The issue was now being aired further afield. Nick Wates, an architectural

7 Following the residents' petition to prevent the field at Wheal Ayr from being used as the site for a police station, another criticism levelled by councillors in the pages of *The St Ives Times & Echo* was that 'organising petitions was a "national sport" in St Ives'.

journalist, wrote articles defending the school for both *Building Design* on 6 July, 1984 and *The Guardian* on 30 July. By the time his second article appeared he reported a fresh and worrying turn of events:

Cornwall County Council is pushing ahead with controversial plans to demolish a Victorian School in St Ives and has banned an architect, hired by the local residents, from entering the building to see whether it could be converted into a community centre...A 24-hour-a-day watch has been mounted to raise the alarm if bulldozers move in.

Despite not being able to enter the school, Joe Poynton produced a report outlining preliminary plans for a community centre based on Silvanus Trevail's original drawings, and updated by residents familiar with the building. He believed it to be 'eminently suitable for conversion to a community centre.' He wrote in the Feasibility Study: 'It looks in very good condition and should be viable for at least another 100 years'.

Support came from yet another source. Patrick Heron, long known for his campaigns to preserve the landscape in the West Penwith area, was asked by members of the Preservation Group to assist in the struggle. He responded by writing, in typically passionate style, a long open letter to Alan Groves, the County Architect, which was published in *The St Ives Times & Echo* on 17 August. He began:

Dear Alan - When you were the Chairman of the Penwith Gallery in St Ives and I was a member of the committee, I had the feeling, rightly or wrongly, that you and I shared the view that St Ives was a very special place...James Joyce had once [said] that St Ives was 'the most interesting town in England. I have always assumed that you would agree that St Ives must be protected from any threat that would destroy its present character...the school's destruction will constitute the greatest single act of vandalism ever perpetrated in St Ives - since that school, because of its size and extreme nobility as architecture, is to the valley of the lower Stennack as important as the Parish Church is to the harbour...[8]

Feelings were running high in St Ives. A few days after Patrick Heron's letter was published a parade was organised by local residents, which aimed to show the town's continuing opposition to the County's scheme. Two hundred residents, including school children dressed in Victorian costume carrying placards, banners and balloons, and accompanied by dancers, musicians and vintage vehicles, made their way from the lifeboat slipway on the Harbour, up the hill to the school. There they linked hands and formed a circle around the outside of the building.

At the end of July another Planning meeting was held in Truro. Richard Carew Pole was no longer Chairman of the Planning Committee, and this time, by nine votes to six, it proposed to continue with construction of the fire station. Angry protesters from the Preservation Group, who had attended the meeting, hung banners in the Council Chamber. They were told that they must be removed.

All this publicity, however, was having an affect. The school was finally saved from demolition on 4 September when, at the request of the Stennack School Preservation Group, the Department of Environment gave the building a Grade II listed status. This was what members of The Group had been trying to achieve over the previous ten months, and they were jubilant at their success. The old building's new status meant that if the Fire and Public Protection Committee wanted to build a new fire station on the site, they would first have to get permission from the DoE. 'Grass roots democracy had done its work', reported *The St Ives Times & Echo* with pride.

Coincidentally, the 'spot listing' that the building received - a method by which buildings in danger of demolition can by-pass the normally slow listing process - occurred on the day that the new Junior School opened at the Burrows.

8 Alongside Patrick Heron's letter in *The St Ives Times & Echo* a drawing was reproduced of St Ives made from a point about eighty yards from the school. It had recently been identified by Roy Ray, Principal of the St Ives School of Painting, as being the work of J M W Turner.

Now that the building had been saved it was important to find a use for it. The

1 Interior of the Stennack School during conversion into the town's medical centre in 1991. Compare with the photograph on page 62. The plaster has been removed to reveal the natural granite.

2 Exterior of the Stennack School during conversion. Compare with the photograph on page 62 which shows how windows were inserted into the slate roof to create natural light for a first floor level. Every slate was removed, checked and replaced.

3 Interior of the Stennack Surgery, opened in the autumn of 1991, showing the stained glass window in the reception area. Depicted in the bottom left panel is the old copper mine that had once been across the road from the Stennack School.

4 Interior of the Stennack Surgery reception area, showing the fine roof timbers that replaced the originals that had to be destroyed.

original Group's aspirations having been achieved, a number of its original organisers withdrew from the campaign. By the end of 1984 a new organisation was formed - the Cyril Noall Community Association, named after the St Ives historian who had recently died. Under the Chairmanship of Bret Guthrie, a local history teacher, the new Association received charitable status and began to raise money to acquire the building on behalf of the town. A number of fund raising events was organised, including an auction held by David Lay in September 1985.[9]

It was not lost on the town, however, that by this time the County Council had no need of a new large police station after all. A central facility had recently opened at Camborne enabling local stations like St Ives to run with a smaller staff and be unmanned at night. It was now clear that a new fire station could easily fit onto a much smaller site. The Paleman Best charity land was eventually chosen, and the enlarged fire station opened on 26 August 1989 by P R Burnett, former Chairman of the Fire and Protection Committee.

In November 1985 the County Council put in a planning application for a change of use for the Stennack School. Their policy now was to sell the building, hoping that by gaining planning permission for alternative uses, the school's value would be enhanced. A smart brochure, produced early in 1986 for prospective buyers, indicated that 'outline planning permission [had been] granted for change of use as: residential, light industrial, use as a tourist attraction'. The County Valuer formally put the building up for sale and asked for sealed bids.

The hard working Community Association felt they were being thwarted in their attempts to obtain the building for local use, because they had to compete with other prospective commercial purchasers. The most they could raise was about £80,000. They felt that there was insufficient time to apply for grants that would have assisted with the purchase, and help pay for conversion. Spirits rose momentarily when, in October 1986, there was a rumour in the local newspaper that 'London's Tate Gallery had made a bid for the school.' But this, of course, was denied by Alan Bowness, the Tate's Director, and so it proved to be a red herring.

The successful bidder was a local businessman. The newspapers reported that he promised the old school would be used for the benefit of the community and remain exactly as it was. Despite the failure of the Community Association to purchase the school, its supporters were now optimistic for its future.

For nearly two years the new owner did nothing with the building and he decided to put it back on the market. The County Council, after considering again whether or not it would be suitable for use as an art gallery, decided against.[10] For a while the school's fate was uncertain.

Help came from an unexpected direction. The three St Ives medical practices had been considering moving from their various inadequate surgeries in the town for some time. All three existing premises had first floor consulting rooms and no parking facilities, which made visits by the elderly and infirm very difficult.

Searching for a single building during the 1980s, the doctors first viewed Talland House, once the home of Sir Leslie Stephen and his family, conveniently located next door to the Edward Hain Memorial Hospital. When its price was found to be outside their range, they resumed the hunt.

The now semi-derelict school caught their eye. They all felt it was just what they were looking for. Planning permission was sought in November 1989 for a change of use, only a few days before Richard Carew Pole made a second visit to St Ives, this time to seek local support for the gallery on quite a different site.[11]

The doctors appointed Barry Ostler from St Agnes, to sympathetically transform the school to a medical centre by constructing a first floor level, thereby considerably enlarging the floor space available. This was achieved in such a way

9 Seven years later David Lay hosted a similar event to raise funds to build Tate Gallery St. Ives.

10 For more information about the County Council's decision not to repurchase the School, see Chapter 8 - The Search for a Site.

11 See chapter 13 - The Local Campaign - St. Ives Tate Action Group.

that the ceiling of the main waiting room area, once the school assembly hall, reached the fine wood roof as it had always done. Windows had to be inserted in the slates for the upper storey rooms. Each roof slate was carefully removed, inspected and replaced around newly created window spaces. The original windows and the roof timbers were burnt because of extensive dry rot. The building contractors were Dudley Coles who started work in the spring of 1991.[12] By 29 November of that year the doctors were able to move in.

The building could not have been used for a more appropriate purpose. As well as providing modern accommodation for the three separate medical practices, the building provides rooms for district nurses, health visitors, chiropodists and mid-wives employed by the Area Health Authority. Containing a large car park, which was once the school playground, the surgeries are serviced by a pharmacy at the rear of the building. A well equipped conference room is used not only by the doctors themselves but by local groups who wish to hire it. (This room was used in 1992 by the local gallery fundraisers for events such as lectures and film shows.[13])

Meanwhile, the efforts of the Community Association were happily not wasted. The money they had raised during their campaign was kept in an account until the medical centre was completed. Part went towards a 'small operations' bed, and a stained glass window for the waiting room, one of whose panels illustrates the old mine on the other side of the road which, in its day, contributed to much pioneering medical work.[14]

But all this is to look ahead. At the same time the Stennack School was put on the market for a second time, in the summer of 1988, Cornwall County Council was setting up its gallery Steering Group.

12 Dudley Coles was appointed to build Tate Gallery St Ives only a few hundred yards away, a few weeks later.

13 In the spring of 1993, before Tate Gallery St Ives was ready for occupancy, the Curator, Michael Tooby, and two of his staff, took offices on the first floor of the old Stennack School. (See Chapter 16 - Dream Becomes Reality)

14 The small balance remaining from the money raised by the Cyril Noall Community Association was given to the local branch of Age Concern who were appealing for funds to increase the size and facilities of their building in St Andrews Street near the St Ives Art Club.

Richard Murphy

A group of schoolgirls pose in Victorian costume before taking part in the town parade opposing the County Council's scheme to demolish the Stennack School, in August 1984.

7   Richard Carew Pole And The Steering Group

Richard Carew Pole, a County Councillor between 1973 and 1993, was Chairman of the Gallery Steering Group from May 1988 until Tate Gallery St Ives opened in June 1993.

From its inception in the late spring of 1988, the County Council's Steering Group, under the chairmanship of Richard Carew Pole, was vital to the successful outcome of the project. Its membership was carefully chosen and its responsibilities clearly defined. It became such a successful forum for overseeing the early planning of the gallery that its members continued to meet regularly until the summer of 1993, when Tate Gallery St Ives opened.

The choice of Chairman could not have been bettered. Richard Carew Pole had been a highly respected County Councillor since 1973 for a region at the opposite end of the county from St Ives, and Chairman of the Council's Finance Sub-Committee since 1985. Although he did not have an intimate knowledge of the St Ives school and its artists, he did have a great interest in the arts in Cornwall, and was a Director of the Theatre Royal at Plymouth. He also had the advantage of contacts and friendships in London.

When Richard Carew Pole was asked to head the Steering Group it took him only a short time to recognise that, despite the economic and financial pressures that the County Council was under, the project would enhance the cultural standing of the county, as well as being of economic benefit to it. He decided that he, personally, would like to be involved in bringing these changes about.

The Group's Chairman, from now on, devoted all his energies to the success of the project. He immediately set to work to choose the members of his team. They included officers of the County Council, councillors and, importantly, private individuals who possessed between them a wide range of professional expertise.

The Steering Group had two main functions - executive and advisory. Its executive role ensured that the project received financial approval from the majority of the County Councillors. For this to happen the gallery needed the confidence and backing of the Chairmen of those Committees that had the power to raise the necessary funds required: the Policy Committee under the Chairmanship of Doris Ansari (who took over that role in 1988), the Libraries and Arts Committee, under the Chairmanship of John Hurst, and the Finance Sub-Committee, of which Richard Carew Pole was its Chairman. Doris Ansari and John Hurst knew that, as Liberal Democrats, they could command the votes of the largest single political group in the Council, which happened to be committed to greater spending in the Arts than at any time in the County Council's history.

But Doris Ansari also knew that there were many competing bids for the County's scarce resources for its capital projects, especially from Education. It was therefore very important for her Policy Committee to be seen to be even-handed with all the departments when annual budgets were being prepared. However, she was aware that if she could get the gallery project approved by the Policy Committee, amongst whose twenty-five members were the Chairmen of the all major committees on the Council, she was certain that approval would be ultimately obtained from the full County Council. As luck would have it, in the summer of 1988, the Deputy Chairman of the Policy Committee was Oakley Eddy, a St Ives Councillor, who was also Chairman of the Cornwall Tourist Board.

Another early bonus for the project was that, as the Liberal Democrats shared the chairs and vice-chairs of all the committees with the other major political group, the Independents, of which Richard Carew Pole was a member, it was believed that sufficient votes could be mustered in the Council Chamber to ensure the project's approval.

The Steering Group had to submit regular formal reports to the Policy Committee. Before each was finalised, Richard Carew Pole always asked Doris Ansari and John Hurst informally whether they thought it likely that their Committees would be able to approve certain proposals. If the answer was 'yes', the project was over its next hurdle, and there was no necessity to discuss the matter with the entire Council, who recognised the executive powers the Steering Group had been granted.

In 1989 John Hurst was succeeded by his Vice Chairman, Barbara Spring, who had joined the Council in the elections of 1985 'especially to be involved in the artistic life of the County; particularly the visual arts'. Barbara Spring for many years played a part in the cultural life of the region; from the 1960s she was a member of the Board of South West Arts.[1]

It was important for the project to be planned and monitered by administrative bodies outside the confines of the County Council. Penwith District Council, covering the St Ives area, was therefore represented on the Steering group, from the summer of 1988, by Des Hosken, Clerk of the District Council. A chief officer of that Council from its inception in July 1973, Des Hosken, who had spent most of his career in local government in West Cornwall, was responsible not only for administration of the District Council itself, but for tourism and the arts.

During the late 1980s he had served on a Steering Group, and then become Company Secretary, of the Trinity House National Lighthouse Centre. That Steering Group was responsible for developing the Lighthouse museum in Penzance. In this capacity Des Hosken worked closely with a number of officers and members of the County Council.

In 1988 the Conservatives were in power in Penwith. Two of its most influential District Councillors at that time were Geoff Venn and John Daniel, Chairmen of the Tourism and Housing Services Committees respectively. Coincidentally John Daniel had another role. He was the Conservative leader of the County Council.

After some initial scepticism for the project, John Daniel came to realise just how important the gallery was likely to be for the district as a whole. In his dual role, therefore, he was able to muster support from the Conservative County Councillors as well as from the District Councillors. This latter cooperation was vital. Penwith District Council not only owned part of the land chosen to be the site for the gallery - the derelict gasworks above Porthmeor Beach - but was landlord of the adjacent Meadow Flats and Barnoon car park. There would need to be discussions, during the course of the project, when the land came to be conveyed to the County Council. Delicate negotiations would be required over access rights with the contractors and the local residents. The District Council also required the assistance of both Geoff Venn and John Daniel to obtain backing for a donation of £75,000 towards the cost of the building operation.

In 1991 the Conservatives on the District Council lost their majority and the Council became hung. The Labour group which took the lead was headed by a St Ives councillor, Alan Harvey. Councillor Harvey not only became Chairman of the Council at this time, but replaced Geoff Venn, who was not re-elected, on the Steering Group. In his third role, as a Town Councillor, Councillor Harvey helped to ensure that the disabled were properly catered for in the new gallery, and he proved to be of special assistance to the Group and to the gallery's curator, Michael Tooby, on local matters during the final stages of the project.

Richard Carew Pole was always anxious to know the feelings of the people in St Ives. He therefore asked that a representative be chosen from the Town Council to join the team once the site for the gallery had been chosen and the Architects' Brief prepared. The Councillors' choice was Beryl James, and she joined the Steering

1 By the time Barbara Spring joined the Steering Group in 1989, her Committee had added 'Records' to its 'Libraries and Arts' responsibilities.

Group in early 1990. A Town Councillor since the government reorganisation in 1974, and three times Mayor, Beryl James liaised between the Town Council and the Steering Group for the remainder of the project. With her encouragement the Town Council responded to a request from Richard Carew Pole for financial assistance, agreeing to donate £15,000 towards the cost of the project over a period of three years.[2]

The Steering Group's other main function, its advisory role, was important to the development of the project from the beginning. Those private individuals who were selected to join the group, some of whom Richard Carew Pole had known for a number of years, provided a range of professional advice. Coming from varying backgrounds, they nevertheless all had an interest in the arts.

John Southern·had direct experience in dealing with all sections of the general public. In 1972 he created the Thorburn Museum and Gallery at Dobwalls, in central Cornwall. Completely redesigned and reopened in 1986 as 'Mr Thorburn's Victorian Countryside', his idea was for children, especially, to enjoy art in an environment in which they felt comfortable, and for his museum and gallery to be fully accessible to the disabled. The venture's success won an award from Sotheby's. In 1987 Southern became Chairman of the West Cornwall Tourist Group, which had direct access to the English Tourist Board.[3] He also became chairman of TDAP, an organisation set up and financed by the County to boost tourism.

While a member of the Steering Group, from which he had to retire due to ill health before the gallery was built, John Southern passed on his passionate commitment to the word 'Tate' being part of the title of the gallery. In his opinion, a suggested name 'The St Ives Gallery' would never have been successful at bringing large numbers of people to the town.

Carol Holland was invited to join the Group by Martin Rewcastle (who also attended meetings during 1988 and 1989). She and her husband Geoffrey, who had worked with Martin Rewcastle on joint schemes connected with employment and training opportunities in the South West, were summer visitors to St Ives for a number of years, buying a cottage near to the Penwith Gallery. They soon got to know some of the artists and gallery owners. In February 1988, they moved permanently to a house just outside the town.[4] Carol Holland had previously worked for Shell for ten years, and then with the charity Arthritis Care from 1972 to 1989, during which time she created and edited a quarterly newspaper *Arthritis News* for which she received the MBE in 1990.

Lady Holland, as she became on her husband's knighthood at the beginning of 1989, joined the Steering Group in June 1988. Less than two years later, she was invited to become a member of the newly formed St Ives Tate Action Group (STAG), which she then represented on the Steering Group together with Toni Carver, proprietor of St Ives Printing and Publishing, publisher of *The St Ives Times & Echo*.[5]

Toni Carver brought to the Group a knowledge of the history of community arts projects in St Ives, both successful and unsuccessful. A sceptic, as far as running any project through a committee was concerned, he nevertheless was aware that it was important to obtain the confidence and continued support of local people. He felt that it was vital for them to be kept in touch with the decisions being made in Truro about an important addition to their own town, by what many thought of as an 'alien' County Council. He ensured, therefore, that communication was achieved through regular articles on the gallery's progress in the local newspaper.

Both Carol Holland and Toni Carver also regularly reported the continuing progress of STAG to the Steering Group. The enthusiastic local response, both in terms of raising money for the gallery and actively providing support at crucial

2 St Ives Town Council's £15,000 contribution towards the building project was the largest single donation that council had ever made.

3 Funding for the West Cornwall Tourist Group was also provided from the government, local councils and private organisations.

4 Geoffrey Holland's work as Permanent Secretary at the Department of Employment necessitated him being in London all week.

5 For the contribution STAG made to the gallery project, see Chapter 13.

Members of the Gallery Steering Group photographed in the new, empty gallery in the late spring of 1993 at their last meeting. Seated left to right: Jane Geraghty, Councillor Oakley Eddy, Councillor Alan Harvey, Lady Holland, Sir Richard Carew Pole (Chairman), Richard Lester, Councillor Barbara Spring, Councillor Beryl James, Councillor David Roberts. Standing left to right: John Farmer, Peter Fazakerley, Jo Jacques, Christopher Petherwick, Peter Wilson, Malcolm Henderson, Ian Martin, Des Hosken, Mark Nicholson, Peter Kendall, Toni Carver, Michael Tooby.

periods in the project's progress, was of great importance not only to the Steering Group itself, but to the County Councillors, many of whom had little personal knowledge of St Ives.

Martin Rewcastle also asked Patrick Heron to join the Group. He knew of the artist's involvement in helping to save the Stennack School, and Patrick Heron had been one of the small group who had visited the empty school with Alan Bowness in the summer of 1986, at which time he had been a Trustee of the Tate. One of the artists whose work would ultimately be exhibited in the new gallery, Patrick Heron was able to bring to the Steering Group a very different perspective on a number of important issues from aesthetic and art historical viewpoints.[6] There were two other specialist members of the Steering Group chosen by Richard Carew Pole. David McKenna had been Chairman and General Manager of the Southern Region of British Railways, and then from 1968, a full-time Member of the British Railways Board until his retirement in 1976. With his life-long interest in the arts, especially music, and his experience in devising and progressing large scale ventures, he had particular responsibility for scrutinising all the documents produced by the Steering Group during the course of the project. Finally, Christopher Petherick who, since 1979 , had run a local office for the auctioneers Christies, completed the team.

The Steering Group met every six to eight weeks at County Hall in Truro. As well as its advisory and executive roles, it oversaw the framework of the project, and played a large part in co-ordinating the fund raising from both the public and private sectors. It later monitored the progress of the building's construction, making sure that the scheme was always kept within its tight budget.

Officers of the County Council, whose responsibilities increasingly involved the actual planning of the gallery, regularly attended Steering Group meetings. This team was headed by Richard Lester, Deputy Clerk of the Council and a trained lawyer. He had joined the County Council in 1982, after previous local government positions in Leeds, North Yorkshire and Shropshire.

From the time the Steering Group was set up Richard Lester (who was released from some of his other responsibilities by the Chief Executive of the County Council, Geoffrey Burgess) coordinated the project on a day-to-day basis, working closely with Richard Carew Pole. Together they, and later Carol Holland, met with Tate Gallery staff in London, to bring together both ends of the scheme. Richard Lester calculates that, at one stage, he was spending about a quarter of his time developing and monitoring the progress of the gallery. An important member of his team was John Cooper, the Principal Solicitor, who took part in negotiating a lease agreement with the Tate Gallery.[7]

Ian Martin's role decreased after Richard Lester was appointed to manage the project, but he continued to be involved in the gallery's long term planning, assessing its impact both on St Ives and the county as a whole. As part of the County's submission to Europe to economically justify a European Regional Development Fund grant, he looked at potential visitor numbers and attempted to assess how many jobs the gallery might create in the area. His staff in the Planning and Economic Development Department played key roles in obtaining grants from both Europe and the Rural Development Commission.[8]

Alan Groves the County Architect was responsible for putting forward the names of prospective architects, writing the Brief, making sure the chosen architects, Evans and Shalev, produced their detailed drawings for the County on schedule, putting the contract out to tender, selecting the consultants and managing the project once construction work started on site. Alan Groves attended the Steering Group meetings, as did his Deputy, Malcolm Henderson in Groves'

6 In order for there to be no chance of a conflict of interest, Patrick Heron stood down from the Steering Group for several months when South West Arts commissioned his daughter and son-in-law, the architects Katharine Heron and Julian Feary, to undertake a Feasibility Study of three sites in St Ives to choose a location for the new gallery. (See Chapter 8 - The Search for a Site).

7 The widening role of the Tate Gallery is discussed in Chapter 11 - Private Funding and Tate Gallery Involvement.

8 A full account of how the County Council obtained both these grants is outlined in Chapter 12 - European and Other Public Funding.

absence, and reported on the progress of the project.

In the early days Jo Jacques, the Assistant County Treasurer, was particularly involved in the financing of the project from County resources. He was also responsible for calculating the costings of developing alternative sites for the gallery, and he collected donations from a number of the charitable organisations before the Tate Gallery took over this responsibility. Later he organised paying the construction bills and fees on behalf of the County Council.

The day-to-day financial monitoring of the project was undertaken by Peter Fazakerley, the Chief Quantity Surveyor in the Architect's Department. Working with Alan Groves, he was responsible for all the contractural and financial aspects of the project, appointing the contractors, subcontractors and the consultants, as well as negotiating their fees. He supervised the works funded by a Derelict Land Grant, ensuring that it was negotiated to the advantage of the project.[9] As building work progressed, and more donations were received, Peter Fazakerley made sure that those items which had originally been omitted from the Contract because of a lack of funds, were re-introduced as soon as possible.

David Goodley, the County Valuer, then Director of Property Resources, was responsible for looking into possible sites for the gallery, as his role was to manage and give advice on the County's land and property. Once the gasworks site had been chosen it was his department's job to negotiate its purchase from both British Gas and Penwith District Council.

John Farmer, Libraries and Arts Officer, was particularly concerned to show how the new gallery fitted into the 'art scene' as a whole in West Cornwall. There was some feeling that the project was swamping other arts initiatives in the county because of the amount of time, and particularly the potential funding - both general and public - that it was taking up. John Farmer felt it particularly important to demonstrate that the gallery would be 'the jewel in the crown' for Cornwall. Existing arts institutions were assured that their funding would in no way be jeopardised, undermined or redirected. The new gallery would only enhance interest in their activities.[10]

As the project progressed, representatives of the Tate Gallery in London came to Steering Group meetings. Occasionally it was the Director himself; at other times it was his Deputy, Francis Carnwath. Peter Wilson, responsible for the building project from the London end, joined the Group on most occasions.

Peter Wilson had West Country connections, and had been employed by the Tate Gallery since 1972, initially as a paintings' conservator, and then for the next ten years from 1980, as Head of Technical Services. In 1990 he was asked by the Director to manage the Tate's buildings, a new position created once the Property Services Agency no longer had that responsibility. On occasions Peter Wilson stood in for the Director at Steering Group meetings in the months before Francis Carnwath was officially invited to attend.

When Michael Tooby was appointed as the gallery's first Curator, he too became a regular attender.

Richard Carew Pole, according to all who worked with him, made the perfect chairman for this disparate group. Probably his greatest skill was understanding and appreciating the worth of everyone involved in the project, encouraging them to take responsibility for putting their ideas into practice. Commanding authority, he was highly respected by all. At the same time he was regarded with affection. As he lived at the opposite end of the county to St Ives, his fellow County Councillors were aware that, politically, he had no personal involvement with the project or particular axe to grind.

Richard Carew Pole consistently passed on to everyone with whom he came into contact, both inside and outside the County Council, an utter conviction in the

9 How the site came to be eligible for a sizeable Derelict Land Grant is told in Chapter 15 - Building Construction.

10 There were worries and criticisms from many quarters about the project. These are detailed in Chapter 14 - Public Concerns.

project's viability, even when the ground was getting rocky. The enthusiasm, efficient manner, patience and yet firmness with which he conducted the Steering Group meetings; the way he planned the project's orderly evolution through its formulation, fund raising, negotiation and execution - winning everyone's approval at each stage of the project - ensured that the Steering Group's role was remarkably effective in bringing Tate Gallery St Ives into existence.

The first major task of the Group was to decide whether the Stennack School, now on the market for a second time, should be converted into a gallery, or whether a new building should be designed and built on a greenfield site.

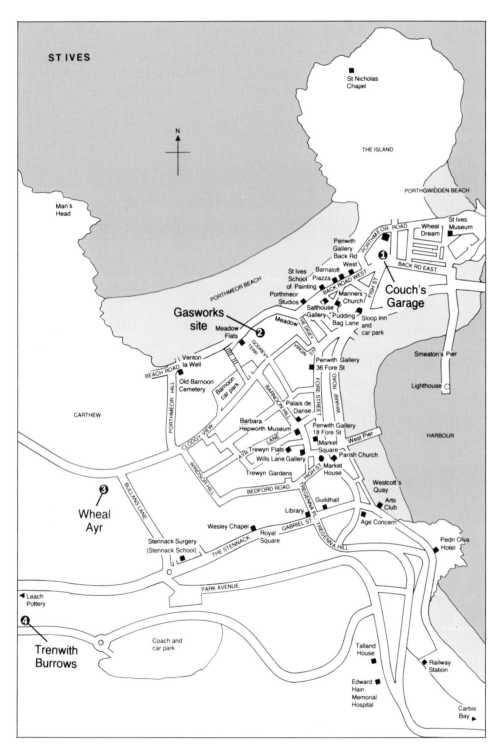

ST IVES

St Nicholas
Chapel

THE ISLAND

N

PORTHGWIDDEN BEACH

Man's
Head

Wheal
Dream

St Ives
Museum

PORTHMEOR BEACH

Penwith
Gallery
Back Rd
West

BACK RD EAST

St Ives
School
of Painting

Barnaloft
Piazza

❶

Porthmeor
Studios

Mariners
Church

Couch's
Garage

Salthouse
Gallery

Pudding
Bag Lane

Sloop Inn
and
car park

Gasworks
site

Meadow
Flats

Meadow

❷

GODREVY TERR

Smeaton's Pier

Venton
la Well

Penwith Gallery
36 Fore St

Lighthouse

BEACH ROAD

Old Barnoon
Cemetery

Barnoon
car park

CARTHEW

PORTHMEOR HILL

FORE STREET

WHARF ROAD

Palais de
Danse

HARBOUR

CLODGY VIEW

BARNOON HILL

LANE

Barbara
Hepworth Museum

Penwith Gallery
18 Fore St

West Pier

AYR

Trewyn Flats

Market
Square

Wills Lane Gallery

Parish Church

Trewyn Gardens

WINDSOR HILL

HIGH ST

Market
House

Westcott's
Quay

❸

BULLANS LANE

BEDFORD ROAD

TREGENNA PL

Guildhall

Arts
Club

Wheal
Ayr

Library

Age Concern

Wesley Chapel

GABRIEL ST

Royal
Square

TREGENNA HILL

Pedn Olva
Hotel

Stennack Surgery
(Stennack School)

THE STENNACK

PARK AVENUE

◀ Leach
Pottery

Coach and
car park

❹

Talland
House

Railway
Station

Trenwith
Burrows

Edward
Hain
Memorial
Hospital

Carbis
Bay ▶

Map of St Ives showing the sites that the architects Julian Feary and Katharine Heron looked at in their 1988 Feasibility Study: (1) Couch's Garage, Back Road East, (2) Derelict gasworks at Porthmeor Beach, (3) Wheal Ayr, at the top of Porthmeor Hill, and (4) Trenwith Burrows close to the Junior and Infants School above the town.

8　The Search For A Site

The choice of site for the new gallery proved to be crucial to the eventual success of the project, but in early 1988 the derelict St Ives gasworks was never even an option, as it was not on the County Council's original list of possible locations. Also, what in retrospect by the summer of 1993 seemed an obvious choice to everyone, was much less so in 1988. For a time there were serious doubts about the wisdom of building an art gallery on a steeply sloping, contaminated piece of derelict ground in an area of St Ives often battered by severe winter storms.

The Stennack School had been a serious contender for the gallery in the summer of 1986 and when, therefore, in May 1988 it again became available, Cornwall County Council for a while considered the possibility of repurchasing it. The newly-formed Steering Group asked John Miller, of Colquhoun, Miller & Partners to look at the building a second time, and update the 1986 conversion costs.

In June the architects reported back to the County Council that their quantity surveyors, Brian Davis Associates, had now estimated costs to be £1,457,500; an increase of £250,000. John Miller pointed out that there would be difficulties in bringing the building up to the required environmental standards and that the large number of classroom windows, especially those facing south, made it unsuitable for displaying paintings; extensive and costly sun screening would be essential. At this time visits were made to the building by members of the Steering Group, and they found it to be in a poor state of repair, some of the floorboards being, by now, completely rotten.

The building's owner had heard about the possibility of using the school as an art gallery, and he let it be known that he was not prepared to sell his property for less than £300,000, which was more than its original purchase price. It was clear to Ian Martin and others on the Steering Group that it might be necessary to take a different approach if the project was seriously to go ahead.

The matter was discussed at length at the Tate Gallery in London on 8 June, when Alan Bowness met with Richard Carew Pole for the first time. Also present were Richard Lester, Ian Martin, Martin Rewcastle and David Harris, the Member of Parliament for St Ives. This was Alan Bowness' final involvement with the project as Director of the Tate Gallery, for in the autumn he was to become Director of the Henry Moore Foundation.

At the London meeting Alan Bowness confirmed that the Tate Trustees were willing to loan about sixty paintings and sculptures to the County for showing in the Stennack School or a building on a greenfield site. That would be the limit of their involvement. However he promised that Tate staff would give technical advice, when necessary, about a suitable building as far as lighting, environmental control and management were concerned.

The Steering Group decided to undertake a site appraisal which would compare the advantages and disadvantages of a school conversion against a new building somewhere else in the St Ives area. David Goodley, Director of Property Resources, who was responsible for buying, selling and managing the County's land and property, was asked to identify County Council and other publicly owned land that might be suitable for development.

The first site put forward was Trenwith Burrows, a piece of land adjacent to the town's main car park, high above St Ives and close to the Junior and Infants'

Colin Orchard

1

Colin Orchard

2

Three of the sites studied in the 1988 Feasibility Study.

1 Couch's Garage, Back Road East. After J & J Couch moved their engineering company to Long Rock, outside Penzance, in order to expand, the property, now owned by the District Council, has been earmarked for public housing.

2 The Ayr Playing Field at Wheal Ayr, with panoramic views of St Ives Bay. Once the playing field for the Stennack School on the other side of Bullans Lane, and owned by Cornwall County Council, the land is used as an overspill car park during the summer months.

3 Trenwith Burrows looking west. The land is owned by Cornwall County Council, and is close to the Trenwith car park above St Ives. In the distance is the parish church of Halsetown, St John's in the Fields.

Colin Orchard

3

Schools. It was available because it had been surplus to requirements as a result of a prior highway scheme. Being in the vicinity of the old Trenwith copper mine the area was known to be full of old mine workings.

The second site, land at Wheal Ayr, had a controversial history.[1] A large open space, close to the top of Porthmeor Hill, it had for many years been the playing field for the adjacent Stennack School. In 1957, the local Scout troop financed and erected a hut at the top end of the field. From that date there was often conflict between St Ives Borough Council and the County Council as to its use outside school hours. With the impending closure of the Stennack School, local residents hoped that the land would remain available to the general public for recreation purposes. The County, for its part, hoped to build elderly people's flats there, but the sewage embargo, in force since 1974 (which prohibited any new residential development until a new sewage system for the area was in place) had prevented this proposal from going ahead. The residents vigorously opposed any possible sale of the land by the County to a private developer and, in 1984, there was a serious attempt to pursuade the Town Council to purchase it.[2] By the end of 1985, however, the County Council decided to hold on to the land for continued use as an overflow car park in the summer months in order to bring in valuable revenue.

Another site identified by David Goodley was part of the Paleman Best Charity land owned by the Town Council, near the Penbeagle Industrial Estate, and which, eventually, became the home for the new fire station.[3] Finally, a piece of land at Balnoon, near Halsetown, off the Coach Road, was added to the list. Originally the site of the Corporation's incinerator, which was demolished in 1950, it had for some years been used by County Highways for storing stone chippings and other road materials.[4]

Shortly after this list had been compiled, the Steering Group was told about a further site - Couch's Garage - in the centre of the old part of St Ives, at the top of Fish Street on Back Road East. The now derelict building and open land adjacent to it was originally developed by John and James Couch as a light engineering factory. The company was an important employer in the town for many years. Some of its products, many of which were exported around the world, were: air compressors, ships' lockers, propellors for fishing boats and a number of pieces of equipment used by the Commandos during the Second World War for rock climbing.[5] The company also operated a large and well-equipped garage and motor repair section accommodating one hundred and fifty cars.[6]

Now the factory was no longer in use. To enable the firm to expand, in 1974 it had transferred to a larger site on the Long Rock Industrial Estate outside Penzance. The land and building in St Ives were later taken over by Penwith District Council for use as a residents' car park, and the Council's intention was to build twenty-one residential flats on the site once the sewage embargo was lifted.[7]

All the selected locations, plus the Stennack School, were visited by members of the Steering Group, following which a report outlining each one's positive and negative aspects was circulated.

It was time to involve St Ives itself. On 16 August 1988 Richard Carew Pole, John Hurst, John Southern, and other members of the Steering Group, informally met with the Mayor and some of the Town Councillors at The Guildhall. They alerted the Council to the progress being made towards finding a location for an art gallery. After discussions, they learnt from the Councillors that Couch's Garage had the greatest potential, as it was close to the Penwith Gallery and many of the artists' studios.

As a result of the appraisal, the Stennack School was finally dropped, and three sites were shortlisted: Trenwith Burrows, Wheal Ayr and Couch's Garage. Martin

1 Wheal Ayr was close to the town's only tin mine. Although very ancient, by the early nineteenth century it had long ceased production. In 1838 there was a proposal to resume mining there, but because its operation would interfere with the only water supply for the Downlong area of St Ives at Venton Ia well, above Porthmeor Beach, there was nearly a riot by the local residents. Work was therefore abandoned until St Ives received its first proper water supply in 1844.

2 As shown in Chapter Six, to the anger of the townpeople, there was a suggestion that part of the land at Wheal Ayr be used as a site for the new police station.

3 Twenty acres of land had been bequeathed to the Council by Mr Best in 1951.

4 On 1 April 1938, *The St Ives Times* reported: 'An important step towards the preservation of the beauty of St Ives coastline and the prevention of the contamination of our beaches, was taken this week when the Mayor formally opened the Incinerator at Balnoon. It will deal with all refuse from the Borough. St Ives was the first town in Cornwall to establish an incineration plant - it could deal with 50 tons of refuse a week.' However, by the end of April the newspaper reported that the Incinerator was not big enough for the town. 'There is far more refuse being collected than there should be', it declared.

5 J and J Couch had a link with the art world. On 7 April 1950 Barbara Hepworth wrote to *The St Ives Times*: 'I would like to make known my extreme gratitude to Messrs. J & J Couch of St Ives, for the fine way in which, at a moment's notice, they undertook to move all the stone for the Festival of Britain sculpture from St Ives railway station to Trewyn Studio and erect the pieces on the site ready for me to carve.'

6 Guido Morris, the printer, designed a fine poster (using Bembow typeface) in black and red to advertise Couch's Garage. He also designed a small booklet detailing the garage's service tariff.

7 In 1976 a proposal for constructing twenty-one private flats with twenty-three parking spaces, was turned down by the Council because they were 'architecturally unsuitable' as well as the sewage embargo being in place.

Dr Roger Slack

The location of the old town gasworks at
Porthmeor Beach seen from Beach Road,
(photographed in the 1970s) owned by
British Gas, was identified by Julian Feary
as being a possible site for the new gallery.
The concrete plinths on the left supported
the cigar-shaped high pressure gas holder.
High above the site is the end house of
Godrevy Terrace.

Rewcastle organised a full site feasibility study, which South West Arts agreed to pay for. The architects Katharine Heron and Julian Feary, from London, were commissioned to assess each site for its suitability in terms of location and potential of a building of which 75% would be gallery space.

Both Katherine Heron and Julian Feary had trained at the Architectural Association in London and had gone into partnership in 1984. Projects that they had worked on included the conversion of buildings into an art gallery for the artist Ian Hamilton Finlay; the reconstruction of Paul Nash's design for a bathroom for Tilly Losch for the exhibition *The Thirties* at the Hayward Gallery and a number of restoration schemes for stone buildings in Cornwall and Yorkshire. Katherine Heron was also responsible for the conversion of pier buildings on Orkney into the Pier Arts Centre.[8]

To assist them with their study, The County Architect's Department provided Katharine Heron and Julian Feary with background information on each of the locations, defining their areas and identifying the available services. The two architects immediately made a preliminary reconnaisance, accompanied by Martin Rewcastle.

It was while walking around Porthmeor Beach that Julian Feary spotted the derelict gasworks. He immediately thought it might make an excellent site for the gallery. Martin Rewcastle was very excited, and suggested that the location be added to their study. The seemingly small and rather desolate area had not been included on the County Council's list because the land in question was owned by British Gas.

While preparing the feasibility study, Peter Wilson recalls that he discussed the project in general terms with the two architects at the Tate Gallery in London, although until that time he knew nothing about the idea of housing a permanent collection of works in St Ives. In 1988 he was responsible for managing the Tate's collections and he had written the gallery's Loan Regulations. He was therefore able to assist in discussions on possible problems that were likely to be encountered when constructing a gallery in an exposed location close to the sea.

Katharine Heron personally presented a preliminary report to the Steering Group on 12 September. The Trenwith Burrows site was excluded from the survey and the gasworks site added. The submission contained a panoramic view of St Ives with the three sites identified, plus photographs of each location, and site plan showing an outline of buildings of comparative size on each, to demonstrate how different configurations could be accommodated at each locality.

The architects' conclusions were, that a gallery at Wheal Ayr was likely to be the cheapest to construct, but was in the least appropriate location, being away from the centre of town and in a Victorian residential area. Couch's Garage was in an excellent position, as far as its proximity to the heart of the artistic centre of the town was concerned, but access to it through the narrow streets surrounding the site might be difficult, as would car parking. It was known, too, that there was a reluctance by the District Council to give up a potentially valuable development area.

As far as the gasworks site was concerned, development costs were likely to be high due to the fact that the land would have to be acquired from British Gas and, because of the use it had been put to over the years, the ground would be heavily contaminated. However, the architects recognised that it was the most exciting location architecturally. Any building there would be a prominent landmark, visible from both Porthmeor Beach and The Island, and would itself command panoramic views. Because of the steeply sloping nature of the site there was the opportunity for entrances to the building at both upper and lower levels.

The architects were asked by the Steering Group to add costings to their

8 The Pier Arts Centre project is outlined in greater detail in Chapter 18 - Links with Millbank, Liverpool, Kettle's Yard and Orkney.

proposal. They appointed Peter Andrews of Andrews & Boyd to undertake this work, which Cornwall County Council agreed to pay for.

While the architects' report was being prepared, and in order to assist the Steering Group make a decision, Ian Martin produced a survey on tourist profiles. He grouped potential gallery visitors into three categories: 'specific' - those who make a special journey to a particular building or event; 'package' - those who go to an area with a view to seeing a number of places; and 'impulse' - those who are in an area and decide suddenly to go to a particular building, perhaps because it looks interesting. He suggested that each of the three sites should be looked at in the light of these profiles, and also as they related to the location of the Barbara Hepworth Museum. Would visitors find it easy or desirable to visit the Hepworth Museum after visiting the gallery?

The Deputy County Planning Officer's conclusions were that none of the sites was particularly convenient for the Tate Gallery's small existing outpost, and he recommended that Wheal Ayr should be the County's choice: it was the least expensive to develop, it was easy to reach from outside the town and car parking would not be a problem.

On 29 September, at a full meeting of the Town Council, the Councillors were brought up to date regarding the results of the Feasibility Study. There was now growing support for building on the gasworks site. Councillor Alan Harvey, who had paid a visit to Patrick Heron, said that he understood the artists, too, would be in favour of this option. As far as the other two sites were concerned, the Councillors believed that Penwith District Council was unlikely to sell Couch's Garage, and Wheal Ayr was thought to be too far from the heart of the town to make it an attractive proposition. The Town Council agreed to send a letter to the Chief Planning Officer at the County Council, with a copy to the new Director of the Tate Gallery, setting out its preference. Shortly after Nicholas Serota replied. He noted with interest the conclusions, and would be visiting St Ives in December to personally assist in making the final choice.

On 17 October Katharine Heron and Julian Feary met the Steering Committee again with their final report. This included the costings that Andrews & Boyd had calculated for each of the three sites. The consultants considered that Couch's Garage would be the most expensive to develop because of the necessity of providing car parking below ground, to compensate for the land lost by any proposed development. The gasworks site would, however, be only marginally less expensive to build on. A copy of the report was sent to Nicholas Serota.

An important addendum to the architects' Feasibility Study was a letter written by John Southern, one of the members of the Steering Group. He had been asked by the architects to look closely, through commercial eyes, at the three sites. He wrote, in what seems now to be a most prophetic way:

...whilst Wheal Ayr and Couch's Garage showed some initial potential this was immediately and completely dwarfed the moment I arrived at the Old Gasworks site. What a remarkable and dramatic location it is, where the very building itself, terraced and clinging to the cliff could, if cleverly designed, become almost as exciting and breathtaking outside as the pictures it would contain within...Furthermore, if adults in commercially viable numbers are to be attracted to the project, their children need to be catered for as well and at the Old Gasworks site the building itself will immediately create excitement for them and a desire to explore it in detail. They will wish to climb its terraces and scale its heights and will I'm sure find it an adventure not to be missed...Finally of course, we should not forget the artists whose work we seek to display, and surely no more marvellous or fitting location could be found anywhere, with the building housing their work looking out across the sea and buttressed against the elements which they loved and painted so beautifully...

Despite the growing support for the land at Porthmeor, Wheal Ayr was still the favoured site as far as the County Planning Department was concerned. Ian Martin voiced his concern over the small area of the gasworks, and the fact that there would be no visitor parking. He would have preferred British Gas to sell the site and donate the proceeds for developing the land at Wheal Ayr.

For their part, British Gas had plans of their own for the derelict site. As early as December 1987 the company had put in a planning application to Penwith District Council for permission to build sixteen flats with associated car parking and a private sewage treatment works. After discussions with the Town Council the application was refused on the grounds that the development was premature pending improvements to the séwage system, and that the flats, as designed, would constitute an overdevelopment of the area.

British Gas could not have been put off by this refusal because, in November 1988, perhaps aware now that the County Council was showing an interest in the site for the purpose of building an art gallery, a second application went before the District Council's Planning Committee. This, too, was disliked by the Town Council. Local residents in the Porthmeor area signed a petition against the proposed development. The revised plans show a complex of units, some as many as six storeys high, with car parking underneath; the top floor coming well above the retaining wall on the south side of the site. Refusal was again given by Penwith District Council on the grounds of overdevelopment: 'The site...would result in the provision of dwellings lacking a reasonable residential environment', it concluded.

Like Ian Martin, Martin Rewcastle hoped that British Gas might donate their land to the County Council, which would greatly reduce the costs of the preferred option. He therefore suggested that the company should not be contacted until the Council had formally indicated that it was definitely their choice.

The occasion that decided the issue took place in St Ives on 15 December. After lunch at the Tregenna Castle Hotel, Nicholas Serota, Sandy Nairn - Director of Visual Arts at the Arts Council, Richard Carew Pole, Martin Rewcastle, Ian Martin, Richard Lester, Patrick Heron, Des Hosken from Penwith District Council and Katharine Heron visited both Wheal Ayr and gasworks sites. Nicholas Serota, making his first visit to the town in his new capacity, told the group that he supported the project whole-heartedly. As far as the choice for a gallery at Wheal Ayr was concerned, he felt that its Victorian suburban setting made it rather unattractive for a prestigious gallery. When the gasworks site was viewed, however, Nicholas Serota reported to his Trustees at their January meeting:

It is a spectacular location overlooking Porthmeor Beach...this site would be an exciting project with a potential which would fully merit the Trustees' support.

On 9 January 1989 the Steering Group met and formally agreed that the preferred location was the gasworks.

The chosen location became an unexpectedly important asset to the project. But this is not the first time that the land close to the centre of Porthmeor Beach had played a vital role in the life of the residents of St Ives. Its modern history went back one hundred and fifty years.

1 Old Market House photographed around 1900 when it was the meat market. During the nineteenth and early twentieth centuries the upstairs rooms housed the Council offices.

2 A view towards Wills Lane with the Market House on the extreme left, dated 1906. The building in the background appears to be a sweet shop. It later became a café and then a gallery, occupied first by Marjorie Par, then Reg Singh, and currently by Henry Gilbert.

3 Early photograph of the gasworks (c. 1913) at Porthmeor, with its two gasholders, looking east, with bathing machines and deckchairs in evidence. In front of the gasworks is what was known as the 'gas cliff'. Below the cliff, washing is hanging on a clothes line.

Percy Quick

1

St Ives Museum

2

William Carr

3

84

9 Porthmeor And Its Gasworks

It is interesting that a comparatively small piece of land, nestling into the hillside on the north and windswept side of St Ives, should have been the home of just two important amenities - the gasworks and Tate Gallery St Ives. It was fortuitous that the site was available for use as a gallery in the late 1980s when the gasworks, which had been located there for one hundred and forty years, was closed by the South Western Gas Board in the mid-1970s. The history of the gasworks, and the sandy beach beside which it stood, serves as a record both of the modernisation of the town as a whole and the development of an increasingly important holiday destination on its north-facing bay; while the story of St Ives' artistic life weaves in and out of these narratives.

> 'The Gasometer'
> In summer-time when the barometer
> Is up as high as it can be
> I love to stroll by the gasometer
> So cool, so fresh, beside the sea
> Especially now it's painted green
> And blends so nicely with the scene
>
> In winter-time when my thermometer
> Means chilly days and chillier nights
> I sit and bless that good gasometer
> That gives me cheerful warmth and lights;
> I'm very glad it's painted green
> Instead of what it might have been
>
> Last night I looked at my chronometer
> And saw 'twas late, and went to bed
> And dreamed they'd painted the gasometer
> A brilliant orange striped with red
> Then woke to recollect, serene
> They'd painted it a lovely green

Thus runs one of numerous anonymous verses printed in *The St Ives Times*. Several 'poems' were written about the town's gasworks, and this strangely scanning contribution, which appeared on 19 September 1930, is a good example of the way residents and visitors viewed its small industrial complex, for so long a prominent feature of one of the country's most beautiful beaches.

The sarcasm engendered by this amenity, which is reflected in the verses above, is in stark contrast to the manner in which the gas undertaking was repeatedly portrayed in official records. From the time the sixty-year old facility was taken over by the St Ives Borough Council, in 1894, until gas was nationalised in May 1949, every decision, every complaint, every detail about the price of gas, coal, coke and tar was faithfully recorded in the minutes of the Council meetings which, from 1910, appeared every month in the pages of *The St Ives Times*.

Reading these accounts now, the painstaking researcher uncovers a history of the town in peace and war: how it was administered and how it coped with new inventions and changing government policy, such as the telephone, electricity,

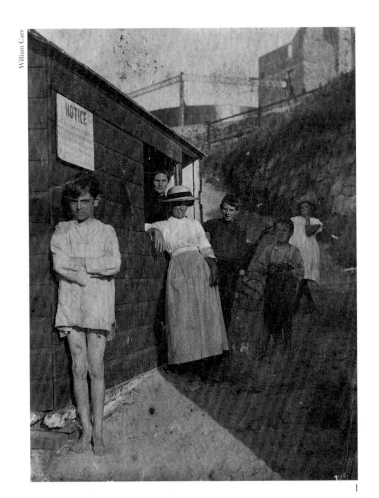

1

2

1 Porthmeor Beach immediately below the
gasworks, with the beach hut that was used
to sell tickets to hire deckchairs, around
1912. In front is young William Care, son
of John Care, who owned the beach
concession.

2 Porthmeor Beach showing the gasworks
and John Care's refreshment kiosk, from
which people could order trays of tea, in
the early 1930s. At the top left can be seen
the brick retort house.

better pay and conditions. But to obtain a more complete picture of the changing face of St Ives, the numerous letters to the newspaper, like the verses above, give a far greater insight into the way the town's inhabitants and visitors viewed the group of men (there were never any women) who ran an increasingly complex operation on behalf of the rate-payers.

It was to bring light to the town that the gasworks was originally built in 1835, three years before Queen Victoria's coronation and only thirteen years after gas lighting first came to Redruth. In those early days St Ives was almost cut off from the rest of the country by road. Before the Great Western Railway linked the town to London, Paddington, via the main rail network in 1877, few visitors hazarded the journey through the county. Goods and services were usually brought in by sea.

Despite its remoteness, St Ives had become a Borough as early as 1639, with a 'Mayor, recorder, town clerk, and a corporation consisting of twelve aldermen and twenty-four burgesses', according to the St Ives historian Cyril Noall. Every decision that involved the town from that date until 1974[1] was in the hands of this group of men.

In February 1835 at a public meeting held in the Town Hall, the upper floor of the recently rebuilt Market House in Market Square, beside the Parish Church, the decision was taken that St Ives should be lit by gas . The person who recorded this event was a Mr John Tregerthen Short, who had set up a Navigation School at the bottom of Barnoon Hill.[2]

Cyril Noall has written extensively about the early days of the gasworks in *The St Ives Times & Echo*. He recorded how, within a week of the public meeting, a committee was formed of some of the town's leading citizens, who wasted no time in putting the plan into action. They quickly purchased a site on part of Barnoon Field near Porthmeor Beach, well away from the town and its harbour, and in a part of St Ives 'little used except by the "Free Traders" who sometimes ran cargoes of contraband in here on moonless nights'.

Barnoon Field, previously used for grazing cattle and sheep, covered the whole area along the coast, including the land to the west of the new gasworks on which the cemetery was later consecrated in 1857. There was a paucity of roads in the area, and the only route to the cemetery was through the town and up steep Barnoon Hill. Below the burial ground the ancient holy well of Venton Ia provided Downlong's main water supply.[3]

Access to the new gasworks from the direction of Back Road, in the east, was also not easy,[4] but by 19 May, 1835 the foundation stone had been laid. The work was undertaken by Camborne masons (the St Ives masons had demanded one third more money to carry out the work, according to Cyril Noall). Apparently, during construction, the extraordinary sight of workmen digging holes in the ground to accommodate gas pipes produced 'crowds of curious sightseers'. It must have been even more extraordinary when, before Christmas that year, the town was lit 'with a most brilliant light' (although this is probably a slight exaggeration). The first public building to be illuminated was the Market House itself.

Except on moonlit nights, each evening lamplighters went around the town with a little ladder to turn the gas lamps on. A few hours later they made a second journey to turn them off again.[5] Unfortunately there was a downside to this 'progress'; in 1841 there were riots in the town because people refused to pay the new taxes to finance their facility. The moon or 'parish lantern' was still good enough for them, they believed. The disturbances led to the town appointing its first policeman.

Hardly any homes were lit by gas, however. Many residents of the town were too poor to change from oil lamps, which continued to be their only artificial light

1 In 1974 major changes occurred in the way local government was organised throughout England. Districts and Parish Councils replaced the old Borough and Rural District Councils.

2 The building that was once John Short's Navigation School was demolished in 1910 to make way for the Barnoon Cinema, later called the Palais de Danse which, in 1961, was taken over by Barbara Hepworth.

3 Venton Ia well was a popular meeting place for the girls and housewives who came daily to collect the precious liquid in their earthenware pitchers or 'particles'. (The well can still be seen at the foot of Porthmeor Hill.)

4 For further information about the land at Porthmeor and the difficulties encountered during construction of the gasworks, see 'The Recollections of Mr and Mrs Edwin Williams, 7 April 1942' recounted by Tre Pol Pen (Brian Stevens) in his article 'Uncovered evidence of a St Ives past' in *The St Ives Times & Echo* 12 August, 1994.

5 In 1892 lamplighters switched from using ladders to poles. This produced a saving in gas consumption as the men no longer had to set out so early on their rounds each evening.

1

1 Bryan Pearce several times painted the coal boats arriving at Smeaton's Pier. This particular painting 'Coalboat in St Ives Harbour' was painted in 1974.

2 A panoramic view of St Ives, around 1938, looking towards The Harbour with Porthmeor, Man's Head and Clodgy beyond. The coal boats came in at Smeaton's Pier (bottom right of the photograph) where they were unloaded. The coal was then put into horse-drawn carts and driven to the gasworks on the opposite bay.

2

well into the twentieth century. The gasworks, or 'gas house' as it was commonly known, therefore operated on a very small scale, and apparently was never very profitable.

In 1863 the company that owned the works sold out to a Mr George Bower. A nineteenth century 'entrepreneur', Mr Bower planned to run both the gasworks and the Ayr water supply that replaced the spring at Venton Ia, for personal profit.[6] Not surprisingly this proved to be a disruptive period for the town. Gas prices escalated and the service deteriorated to such an extent that the Council, after first unsuccessfully attempting to light the town with paraffin, decided to abandon public lighting altogether during the summer months. But it was finally pursuaded to take over the gasworks in 1894, when it acquired the land, buildings, coal and tar for about £2,000, and appointed a manager. From that day until Nationalisation, over fifty years later, the Council attempted to run the operation in a business-like way for the benefit of the town.

Coal for the gasworks regularly arrived by boat from all parts of the country. (As recently as the 1940s, the painter Bryan Pearce can remember ships, with their brightly coloured funnels, arriving at Smeaton's Pier.) The coal was shovelled by 'trimmers' onto the back of horse-drawn carts, and weighed on the weighbridge near the Sloop Inn. Here the appropriate dues were calculated and paid to the Harbour Master.[7]

The coal was taken through the narrow streets to the coal stores at the gasworks. Some of this fine quality coal, however, never reached its destination. A small quantity always fell between the ship and the pier during unloading. At low tide children went out with their buckets to pick up what they could find, to take home for burning on the family's Cornish range. Youngsters could also be seen following the carts through the town ready to pick up any coal that fell onto the road, as the wheels of the carts rattled over the uneven cobbles.

At the gasworks itself, where teams of men worked three shifts throughout the twenty-four hour period, the coal was taken up in a lift to the top of the hopper where it was baked by a furnace under the retorts. The gas was passed through water and beds of iron oxide in vertical coolers which extracted the impure sulphur. The residue of tar was piped away and coke was left at the bottom. The coke was then cooled down with water.

Both coke and tar were sold to the public. The bakers in town made regular journeys to the gasworks, some with wheelbarrows, to take away the coke for their ovens. And as it was light in weight, the children, too, were often sent to fetch coke for their parents. The tar was bought by the fishermen for their boats. Joe Plummer remembers buying tar for six pence a gallon.[8]

From only reading the Council minutes, the reader would be forgiven for believing that the gasworks was generally a success story, although it was suggested there was sometimes a certain amount of 'hot air' produced by the councillors in their interminable meetings. A more interesting and evocative picture of how a number of residents of the town thought of the 'progress' being made by the town's 'fathers' can be seen repeatedly in the letters to *The St Ives Times*. A 'Member of Cocking Court' (an area just off Fore Street) responding to one of the regular increases in the price of gas, was very outspoken in August 1919:

Sir - As a representative of the Downalong and the fair half of St Ives as don't use gas and don't want to, I should like to know what the other half as kicking up all the rumpus about paying eight shilling and six pence for gas and meters according. They've got the remedy in their hands all right, let 'em cut off their gas and get their light and heat same as we do which will oblige the Corporation to shut down their rotten old gas works and give the hard working gas committee a rest poor dears. And the sooner they do it the better for we shan't get electricity till they do...

6 See note 1, Chapter 8, about earlier problems with the water supply.

7 Details of these dues, covering the years 1930-1933, are listed in a small book in the possession of the current Harbour Master.

8 When the new retort house was built in 1933, the tar was no longer of the right quality for use on the fishing boats. Supplies were ordered from Hayle instead. Not surprisingly, the sale of tar from the St Ives gasworks plummeted at that time.

Aerofilms

1

Studio St Ives

1 An aerial view of the gasworks at Porthmeor Beach, 1938/9. Clearly visible to the right of the brick retort house are Number One and Number Two gasholders, while behind is the cylindrical high pressure holder that provided gas for Carbis Bay. Compare this view with the frontispiece photograph of Tate Gallery St Ives from the air.

2 A close-up view of the brick retort house as it appeared just before World War Two.

2

This was an interesting point. Gas supplies appear to have been intermittent, in this case probably because of difficulties in obtaining supplies of coal during and after the First World War. Despite the problems, electricity was slow in coming to the town, unlike neighbouring Hayle. The new form of power is mentioned little in the pages of *The St Ives Times*; it would seem that the Council did not welcome serious competition. Their nervousness can be detected from reading the Council minutes of early December 1922:

The Council had allowed electric light into the town, and the people behind it intended to advertise it and obtain as much custom as possible. It would therefore be the duty of the Gas Committee to take measures to maintain and increase the consumption of gas if the Gas Company was to be lifted completely out of the rut into which it had fallen, and from which it was lifting its head.

The Councillors gave approval only slowly, throughout the 1920s, for the Cornwall Electricity Power Company to lay underground cables around the town, one section at a time. Even Borlase Smart had difficulty getting electricity installed in the galleries of the St Ives Society of Artists, on Back Road West, but this had more to do with apathy. At the Society's AGM, in 1935, he told members that sales were being lost through inadequate lighting. Although, apparently nearby Newlyn Gallery had found it absolutely necessary to install such an amenity, the committee nonetheless decided that the question should be deferred until the autumn.

It took time for many people to be connected to the system, and electric street lighting was not installed in St Ives until after the Second World War.[9]

Meanwhile, after the First World War, the gasworks increased in size to cope with extra demand, and more public lamps were erected. However there were constant complaints about lamps not being lit, and visitors wrote regularly to *The St Ives Times* lamenting that they had fallen over on the way back to their hotels, after an evening out. Some angry correspondents suggested that the only lamps lit were those outside the homes of the councillors! There were other problems. During the coal strike of 1921 supplies were again in short supply, and five years later pressure had to be severely reduced at the time of the 1926 General Strike.

The gas facility was very smelly. Mary Quick, whose father worked at the gas-works, before and during the Second World War, wrote in an article 'The town lit-up for Christmas 154 years ago' in *The St Ives Times & Echo* of 15 December, 1989:

...the stench of sulphur could be nauseating to those living nearby, especially when the wind was in the north west. On such occasions even venturing into the Digey invited a serious assault upon the nose!

For some people, however, the fumes could be of benefit. Beryl James remembers, as a small child, being taken out to Porthmeor in her pram to breath in the tar from the works when she had whooping cough.

Finance was a regular concern. In 1922 the councillors were embarrassed when the unfortunate gas manager, Mr Grant, wrote to the newspaper asking for a pay rise. His employers were not keen to raise his salary by £40 to £275 a year. Even after the gasworks had been expanded in the 1930s, John Thomas, who joined as an apprentice fitter in 1935, still remembers that on being granted an increase of three shillings and fourpence an hour, one of the Councillors said: 'These rises have got to stop'. In 1924 there were complaints from some councillors at the proposal to install a telephone at the facility because it was thought to be an unnecessary expense.

In December 1928 the Mayor opened a gas showroom in Fore Street which proved very popular with the town as consumers no longer had to pay their gas bills at the Town Hall on the top floor of the Market House. It was originally sited

9 Public lighting, however, was not welcomed by all. A Mr K O Harris, from Keynsham, who as a visitor probably saw St Ives through rose-coloured spectacles, wrote to *The St. Ives Times* on 4 October 1946: 'Gone will be those quiet dim gurries hiding secrets (real and imagined) perhaps for hundreds of years and always offering to the visitor a different way home. What, in England, can replace Virgin Street, with its wheezing gas lamps, whispering in doorways and scuttling cats?'

HOME MANAGEMENT CORNER

Conducted by | Miss Switch

LET'S HAVE A VEGETARIAN MEAL!

Meat rationing is here. Well, we needn't worry much about that. Offal, the rather unpleasant official name for liver, kidneys, breast, sweetbreads, etc., remains unrationed but they are likely to be fairly scarce (and perhaps dearer than they were) · because they are much sought after. So we shall have at least one fish meal every week and why not at least one *vegetarian* meal? I can promise you that a vegetarian menu can be tasty, filling and nourishing and any of the following recipes will bear me out. They are all quite substantial dishes and may be substituted for the entree course.

BEAN STEAKS

4 oz. flour. ¼ teaspoon bicarbonate soda.

SMALLER SUGAR RATIONS

The next of the official

MINISTRY OF FOOD WARTIME COOKING DEMONSTRATIONS

at your Electricity Service Centre will be devoted to sugarless recipes and ways of making your sugar go further.

ASK FOR DETAILS AT THE

ELECTRICITY SERVICE · CENTRE

melted margarine. Milk for mixing. Salt and pepper.

Mix the bread-crumbs, walnuts, margarine, egg and just a little milk in a basin. Drain the peas, rub through a sieve and mix in the resulting puree with the rest. Season, add onion and mix thoroughly, then pack the mixture into a small buttered tin. Cover with greased paper and bake for about 40 minutes in a moderate oven (350° F. in electric oven). Serve with tomato sauce and peas.

VEGETABLE PUDDING

1 small spring cabbage. 2 ozs. margarine. 1 egg. 1 teaspoonful milk. Breadcrumbs. Seasoning. 1 oz. grated cheese.

1

1 The Cornwall Electric Power Co. regularly advertised in *The St Ives Times* before and during the War. These wartime recipes for vegetarian meals appeared on 31 May 1940. As a result of this campaign, the Borough Council, who owned the gas concession, organised rival cookery demonstrations in the Gas Showrooms in Fore Street.

2 Thomas Paynter, also known as 'Man Friday' spent many years living at the gasworks, where he kept himself warm. There he recounted extra-ordinary tales to passing visitors. He died in 1941.

3 A view of the gasworks on Porthmeor Beach, looking west, soon after it was enlarged in 1933. Its distinctive brick retort house and chimney dominated the beach which, even then, was a popular bathing area. To the right of the retort house the cemetery can clearly be seen.

2

3

in a small workshop opposite the Castle Inn. In 1938 the showroom moved to larger premises, a little further down Fore Street.[10] As well as providing workshops for repairing pipework, there was enough space to store the equipment the gas fitters required when they went out to install cookers. Here also customers viewed the very latest gas appliances which, in turn, boosted the sale of gas.

The showroom assumed a wider role when it was utilised for demonstrating austerity cooking during the Second World War, as part of the government's 'Kitchen Front' campaign. The sessions were run alongside rival demonstrations organised by the Cornwall Electric Power Company, often at the Palais de Danse, that complemented their expensive advertising campaign begun in 1939. Each month *The St Ives Times* reproduced a smart looking 'Miss Switch' who extolled the virtues of clean inexpensive electric appliances and who, after 1939, helped war-worn housewives make the best use of heating, lighting and available food.

The gas showroom, which for a while was managed by Mrs Langford, the gas manager's wife, remained at the same location in Fore Street, until the South Western Gas Board closed it down in 1984, much to the anger of residents.

One of the more colourful anecdotes about the gasworks concerns a 'Cap'n Paynter'. Eddie Murt told the tale in his posthumously published book *Downlong Days*:

...the main attraction at the gasworks was a man called Cap'n Paynter, known as Man Friday to the general public. He slept in the works and no doubt the dust helped him to earn his nickname. His stories were told in all seriousness to any who would listen. He had sailed in ships with cargoes of small green men, umbrella seed etc...His most famous story was when the mate with a full set of whiskers went on to the foredeck and the wind blew his whiskers off, only to stick to the chin of Cap'n Paynter who happened to be on the bridge. His face still survives in pictures and a well-known Kodak advertisement, but alas most of his stories have been lost. Thomas Bassett Paynter died in March 1941 aged 76 years.

Many St Ives residents still recall the gasworks as it looked after it had been enlarged in 1933. Major expansion was necessary because the demand for gas had increased substantially, following the incorporation of Carbis Bay and Lelant into the Borough. There was also a steady increase in the number of summer visitors coming to the area.

A new vertical retort design was the radical solution chosen to increase the production of gas. Any other development of the works would have meant purchasing extra land and rehousing people living in The Meadow to the east. The new facility, apparently 'the most up to date plant in Cornwall', was built by Woodall Duckham & Co at a cost of about £10,000. Many who helped build it were local fishermen glad of earning extra money.[11]

The expanded works, which took eight months to build, was opened on 11 January 1933, by no less a person than the President of the Board of Trade, Mr Walter Runciman. There was tremendous pride in the town.[12] On the way out of the works 'the old plant was seen', said that week's newspaper report, 'and a sorry spectacle it presented, after seeing its modern successor'. But it was like the emperor's new clothes. Any photograph of this 'fine addition' to the town clearly shows that the Mayor and Corporation's 'pride and joy' were misplaced. As a letter from Miss F Lynn-Pitt, whose brother had had an artist's studio on Porthmeor Beach, revealed only nine months after the grand opening:

Would not the Council be doing far better for the town by using the ratepayers money in removing the odious gas works, especially the recent atrocious addition, to some remote part of town?

And later, a Marcus Adams, calling himself 'A lover of St Ives', was even more forthright. In September 1938 he wrote: 'I should like to see the gasworks blown up'.

10 The second gas showroom occupied a site, with cellars below, which had for the previous ten years been let to a butcher named Cocking.

11 During the winter months the fishermen were often unable to go to sea, and there was, of course, no social security benefit available to them on those occasions.

12 The Mayor, Alderman G Warren, in his speech at the lunch after opening the new facility, extolled the virtues of the gasworks: 'The reputation of the Cornish Pasty in the past is well known; I venture to say that a Cornish Pasty cooked by heat with the St Ives Gas is a feast (and I was going to say washed down with the radio-active water from Trenwith) fit for Kings.'

1

Colin Orchard

2

1 Porthmeor Beach looking towards Mans Head with tents and bathing machines much in evidence, taken in the early 1930s. John Care's snack bar can be seen on the left.

2 A contemporary photograph of Man's Head, the distinctive granite rock formation that is to the west of Porthmeor. This unusual shot shows Porthmeor Beach in the background.

And that is the truth of the matter. What had once been a small industrial site, hidden from the public gaze, was now a prominent building, dominating an increasingly popular tourist area. It was regularly called 'a monstrosity' by the general public until the day it was finally pulled down in 1958.[13] The red brick retort house, with a tall chimney in its pitched roof rose, above the surrounding buildings like a 'carbuncle', and commanded the entire Porthmeor Beach. As well as its appearance, residents still had to contend with the smell which, in certain winds, permeated the whole town.

The gasworks was further updated. Shortly after the retort house was built, a large distinctive cylindrical high pressure gas holder (apparently 'the second of its kind in the country') was constructed to the rear of the works to store gas for Lelant and Carbis Bay.[14]

Once located on a road to no-where, whether the residents liked it or not, the gasworks became an integral part of the expanding town, which was gradually being opened up on its northern side. A road past the gates was built in 1893, and a footpath to Man's Head and Clodgy, at the edge of the moors to the west, became popular with walkers.

In 1911, in order to generate extra revenue from those taking exercise in that area, the Council decided to install chocolate machines along the path, hoping to entice even more tourists to visit this beauty spot. One angry letter writer, a Mr John Abbot, complained bitterly of the unsightliness of these machines in such fine surroundings. He did concede, however: 'My annoyance was tempered by the satisfaction derived from noticing that most had effectively been put out of action'. Even at this early date, some people could foresee that St Ives might possibly degenerate into a 'commonplace tripper's resort of round-abouts, blatant noises and chocolate machines'.

It would be wrong, however, to imagine that neither Porthmeor beach nor the more popular Porthminster beach, facing St Ives Bay, were unspoilt. Another letter writer of that year, Mr G Walton Evans, said:

...frequently the sea is unfit to enter, owing to the sewerage which drifts, at certain states of the tide and wind, inshore...judging from the amount of potato peelings, cabbage leaves, lemon skins, old boots, etc. floating about, it is evident that the authorities permit rubbish to be thrown into the sea...[15]

Despite constant criticisms, the outside world read eulogies of the town's amenities. The painter Frank L Emanuel vividly described Porthmeor, with its growing importance to artists, in *The Architectural Review* of 1920:

...a semicircle of lovely clean sand out of which rise here and there tawny shaggy rocks. Into this bay ride in magestic ranks the magnificent crested rollers of the Atlantic. At the town end of the bay along a segment of the circle rises straight out of the sand an unbroken line of lofty stone walls. A few years ago no windows opened from these 'cellars' on to the Atlantic; but now, braving the storming of the seas, great studio windows and top lights have broken out all along their upper portions. Even this alteration has not removed the likeness of this spot to a bit of Tunisian or Moroccan coast town.

Porthmeor beach, unlike Porthminster, was used, almost exclusively, by the local people. Before the First World War, children spent every idyllic day of their summer holidays 'camping out' on the side of the ancient hill fort on The Island, leading up to the battery. Here they played in makeshift tents made out of washed potato bags and broom handles. For the adults the area had more utilitarian uses. The beach itself was used, for many years, for the setting of nets to catch small fish. And as recently as the 1930s both the sand and the blue elvan rock, which heated up quickly, together with the grass on The Island, were utilised to lay out the

13 During construction of Tate Gallery St Ives, local people called the grey building emerging under its scaffolding a 'monstrosity' as well as a 'hideous blight' and an 'eyesore'; forgetting, no doubt, the edifice it was replacing!

14 The high pressure holder joined the large Number One low pressure holder (site of the Tate Gallery's Loggia) and the smaller Number Two holder, as well as coke hoppers, compressor house and meter house to the east of the retort.

15 According to Cyril Noall in his book *Yesterday's Town : St Ives:* 'Sadly, in 1899, the Council was itself accused of dumping ashes from the municipal gasworks and other refuse on the beach, while bathers and picnic parties were subjected to a dangerous bombardment of stones during blasting operations in the nearby quarry'.

1

1 Three washerwomen making their way down onto Porthmeor Beach with their baskets of washing, in order to lay the wet clothes out to dry on the rocks. More washing can be seen on The Island in the background. This photograph was taken after 1904 (when the War Office demolished the old chapel on The Island after it no longer needed the building to store its munitions), and before 1911 (the date when the chapel was rebuilt by Sir Edward Hain).

2

3

2 The Sloop Inn and, to the right, Pudding Bag Lane, whose old houses were demolished in 1935 under a Government Clearance Order. It was believed that the old cottages were unfit for human habitation, but the area's demise divided the town. Despite an outcry from the artists and the Council for the Protection of Rural England, many of the councillors believed that the Sloop Car Park, built on the site, was a vital addition to the town's amenities. The stones from the houses in Pudding Bag Lane were used to construct a retaining wall near the cemetery at Porthmeor.

3 Porthmeor Beach in the mid 1950s. (Compare with 1.) By now the area had gained in popularity, due to the fact that the gasworks was no longer producing gas. The large building to the right of The Island is Hampton's Mattress factory which, between 1926 and 1941 had been the site of Crysede Ltd, a company that dyed and printed silk and manufactured fine clothes. St Nicholas' Court is now located on the site.

Monday washing.

In 1912, facilities were first provided to encourage holidaymakers to come to Porthmeor. Mr John Care and Mr James each rented a portion of the beach and supplied amenities such as tents, bathing machines (by the day or week) and deck-chairs. They also provided the holiday-makers with trays of teas.[16]

Twenty years later the Borough Council decided to purchase the land along the edge of the beach, part of which was used for allotments by the fishermen between April and September.[17] The Council had the idea of improving the facilities, as well as increasing its own revenue by providing car parking and a bowling green. Miss F Lynn-Pitt was very angry. Her brother, the artist James Lynn Pitt, who had died in 1922, had 'developed Porthmeor as a bathing place', presumably for his own profit.[18] Miss Lynn-Pitt's opposition to the land being compulsorily purchased, coupled with opposition from the beach's other owners, led to a public hearing in May 1934. When compensation payments were being discussed, a Mr Jenner, for the Council, said that he did not think the beach was likely to get more popular. 'If £45 or £50 was a fair rent now', he predicted 'I do not think that in 1950 there would be any increase'!

At the beginning of 1935, an improved road was constructed from Ayr down Porthmeor Hill to link up with Beach Road at the bottom. A large retaining wall, thirty yards long, below the cemetery, had been created in 1933 from the stone that had come from the houses recently demolished in Pudding Bag Lane, under a Government Clearance Order.[19] During the war, the high wall, hung with a huge net, was used as a training ground for the American soldiers prior to the D-Day landings.

A sea wall from the Meadow in the east, past the gasworks, was erected in 1936. St Ives was now well and truly on the tourist map.[20] Borlase Smart himself was commissioned by the Council to paint a panoramic view of the Borough that was made into a poster.

Porthmeor Beach will long be remembered as the graveyard of the 3,700 ton Panamanian steamer *Alba*, loaded with coal which, on 31 January, 1938, ran aground on the rocks on the north-west side of The Island. Most of the crew were rescued by the St Ives lifeboat *Caroline Parsons*, with the assistance of many of the townspeople who risked their lives to haul them out of the water. Sadly, three crew-members were brought ashore dead. Two were buried shortly afterwards in the Barnoon Cemetery. The *Alba's* boilers can still be seen at low tide.

Before the Second World War a build-up of sand at The Island end of Porth-meor Beach began to cause concern. Cynics blamed it on the new gasworks, but it was actually caused by the tides and the currents. During the war little was done, although American Army GI's were made to shovel the sand as a punishment. Wilhelmina Barns-Graham, who had a Porthmeor Studio, recalls that: 'The Americans hoped to see nude models when they were clearing the sand. One day they cracked a window!'

It was during the war that the gasworks became memorable in a different way, although readers from out of the area would have found it difficult to know the reason from the newspapers reports. On Saturday 5 September, 1942 *The Western Echo* heralded:

South West Town Bombed...One person killed - many others injured. Beaches and streets machine-gunned. Much damage to property.

What was being censored from everyone who had not witnessed the event was that:

Two bombs...fell at St Ives [on Friday 28 April at 3pm] demolished two gasometers, [sic] wrecked four houses, severely damaged twenty others and caused slight damage to nearly four hundred others...fifty-four people were injured.[21]

16 Nevertheless a Councillor in 1938 bemoaned the difference between the town's two major beaches. 'Porthminster Beach looks like a parlour after it has been spring-cleaned, and Porthmeor looks like a scullery during lime-washing'.

17 Kit Law remembers the path along Porthmeor being called the 'gas cliff' at that time.

18 James Lynn Pitt's paintings, many of Porth-meor Beach itself, were exhibited in his 'White Studio' at Porthmeor.

19 The desecration of Pudding Bag Lane was thought by many to be a scandalous operation. Borlase Smart and other artists were very angry that such a picturesque part of old St Ives should be destroyed to make way for the Sloop Car Park. Their anger did not abate. Borlase Smart wrote in a letter to *The St Ives Times* of 4 June, 1937: 'When I look around St Ives and see what has happened to certain parts of the town and neither the inhabitants nor the [Council for the Protection of Rural England] have apparently raised a finger or a voice to question such vandalism, it is beyond belief'.

20 Holiday makers sometimes had to contend with unexpected occurrences. On August Bank Holiday in 1938 a thunderbolt fell within a few feet of the water's edge at Porthmeor 'like a streak of fire'.

21 The death occurred to a Mrs James returning to her house at the top of Porthmeor Hill after shopping in the town.

South=West Coast Town Bombed.

One Person Killed— Many Others Injured.

BEACHES AND STREETS MACHINE-GUNNED.

MUCH DAMAGE TO PROPERTY.

A South-West Coastal town had its first daylight air-raid last Friday afternoon, when two enemy 'planes made a sudden sweep over the town.

Coming out of the sky with a suddenness that startled the visitors and inhabitants, they flew very low before dropping two bombs—one on an industrial building and the other in a residential part of the town.

Despite the suddenness of the attack, accompanied as it was with terrific machine-gunning and cannon-gunning, the inhabitants behaved in a remarkably stoic manner, and the true spirit of "one and all" prevailed in their efforts to render succour and aid to the many injured.

All the services were quickly in action, and officials and personnel deserve the highest praise for their indefatigable work.

Since the bombing, too, working parties have been very busy. Without being invidious, high praise must be paid to the Surveyor and his staff; to Mr. Young and the men under his charge; and to Mr. Casley Langford and his men. Appreciative work has also been done by members of the W.V.S., Ambulance, First-Aid Parties and the A.T.C. lads.

Unfortunately—although the severity of the raid might have caused even more casualti...

1

2

1 The headline of *The Western Echo* of 5 September 1942 reported that a south-west coast town had been bombed. Because of wartime censorship there was no mention of the fact that the town in question was St Ives. However, everyone who had been injured was named in the article, and their injuries detailed. There was, of course, no mention of the fact that the gasworks had been severely damaged.

2 A group of St Ives children sitting on Porthmeor Beach, about 1946, showing clearly how the gasworks dominated the area. The three girls with dark hair, from left to right: Joan, Vivien and Pam Hawkin. In front of Joan is Mary Pearce, Bryan Pearce's younger sister. The building up of sand in the background can be seen.

3 A rare photograph showing damage done to one of the gasholders after the facility had been bombed on 28 August 1942. Compare this with similar photographs on page 172 of workmen looking into a hole in the same place while constructing Tate Gallery St Ives.

3

John Thomas remembers the occasion vividly. He was undertaking repairs to the east of the retort house. Two German planes flew low towards St Ives from the direction of Hayle, and both carefully aimed their bombs. The first hit the top of the retort house; the explosion in Number Two gas holder blew up Number One holder, while the force of the blast deflected the path of the second plane so that its bomb fell near the top of Porthmeor Hill. The planes turned and fired cannon shells, which pierced the high pressure holder. Then before they left the area they fired on the beach, (luckily close to the edge of the sea), as well as the town. They then flew over the main road to Penzance, which they also machine-gunned, before returning across the Channel.

The high pressure holder rapidly lost its gas, and a very explosive mixture built up inside. If a fire engine had not been fairly close by, John Thomas believes that the holder would have blown up, severely damaging the town.

It was a very sunny afternoon. There were many people on the beach, which is why the number of casualties was so high, for the force of the explosions led to debris from the gasworks being flung as far as Smeaton's Pier to the east and Orange Lane in the west. A young John Cock, playing with his brother in a garden at Carthew, remembers vividly the roaring of the burning gas holders, as the two boys ran into the house to escape the lumps of debris falling into the garden. And Joe Plummer, in a fishing boat with his son, out in the bay, recalls 'the empty shells falling about us like rain' and people on the beach being smothered with tar from the gasworks.[22]

The facility was out of action for six weeks. Everyone in the town was told to turn off their gas supply. Staff worked fourteen hours a day, seven days a week, to make the repairs, under the direction of the Manager, Mr Langford. He used highly unauthorised methods to return the gasworks into proper working order. The main at the top of Porthmeor Hill, which was also damaged, had to be repaired at the same time. Before the town could be reconnected to the supply, staff visited everyone a second time to make sure that there were no gas appliances still turned on.

The buildup of sand on Porthmeor Beach continued to be a menace. It was shifted, first in 1944, after pressure was put on the council by the redoubtable Borlase Smart. His letter not only pointed out the menace itself but, he asked, 'who wants to have to gaze at an ugly gas works when you face the sun in your deck-chair?' Then, in 1945, a petition was signed by 240 residents to persuade the Council to take more positive action.

The situation was not improved when, in September 1948, a gale from the North-North-West, accompanied by high tides, removed hundreds of tons of sand from the western end of Porthmeor; at the same time doing considerable damage to neighbouring property.

By 1950 the problem still had not been solved. The sand was invading people's homes and studios. The Council did nothing; they were unwilling to take full responsibility for the large clearance bill. Finally, in the spring of 1952, 'The Battle of the Beach' was won. Two powerful bulldozers shifted about 40,000 tons of sand to the satisfaction of local residents and holiday makers alike.[23]

It was a sad day when, in April 1949, the gasworks was acquired by the South Western Gas Board. The Councillors were greatly upset by the socialist policy of nationalisation; they were justifiably proud that their facility was now operating efficiently and profitably. Alderman J Daniel thought it 'a form of legalized robbery'. But there was nothing they could do. The Board paid the Borough £22,000, and accepted a loan debt of the same amount. Mr Langford, the Man-

22 Part of the bomb that landed on the gasworks, as well as other memorabilia, may still be seen in the St Ives Museum at Wheal Dream.

23 Part of the cost of removing the sand was met by contributions to a 'Sand Fund' organised by *The St Ives Times*. The largest single contribution of £50, came from the Arts Council of Great Britain.

1

2

3

1 'The Battle of the Beach'. Two bulldozers move 40,000 tons of sand on Porthmeor Beach in 1952, after several years accumulation, which led to some of the studios along the beach having sand half way up their windows. The long building without windows, to the left of the photograph, is 'Barny's Loft'; next to which are the Piazza Studios, with Porthmeor Studios (still in existence) beyond.

2 The spectacular scene of the chimney stack belonging to the retort house at the gasworks, when it was demolished in December 1958. It accidentally fell in the wrong direction. This series of photographs was taken by a local resident, Miss Alfreda Perkin (who lived in The Meadow) and was reproduced in *The St Ives Times & Echo* on 5 December 1958, at a time when illustrations in that newspaper were few and far between.

3 Demolition of the retort house in 1958 seen from above.

4 The rusting gasholder as it looked in the late 1970s, sandwiched between the blocks of Meadow Flats.

4

ager, was praised for his success and for the way he had worked with his staff.

Nevertheless, for John Thomas and his colleagues, working conditions now improved greatly. Under the old regime, Thomas recalls that he 'had been gassed several times, until Dr Lockart insisted that respirators must be worn when working in dangerous areas'. The staff's pay increased, and for the first time they were able to travel to the gasworks at Penzance and Hayle. A few months after nationalisation the price of gas rose throughout the region. Members of the Council, of course, were angry, but they were no longer in control. Neither, apparently, was the new owner able to eradicate the strong smell of gas that still permeated the area.[24]

It was the beginning of the end. Despite an increase in demand for gas, first Penzance and then, in 1957, Truro became the area's local supplier. Most of the gasworks in Cornwall closed down. The ugly vertical retort at Porthmeor Beach became obsolete. The Council hoped to buy back the land, initially for use as a car park, but the Gas Board said it would be retaining the gasholders for storage purposes, and purchase was therefore out of the question.

Residents could not wait for its demise. An angry Mr E H Richardson wrote to *The St Ives Times & Echo* on 1 March 1957:

Take away this lofty eyesore. The gasworks overlooking Porthmeor Beach, St Ives tallest and ugliest building, have been a useless *monstrosity* for some years.

It was to be the following summer, when part of the redundant eastern area, measuring about a quarter of an acre, which contained the retort house and chimney, was sold back to the town for £600 and demolition took place.[25] The retort did not fall without one final drama, however. The chimney stack apparently fell the wrong way, and crashed through the roof of the compressor house below (one of the facilities that the Gas Board was hoping to retain!).

The Gas Board arranged to clear the site. In 1961 the first block in the Meadow Flats complex was built there, containing eight one-bedroom units for elderly people. Designed by Henry Gilbert, it stood at the eastern end of the gasworks, which now contained only two gas holders and the meter house by the gate.[26]

The closure of the gasworks seems to have signalled a new lease of life for the Porthmeor area. During the 1960s the bay became more popular than ever with holidaymakers, who were now pouring into the town, but it never developed into a second 'harbour front'; it remained the home of apartments and artists' studios, rather than shops and other commercial activities.

The first housing development along the beach was the construction of 'Barnaloft', residential studios on the site of 'Maid Betsies cellars'. These cellars, which had no windows onto Porthmeor, consisted of old net lofts and stores where since the early nineteenth century pilchards had been cured in salt and packed for export. Part of the building, opposite the Bible Christian Chapel on Back Road West, was owned by Barney Stevens, and had once been a coal yard, known as 'Barny's Loft'. This was another complex designed by Henry Gilbert. The builder was Percy Williams & Sons of Redruth. Consisting of twenty-two units, all facing the sea, the block was completed in 1963. A year later the scheme won a gold medal for good design from the Ministry of Housing and Local Government and the RIBA.

Just to the east of Barnaloft was the recently opened Penwith Gallery. To the west, Henry Gilbert designed a second block of beach-side flats and maisonettes on the site of the old three-storey wooden Piazza artists' studios and the large garage that had been owned by a Mr Sam England. This new complex of twenty-seven flats, cottages and split-level studios, also built by Percy Williams & Sons Ltd., was completed in 1967, but not without a certain amount of controversy.

24 There must have been other problems with the nationalised gasworks, because in January 1951, the Hoteliers wrote a letter to *The St Ives Times* complaining of the quality of the gas supply.

25 The land would revert to Penwith District Council when the Borough came to an end in 1974.

26 Above the site, in 1956, the first section of the Barnoon car park was laid out to ease the severe traffic problems encountered every summer. Car parking facilities in the town, were then so poor that it became the practice to park on a large area of The Island. It took some time, however, to extend Barnoon Car Park to its present size, as councillors and residents alike felt it inappropriate for holidaymakers to put their cars so close to a cemetery.

1

3

2

4 Porthmeor Beach Development between 1963 and 1967. Viewed from the west, the design incorporates a pedestrian walkway with seating above, and small beach huts on two levels below. To the west, and out of view, is a building for The Surf Life Saving Club which houses the town's lifeguard. In the 1960s much of The Island was used for parking cars in the summer months. There were plans to tarmac much of The Island for a permanent car park, but there was such an outcry that the proposal was greatly toned down.

1 The pilchard packing cellars and net lofts before they were demolished to make way for the Barnaloft studio flats on Porthmeor Beach (completed in 1963). Behind the roof can be seen St Nicholas' Chapel on The Island.

2 The newly built Barnaloft studio flats, completed in 1963, and the first new building scheme in the area following the demolition of the retort house at the gasworks. Each of the twenty-two units in the three-storey building has a balcony facing Porthmeor Beach.

3 The Piazza Flats, that replaced the old wooden artists' studios, constructed alongside Barnaloft, were completed in 1967. This photograph shows a view of the four storey building from the back with its enclosed courtyard. The complex contains twenty-seven flats, cottages and split-level studios, each with a balcony overlooking Porthmeor Beach.

4

The new development, being five storeys high, was taller than neighbouring Barnaloft. There were lengthy discussions between the councillors about this discrepancy in height, and angry letters appeared in the newspaper. One correspondent suggested that local residents were losing their privacy and 'will now have to curtain their windows'. Nevertheless, both Barnaloft and Piazza soon became highly sought after, often as second homes, by distinguished professional people.[27] In 1969 the Piazza development was awarded a diploma in the Minister of Housing's awards for Good Design in Housing, the only scheme to do so in the South West Region that year.

At the same time, the beach facilities themselves were improved by the Borough Council, again not without a certain amount of contention. The then owner of Seal Cottage, on Back Road West, thought that the development would:

certainly not be appreciated by the artists...and the Council will succeed in driving away from St Ives the many holiday-makers who are thankful to get away from the noisy crowds and ice-cream kiosks, and who come to Porthmeor Beach as one of the few places where they can enjoy the sea from an unspoilt beach.

The beach huts, tea room, shop and shelters, again designed by Henry Gilbert, and occupying the central section of the beach, did not become the expected eyesore. Erected in stages, as public funds became available, they were designed in such a way that they tucked in below the level of the existing road. The highway itself was given a new pavement to allow pedestrians easy access along the central and western end of the beach.

Porthmeor was used several times for hosting the National Surf Championships, the first occasion being in August 1963. The event was billed as 'the biggest open air event in Cornwall this year'. The Surf Life Saving Club's facilities, originally a small hut, were now improved and incorporated into the rest of the beach development.

There was only one occasion when the beach had to be closed to the public, and that was at the time of the Torrey Canyon disaster. In April 1967, gallons of crude oil poured from a holed tanker wrecked on the Seven Stones reef off Lands End, some of which was washed onto Porthmeor. A sickly smell permeated the entire area and, apparently, all the bees were killed off. A team of British and American troops using heavy equipment, together with volunteers from the town, successfully battled for nine weeks with large quantities of detergent to ensure that the sands were clean in time for the summer season. They also constructed a long boom across Porthmeor Beach, the Harbour and Porthminster.[28]

Finally, the steeply sloping plot of land to the west of the gasworks, known as Johnny Hollow's Field, became another phase of the Meadow Flats scheme, developed for elderly people by the Borough. Twenty flats in three blocks were planned. But this was a problematic development. Construction costs were very high due to the fact that large quantities of rock had to be excavated from the site in order to provide level tiers for each flat to have an unrestricted sea view. During building operations a retaining wall on the site collapsed, and costs soared, which provoked anger in the Council chamber. Nevertheless the flats were completed in the summer of 1969, and they became very popular with their elderly owners.

It had been hoped that the South Western Gas Board would clear the remaining installations from the site so that the Meadow Flats development could be completed. But in July 1975 it was announced that the Board wished to overhaul and renew its equipment at Porthmeor. The Borough's Housing Committee realised that the Meadow Flats scheme would never be completed.[29]

When North Sea Gas was brought to St Ives direct to the mains, the final buildings became redundant. For a short time the gas was brought by road from

27 Artists who took apartments in the Barnaloft and Piazza flats included Barbara Hepworth, Bernard Leach, F E McWilliam and Merlyn Evans (father of the architect Eldred Evans, who with her husband David Shalev designed Tate Gallery St Ives.)

28 The photographer Sam Bennetts, whose house overlooks Porthmeor Beach recalls, however, that 'The boom soon broke up because of the fierce currents.'

29 The Borough then turned their attention to the possible redevelopment of the recently vacated Couch's Garage on Back Road East (See Chapter 8 - The Search for a Site).

1 Johnny Hollow's Field, between the gasworks and the cemetery at Barnoon, in 1967, was earmarked for the second phase of the Meadow Flats complex. The turning space in the road in the foreground had just been made.

2 Construction of the second phase of Meadow Flats, adjacent to the gasworks, as seen in 1968. Complications arose during the building work because of the very steeply sloping site. Many of the flats' new residents moved from Ayr and Penbeagle to be much closer to the centre of town.

3 The completed Meadow Flats development, as seen from the air in 1969. At the top of the photograph is the newly laid out Barnoon Car Park, built to accommodate the growing number of holiday-makers. To the right is the cemetery; to the bottom the Surf Life Saving Club and to the left the gasworks.

the Isle of Dogs terminal to the high pressure holder, then, this too was no longer needed.

The end came. The remaining low pressure holder was removed in October 1984, and the high pressure holder was demolished the following spring leaving only the foundations in place. This last event took place, coincidentally, as the 'St Ives' exhibition was being held at the Tate Gallery in London. *The St Ives Times & Echo* prophesied: 'The removal of the gas holders will disclose an extremely valuable piece of real estate'.

By this time, however, there was a sewage embargo in place, and no new development was allowed until the area had its new sewerage system, which was anticipated to be completed by the early 1990s. The site was destined to remain derelict.

All that remained of use on the site was the gas governor, converting the high pressure North Sea Gas to low pressure gas for the town. When the site was finally sold by British Gas to the County Council in 1990, it was arranged for the governor to be moved to the Ayr Playing Field.

The choice of the gasworks site for the new gallery was therefore a happy and entirely appropriate one. The perfect addition to Porthmeor Beach. The County Council realised that it was essential that any building designed for this unique position should be selected with care.

The last facility at the gasworks, then owned by South Western Gas, is finally demolished. In the spring of 1985 the 'Zeppelin'-shaped high pressure gas holder and the building in front of it were removed. However one eye-sore was replaced by another, as the derelict site was not cleared; it retained much of the concrete that had supported the gas holders. The land was used for storage purposes until it was sold to Cornwall County Council in April 1990.

Sam Bennetts

1

2

1 A view of the western end of the derelict gasworks site from above, with the beach and sea behind. The photograph was taken by Malcolm Henderson, Deputy County Architect, while preparing the Architects' Brief in the summer of 1989.

2 The architects' impression of the gallery, seen from the front, was used extensively during the planning and construction phases. A number of features, such as the windows at the left-hand end were changed in the final design.

10   Design For A Gallery

Having selected a site for the gallery, the Steering Group's next task was to find an architect to design a building that would complement its unique yet problematic location, and which would have to pass the necessary planning consents. This process entailed the project coming under intense public scrutiny for the first time. The unusual and exciting building eventually chosen caused a certain amount of criticism in some circles, but in others, it received the highest accolades.

In the spring of 1989 the County Council began discussions with the gasworks site's owners, British Gas. The company, from the outset, did not wish to donate the land to the County, but they agreed to dispense with their normal policy of inviting competitive tenders when disposing of property. It offered the site to the County Council for £200,000, and promised not to do anything with it for the next six months, while the County obtained its necessary consents. At the same time it agreed to donate a sum of money towards the fitting out of the building.

David Goodley, the County Valuer, confirmed that the purchase price was a fair one, and that he would seek outline planning permission from the County Council for use of the site as an art gallery. The Steering Group was glad of the six-month breathing space because the County Council, at that time, was in no position to buy the land. There was, as yet, no authorisation by the Council to allocate any funds for the purpose.

Both Richard Lester and Alan Groves knew that there were problems with the site. The soil was polluted and the vast retaining wall on the south side was in need of repair. In the summer of 1989, therefore, Malcolm Henderson, the Deputy County Architect, arranged for a site survey; an engineering report on the retaining wall; a soil analysis, and the digging of several trial pits to learn more about the land the County Council hoped to acquire.[1] The resulting report indicated that, in order to clear the pollution, soil and subsoil needed to be removed to a depth of up to one and a half metres. However no problems were revealed that could be seen to affect the site's value.

The way was now clear to select an architect.

Katharine Heron and Julian Feary, after their Feasibility Study recommendations were accepted in January 1989, prepared another, more detailed report on the gasworks site itself for use by the County Council when preparing their Architects' Brief. They wrote:

The potential is there to create a new building with panoramic views, totally relevant to the art shown within the museum, and for north light to the galleries.

The architects looked at the overall size of the gallery, its amenities and standards of design, such as temperature and humidity control and unloading facilities. They outlined the next steps to be taken:

...it is proposed to select an Architect for the project by means of a limited competition of six firms of invited architects with a national/international reputation. The intention is to make this a major national event to attract publicity for the project and future sponsorship. The winning scheme will provide a further ingredient for the serious fundraising that will follow - an idea of the building in its context.

Malcolm Henderson wrote the Brief. In preparing this he sought the assistance of Martin Rewcastle for background to the project and John Southern for his ideas

1 The soil analysis was organised by Lawrence Holmes, a mining engineer, who worked in the County Architect's Department.

on how a gallery might produce income, such as the positioning of a bookshop and restaurant. He visited Sadie Cole at Arnolfini and Jenny Bowden at Watershed in Bristol, where he learnt about the storage, delivery and hanging of works of art and the layout of bookshops. He visited the newly refurbished Whitechapel Art Gallery in London, and consulted various books on the St Ives artists, including the Tate Gallery's own catalogue for the 1985 exhibition 'St Ives 1939-1964', obtaining permission to reproduce some of the paintings in the Brief. He also had to hand Katharine Heron and Julian Feary's final report.

In order to illustrate the remarkable views of Porthmeor, available from various levels of the site, Malcolm Henderson scrambled around taking a series of panoramic photographs. He recalls:

The most challenging was from what would be the café on the top floor, at the north-east corner, where the view covered the coast from Clodgy Point round to Godrevy Point, about five miles away. This could only be reached by clinging on to the wall behind with one hand, camera in the other, and inching along the narrowing top of the old retaining wall, while my wife stayed on the beach below, completely unaware of the strenuous and dangerous efforts being made behind her.

A list of twelve architectural practices was drawn up by Alan Groves, in conjunction with Alan Meikle of the Architects Advisory Service at the RIBA.[2] This Service holds folders of information about all architects, and it was these that the County Architect consulted in order to arrive at a final shortlist of five practices. These were :

Colquhoun, Miller and Partners (who had refurbished the Whitechapel Art Gallery in London, and undertaken the feasibility study of the Stennack School)

Evans and Shalev (who had designed Truro Crown Courts)

Michael Hopkins (who was later to withdraw due to ill-health)

Julian Feary (who had undertaken the Feasibility Study)

Stanton Williams (who had designed the RIBA extension in London)

On 17 November 1989 the County Architect's Department issued its 'Competition Conditions' which set out submission guidance to the chosen shortlist. This document included the names of the assessors, the timetable for the project and details of the successful architect's appointment. The project's objective was simply:

...to provide exhibition space for 40 or 50 of the Tate Gallery examples of the Cornish works of art mainly of the St Ives School, 1939-75, mostly painting and some sculpture.

Each practice was given an honorarium to cover its submission costs. (A special resolution from the County's Policy Committee was needed to be taken before the County Council would agree to release funds totalling £10,000 for this purpose.)[3]

Meanwhile, the six-month breathing space period promised by British Gas had expired. But realising that the County Council was sincere in its plans to develop the site, the company agreed to a further postponement of three months before negotations had to be concluded.

The Architects' Brief was itself brief. It outlined the background to the project, details of the kind of gallery that would be required, the results of the trial holes made on the site from the County Surveyor's Department, as well as the Tate Gallery's instructions on loaning works of art and security policy put forward by the Museums and Galleries Commission. It was stated that the total area of the building, including circulation, storage and services, would be 743m² (or 8,000 square feet).

Peter Wilson recalls that, as the County Council was not willing to take on a 'millstone' as far as running costs were concerned, the Brief concentrated very much on those aspects of the gallery that were likely to yield revenue, such as the café and shop. There was much less direction given on the galleries themselves.

2 Before his retirement, Alan Meikle had been the County Architect for Hereford and Worcester.

3 It is probable that such approval was given because the Henry Moore Foundation had recently announced its support for the gallery by promising to donate £250,000 (See Chapter 11 - Private Funding and Tate Gallery Involvement).

The Brief made some perceptive suggestions for the applicants to take special note of:

Apart from the obvious attraction of the exhibits, the Gallery should attract visitors in its own right in the way that the Pompidou Centre and the Lloyds Building do...the building should be stimulating, imaginative and excellent. It should be equally attractive to the art enthusiast and to the family on holiday...The view from the site is considered to be a major asset, and this should be enjoyed from both inside and outside the building...It is important that the building has a 'cheerful' atmosphere. Parents should feel easy about bringing their children knowing that they will find plenty to interest them.

The Assessors Panel was set up. It consisted of :

Nicholas Serota, Director, Tate Gallery
Sir Alan Bowness, Director, Henry Moore Foundation
Colin Amery, Architectural Correspondent of the Financial Times
Richard Rogers, Architect
Richard Carew Pole, Chairman of Cornwall County Council Steering Group
Alan Groves, County Architect and Former Vice President of the RIBA

Under the Chairmanship of Richard Carew Pole, the assessors met for the first time, in November 1989, in the President's Room of the RIBA headquarters at Portland Place, London. They discussed the Brief and confirmed that their responsibility was to select an architect who had 'the best approach to a design solution for an art gallery in St Ives'. Each architect was given forty-five minutes to make a presentation of what was expected to be rough outline plans.

The selection of architect took place before the Panel on 11 January 1990, again at RIBA headquarters. Members of the Steering Group were allowed to be present, but were not able to participate.[4]

The winning design was put forward by Eldred Evans and David Shalev, a husband and wife team who had been in partnership since 1965. Eldred Evans had studied at the Architectural Association and at Yale University; David Shalev at the Technion School of Architecture, Israel. They were well known in Cornwall for their design of the Truro Crown Courts, completed in 1988 for the Property Services Agency. So successful was this project that it won a number of prestigious awards.[5]

The reasons put forward for choosing Evans and Shalev were that the assessors believed their design, with its variable external facade, was the most architecturally sympathetic for Cornwall, and they had made the most imaginative use of the site. However, there was some concern over whether or not the architects could deliver their rather complex building within the total cost laid down in the Brief, which was £2 million, a figure which had to include the cost of buying the site from British Gas and consultants' fees.

Both architects had a good knowledge of the area, not only because of their recent project at Truro. They were regular visitors to St Ives where they owned a flat overlooking Porthmeor Beach, only a short distance from the derelict gasworks site.[6] Eldred Evans knew, personally, many of the artists whose work would be hung in the new gallery. In a statement about their design the architects later wrote:

The experience of visiting the gallery ought to be a natural extension to visiting St Ives, and thus provide some insight into the artists' inspirations and aspirations on this remote and magical island.

They described themselves as being: 'Single minded modernists with a conviction that a building, built to last, is rooted in its time and place.'

There was great enthusiasm for the choice of architect. In the first serious article

4 Richard Rogers did not actually take part in the final selection of the architects. He was replaced by Michael Davies from his practice.

5 The awards for the Truro Crown Courts were presented by : The Civic Trust; RIBA (both national and regional); Financial Times; Royal Fine Art and Sunday Times; Structural Engineers; Cornish Builders' Federation and Concrete Society.

6 Eldred Evans' father, Merlyn Evans, a painter and printmaker, who had exhibited in major surrealist exhibitions before the war, had taken a Barnaloft Studio and worked regularly in St Ives from 1963 until his death ten years later (See Chapter 9 - Porthmeor and its Gasworks).

Barry Swaebe

Colin Orchard

2

Colin Orchard

3

Richard Bryant

1 Eldred Evans and David Shalev, the husband and wife team appointed in February 1990 to be the architects for the new gallery on Porthmeor Beach.

2 Eldred Evans and David Shalev were already known locally for their design of the Crown Courts in Truro, which had been completed in 1988. Many of its features, such as the circular areas, the finish of the exterior walls, and glass bricks were later used to great effect in Tate Gallery St Ives.

3 An exterior view of the Crown Courts from the garden. The main entrance is on the left. Two circular roof areas have a glass apse, as in Tate Gallery St Ives' Loggia. The Courts welcome visitors into the public areas.

4 A view of the inside of the main foyer at the Crown Courts. Similarities between it and Tate Gallery St Ives are easily discernible: the circular meeting area, slim triangular pillars, glass bricks and plain white surfaces.

4

about the gallery to appear in a national newspaper, Rory Coonan wrote in *The Observer* on 1 April 1990, under the heading 'A cliffhanger set in St Ives', that the architects would have:

an opportunity...to justify their reputation for dazzling manipulations of space, form and light...with Evans and Shalev you don't get a pastiche, but a forceful argument sustained by visual logic...architecture here is deadly serious, an earnest seeking after truth...The application of genius might just make of the Tate of the West a most remarkable thing: an architectural oxymoron, an open secret.

In an early interview the architects gave to the film maker Tony Mangion, David Shalev said that the building should be 'in dialogue with the landscape and seascape of the place'.

Time was running short. Construction was scheduled to commence in less than twelve months time, with the building optimistically to be completed during the summer of 1992.[7] As soon as the architects had been appointed, therefore, detailed designs were immediately developed. At the same time discussions took place with the County Architect's department and the Tate Gallery. A major decision about the gallery's entrance had to be resolved.

Originally Eldred Evans and David Shalev had conceived their building from the top down. In line with the Brief that 'the café may be on an upper floor in order to take advantage of the views', the architects had stood at the end of Godrevy Terrace and imagined the position of the café suspended high above Beach Road. They hoped that the main entrance might be at this upper level, and their initial designs reflected this. They planned the galleries on a single floor, underneath the restaurant, leaving the Beach Road level until the last. The circular area adjacent to the beach, which they called the Loggia, would still have existed under this plan, but would have been a 'townscape for St Ives' standing on its own, not an entrance into the building.

It quickly became apparent that access from Godrevy Terrace was not possible, as the land was privately owned. The architects, therefore, rapidly changed their plans and designed an access into the gallery from the Loggia itself. The area now created between the entrance doors and the small circular foyer at the eastern end of the building (the Rotunda) became known as the Mall.

The Assessors Panel had, in fact, chosen the most 'worked out design' according to Peter Wilson, who was asked, soon after Evans and Shalev had been chosen, to assist the architects with the detailed planning.[8] Wilson recalls that the architects 'were really helpful and I spent long working sessions out in their studio...we would walk through the gallery on paper and I would say: "Have you thought about security considerations?".' One of the alterations Peter Wilson suggested was moving the doors in the back run of galleries from the centre line further over towards the outside wall, so that there was a large hanging space adjacent to each door.

As predicted, there were problems with the costings from the beginning. As discussions proceeded and detailed plans became refined, both Peter Wilson and Cornwall County Council added costs to the project, particularly in the areas of air conditioning and security. However the project was strictly 'cash limited', which meant that to keep expenses down certain items had to be omitted from the design.

With both the site and the architect chosen, the Policy Committee was now in a position to produce a report to go before the County Council at its forthcoming annual budget meeting, formally asking for funding for the gallery. To justify its application the report, dated 8 February 1990, concluded: 'It is a unique opportunity which is most unlikely to present itself again', and recommended that:

7 The reason for the urgency was that the County Council learnt that it would only be eligible for a European Regional Development Fund grant if the gallery were substantially built by the end of 1991. (See Chapter 12 - European and Other Public Funding.)

8 Although the Tate Gallery was not managing the gallery at the time the Assessors Panel met, in the absence of a curator Nicholas Serota asked Peter Wilson, his Head of Gallery Services, to assist 'as a gift to the project'.

The County Council's capital contribution to the project is £410,000, i.e. the cost of land acquisition and architects' fees to tender stage. [It proposes that] the County Council review the position at its November 1990 meeting when the decision whether or not to proceed with the construction of the gallery will need to be made.

The Policy Committee's report went before the full Council on 28 February 1990. Despite some concerns that perhaps the money might be spent on something that was seen to be less extravagant, Richard Carew Pole was warmly congratulated on his efforts, and the Councillors approved the spending of £410,000 by 49 votes to 10, with 14 absentions.

Shortly afterwards consultants for the project were appointed. As well as Evans and Shalev, the team consisted of Quantity Surveyors Monk Dunstone Associates, Structural Engineers Jenkins & Potter and Mechanical & Electrical Engineers Max Fordham & Partners.

During this time, it was thought helpful to have the assistance of a consultant who had experience with the design and running of art galleries. Martin Rewcastle recommended that Loveday Shewell be appointed to assist at this crucial stage.

Between 1979 and 1988 Loveday Shewell had been Administrator of the Whitechapel Art Gallery in London, where Martin Rewcastle was employed. She was responsible to the Director, Nicholas Serota, for all aspects of financial and general management, and had been particularly involved with the Whitechapel's building renovation scheme, completed in 1985. She left at the same time as its Director to become an arts management consultant, specialising in financial and general management advice to visual arts organisations and the planning and feasibility of art gallery buildings.

In her new capacity, in 1989, Loveday Shewell assisted a Steering Group set up in March of that year in Norwich to look at the possibility of setting up a 'Tate in the East' in that town. After the success of Tate Gallery Liverpool, the Tate's Director and Trustees were considering showing works from the collection in other parts of the country. Norwich was already the home of the Sainsbury Centre, and work was then underway to build an extension. (The Steering Group's first Newsletter, published in 1989, described the Centre as housing 'one of the finest collections of twentieth century and tribal art in the country').[9]

Loveday Shewell ultimately did not play a significant part in the detailed planning of the gallery in St Ives, due to the fact that her participation came rather late. However she commented on such items as: displays and exhibitions; access and flow of visitors; staffing requirements; position of the café and restaurant; security systems; education provision and, most importantly, budgeting for running costs.

After discussions throughout the spring of 1990 with Alan Groves and other County Council staff; the Director and staff of the Tate Gallery including Peter Wilson; members of the St Ives Tate Action Group and others, Loveday Shewell submitted 'A report on estimated running costs' in July of that year. Two sets of figures were produced because it was not known whether the gallery was to be managed by an independent trust or directly by the Tate Gallery. The report concluded that the building would cost less to run if it was managed by the Tate Gallery.

With the required funds approved by the Councillors, on 9 April 1990 the County Council was able to acquire the site from British Gas. A few days earlier, a small portion of land at the east end of the site, originally owned by St Ives Borough Council, and transferred to Penwith District Council at the time of the local government reorganisation in 1974, was made over to the County Council.

9 The report that Loveday Shewell produced for the Norwich Steering Group outlined possible sites for a 'Tate in the East'. However, due to the fact that property prices took a nose-dive shortly after it was produced, which would have made a joint gallery and commerical complex - the preferred choice - less viable financially, the project was shelved. Another reason for it not coming to fruition may have been that the efforts being put into developing the gallery in St Ives, especially once Tate Gallery staff had become actively involved, meant that there was not enough manpower or funds available to work on two major projects at the same time.

The transfer took place only after the District Council had applied for and received the Consent of the Secretary of State at the DoE, under Section 123 of the Local Government Act, 1972, which granted the District a certificate allowing a transfer to take place for 'a nil consideration' (a figure below its market value).

The County Council had obtained outline planning permission for the gallery on 15 January 1990, four days after the architects had been chosen. Under local government rules in operation at that time, permission was required only from the County's own Planning and Economic Development Committee, as the gallery was to be erected on County Council-owned property.

Detailed planning consent was sought from the County on 9 May. But first, out of courtesy, the application went before Penwith District Council on 1 May and to St Ives Town Council two days later for their comments.

At Penwith District Council the plans were presented to the full Council by the Planning and Economic Development Director, Keith Giddens, who expressed anxiety at the way in which the building was likely to impact on the roofscape of the town. *The Cornishman* for Thursday 3 May reported the Director as saying:

It is a cause of some concern that the eastern end of the building which overlooks this critical [conservation] area, is proposed with relatively large areas of flat roofs, which it is felt could be discordant in townscape terms...Negotiations have been initiated to secure modifications to the proposed roof design in this area, and it is hoped that they will be satisfactorily resolved.

Harry Storer, representing St Ives, was concerned for the welfare of the elderly people living in the adjacent Meadow Flats, especially if the proposed pathway linking the upper and lower levels of the site was very close to their homes.[10] Despite the criticisms, Penwith councillors praised the scheme. Geoff Venn, who represented the District Council on the Steering Group, called it 'an exciting development'.

In St Ives, on 3 May, the Deputy County Architect, Malcolm Henderson, took the plans to The Guildhall, and talked the Town councillors through the proposed building, floor by floor. He had a good response from them, and felt they were very positive towards the scheme. Some councillors believed, however, that it would have been useful to see a model, and there were queries concerning possible noise from the plant room to be located on the roof, facilities for the disabled, especially car parking, and worries about the possible lack of privacy for the properties nearest to the restaurant windows. Councillor William Thomas, summing up his colleague's feelings, described the project as 'a very big bonus to St Ives which is exciting and interesting'.

A week later the design went before an Examination Committee of the Royal Fine Art Commission in London which, coincidentally, took place on the day the Planning and Economic Development Committee first looked at the detailed design at County Hall in Truro.

The Royal Fine Art Commission had been set up to advise on matters of artistic importance, especially architectural schemes on sites of national sensitivity. The Commission's aim was to encourage local authorities to become aware of aesthetic issues when passing plans in areas of special character, such as St Ives, without producing actual blueprints as to how an area might be developed.

The presentation was attended by Richard Carew Pole and Ian Martin from the County Council; Keith Giddens, Planning and Economic Development Director for Penwith District Council; Eldred Evans and David Shalev and David Warren, who represented English Heritage. After an initial presentation from Richard Carew Pole and Ian Martin, Eldred Evans outlined, by means of plans and elevations, the proposed design. Members of the Commission were then informed of the concerns that a number of local residents and Penwith District

10 In the event a pathway linking the lower and upper levels of the site was never constructed. The plans for a public entrance to the gallery from the Barnoon Car Park were shelved fairly late on in the project.

councillors had raised, especially regarding the design of the eastern end of the building.

Members had an opportunity to ask a number of questions; following which David Warren, on behalf of English Heritage, said that he believed the design to be 'subtle and interesting'. He predicted that it would be an asset to St Ives, both culturally and environmentally. He also pointed out that to make any changes in the roof design of the 'uncompromisingly modern' building would not properly be appreciating the gallery's overall style.

A few days after the presentation, a letter written to the Chairman of the Steering Group from the Commission, said:

...the Commission warmly welcomes the proposals, and congratulates Cornwall County Council for the enlightened way in which they have selected their architect. It believes that the resulting design is of a very high quality, and one which makes a positive improvement to the site and its environment. The Commission believes that the design makes a sensitive relationship with the heart of St Ives. It also believes that the scheme successfully integrates with the neighbouring sixties buildings...

It had been expected that the building design would be passed by the County's Planning and Economic Development Committee without too much difficulty. However the scheme, as submitted by the Libraries Arts and Records Committee on 9 May, encountered criticism from a number of councillors. In particular the design itself was not liked by everyone. It was described as being 'Odeon-style' and 'old fashioned', as well as 'incorporating the worst features of modern architecture'. There were three major areas of concern: the flat roof was thought to be in need of redesign; there was not sufficient granite on the outside of the building[11] and the restaurant windows overlooking houses in The Meadow were thought to be 'unneighbourly'.

After much debate it was decided that there was insufficient information for the councillors to make a decision. The Committee's Chairman, therefore, organised a special meeting to discuss the application again, setting a date after the Royal Fine Art Commission had an opportunity to comment on the design.

A great deal of preparatory work went into ensuring that at the reconvened meeting, on 22 May, the members of the Planning Committee understood exactly what the gallery would look like, and how much support there was for it.[12] Members of the St Ives Tate Action Group organised, very hurriedly, twenty-two individual letters of support and, even more significantly, with the help of two of the residents of Meadow Flats next to the site, Mr and Mrs Lugg, twenty-seven signatures were obtained from an overwhelming majority of the flats' occupants. Individual councillors on the Committee were canvassed by telephone. Three members of STAG attended the presentation, as did David Shalev. Tony Mangion's film crew was there to record the proceedings, and outside the meeting room photographs of the site were displayed, several showing the area as it had looked when it was a gasworks.

Ian Martin set the scene by reminding the Committee that outline consent had already been given for the site to be used as an art gallery. He told them that significant financial support from Europe was likely due to the fact that the facility would be a major tourist attraction, extending the holiday season and thus bringing economic benefits to the town.

Generally the comments made against the proposed design were again concerned with the flat roof, the lack of granite on the outside of the building, and the loss of privacy suffered by nearby residents. In addition other criticisms were raised, such as difficulty of access because the gallery was located on the town's one-way system, and the problems of whether the building was in breach of the

11 For some reason, councillors believed that any new building constructed in an old town like St Ives should be faced with granite to blend into its surroundings. Many of them, not knowing the site, were unaware of the white Meadow Flats adjacent to the gallery, designed in the 1960s.

12 The County Council received nine letters of objection, most from residents in nearby Godrevy Terrace immediately above the site. Complaints ranged from lack of car parking, excessive size of building and waste of tax payers money, to a possible breach of the town's sewage embargo.

sewage embargo.[13]

Malcolm Henderson showed the Committee slides of the site and samples of the materials that were proposed to be used in the construction of the gallery. He took Members on an imaginary tour of the building, explaining its complexities and exciting features. He recalls that he:

dealt in a constructive and positive way with the concerns that some of the councillors had raised, and he ended by encouraging Members to have confidence in the outstanding design which had been prepared by architects of international repute.

One of the county councillors for St Ives, and a member of the Steering Group, Oakley Eddy, was at the meeting. He pointed out that the sewage embargo did not apply to non-residential properties, and he went on:

By and large the whole town is totally supportive of it. Let's have it. I think the architects have been totally sympathetic to the site. Its affect on the county as a whole will be major, especially for the year-round business. If this goes ahead we are not only going to be known in this country, but also around the world - it will be in the top ten galleries.

A dissenting voice, however, suggested that the proposed gallery might look all right in the south of France, but not in Cornwall.

One councillor, representing an area in the east of the county, became rather exasperated by the criticisms being levelled. He told the group sharply: 'If you don't want the gallery in St Ives we will have it in Saltash!'

Richard Carew Pole, summing up, reminded the Committee:

You can have one hundred people looking at an art form. Fifty will say they like it and fifty will say they don't...Our job today is to accept this scheme which will involve an act of confidence in the architect and bravery by us who are the clients of the scheme...the Royal Fine Arts Commission has thanked the Cornwall County Council for their enlightened choice of architect. That is what I like to hear people at the centre say about Cornwall.

By the end of the meeting there was overwhelming support for the design, the councillors voting 14 to 1 in favour. Another landmark had been reached.

Having selected an outstanding design, Richard Carew Pole and the Steering Group found it easier to raise funds to pay for constructing the gallery, especially from the private sector.

13 The subject of the sewage embargo was later taken up with the National Rivers Authority who, in June 1990, expressed concern at the likely extra burden to the town's sewerage system, particularly when the restaurant was in use. Nevertheless, the NRA wrote to the Chairman of the Planning Committee, Mrs Joan Vincent, that it was keen to support community projects and decided to leave the final decision to the County Council.

Colin Orchard

1

Andrew Besley

PENWITH GALLERY

2

1 A view of the main concourse of County Hall in Truro during the showing of the exhibition 'A Century of Art in Cornwall 1889 - 1989'. Pictured are works by the traditional Newlyn painters as well as sculpture and ceramics from the avant-garde St Ives artists.

2 Nicholas Serota, Director of the Tate Gallery and Richard Carew Pole, Chairman of the gallery's Steering Group, standing outside the Penwith Gallery in June 1990, on the Director's first official visit to the town to discuss the scheme with local residents and artists.

11 Private Funding And Tate Gallery Involvement

There were major milestones throughout the planning of the project that helped convince the councillors and, most importantly for its long term success, the Tate, that there was genuine support for the gallery in St Ives. 1988 had been devoted, in large part, to finding a site. The surprising choice had suddenly thrown open the possibility of creating a more interesting building than might initially have been thought possible. It gave Richard Carew Pole and his Steering Group a new perspective on the project, and assisted greatly in the search for private funding. It also alerted the Tate Trustees to the fact that the gallery was likely to have a higher profile than originally envisaged. From playing a supporting role, the Director and Trustees gradually became more involved in the decision making. This 'volte face' had far reaching results.

In 1989 the sponsorship campaign got underway. With a target of £1 million to reach, the Chairman of the Steering Group devoted a great deal of his energies to achieving this goal before February 1990, the date when the full County Council formally approved the spending of £410,000 to pay for the site and fees. It says much for Richard Carew Pole's dedication and tenacity that, in the space of only six months, and before a building design had been chosen, around £600,000 had already been promised.

The first offer of private funding was by far the largest and most significant, in both real and political terms. It was a turning point in the project because it gave the gallery credibility, a signal to businesses and trusts, as well as to the councillors themselves, that the proposed project was worthy of support.

Alan Bowness had received a knighthood in January 1988, a few months prior to his leaving the Tate Gallery. In his new position as Director of the Henry Moore Foundation, a charitable organisation distributing thousands of pounds each year to various enterprises, especially projects associated with sculpture, Sir Alan was in an excellent position to give advice and guidance. Richard Carew Pole, at the suggestion of Martin Rewcastle, approached Sir Alan one warm afternoon in July 1989. Sir Richard recalls:

We sat out in the garden. I started off the conversation by discussing the project and asking if I could put in an application for £100,000? Then we had a cup of tea, and by about half-past four I thought I must go. Then I said 'What would be the Trustees' view if I put in an application for £250,000?'. Sir Alan's response was cautionary. He said 'You can certainly do so, but, you will be unlikely to get it.' I put in an application for that amount and we got it![1]

By a happy coincidence, 1989 was the Centenary of the founding of Cornwall County Council. A number of events was organised to celebrate the occasion, one of which was a major art exhibition. 'A Century of Art in Cornwall' was organised by John Halkes and Elizabeth Knowles of Newlyn Orion Gallery. They divided the large and ambitious show, which was sponsored by Barclays Bank Plc, into two parts: 'An Historical Perspective 1889-1989' at County Hall and 'A Contemporary View' at the Royal Cornwall Museum in Truro.[2]

At the opening ceremony in the foyer at County Hall, on 30 September, Sir Alan Bowness spoke to a large gathering, during which he publicly spoke of the generous contribution the Henry Moore Foundation was making to the proposed gallery. For most people present, this was their first intimation of the project. The

1 Sir Alan Bowness recalls that the £250,00 contribution to the gallery from the Henry Moore Foundation was 'the largest single donation the Foundation has ever made'.

2 The historical section of the exhibition 'A Century of Art in Cornwall' consisted of eighty-eight works of art borrowed from many sources, mostly in Cornwall, which charted the development of the Newlyn and St Ives 'schools'.

announcement could hardly have occurred at a more propitious moment, with the works of the St Ives artists so prominently in evidence.

Again with the help of Martin Rewcastle, Richard Carew Pole next approached Lord Palumbo, Chairman of the Arts Council, a collector of modern art, and from the very beginning a staunch supporter of the gallery. With Lord Palumbo's assistance a meeting was held with the Secretary of the Sainsbury Family Trusts, which resulted in a commitment of £100,000. At the same time, it was known that the John S Cohen Foundation was looking to fund five major arts projects around the country that year. It chose the new gallery in St Ives as the Foundation's contribution to the visual arts, making a donation of £50,000.

At a later stage in the campaign, Lord Palumbo organised a lunch at the Arts Council for potential sponsors, which he personally hosted. As a result of this initiative nearly £50,000 was raised.

The largest single local contribution came from Northcliffe Newspapers, a group publishing a number of newspapers in the South West that included *The Cornishman, The Western Morning News,* and *The West Briton.* One evening, at a performance of 'The Marriage of Figaro' given by the Glyndbourne Touring Company at the Theatre Royal in Plymouth, Richard Carew Pole found himself sitting next to the Managing Director of the group, Ian Park. During the interval, they spoke about the gallery. Ian Park, who had an interest in the visual arts, suggested that a formal application for funds should be made. As a result £25,000 was added to the growing total.

Richard Carew Pole was indefatigable in his pursuit of private funding. Cornwall has no major charitable trusts, indigenous foundations or potential patrons of the arts. Neither does it house large companies other than English China Clays. The Chairman of the Steering Group always made this case when he spoke to people outside the county asking for financial help. Charities, trusts and companies were contacted with great vigour, and his untiring efforts brought extraordinary results. By the time the gallery opened, in June 1993, the final private sector total reached £1.4 million.[3]

The greatest proportion of the money came not from companies, but from trusts and charities who had a direct interest in the arts. Commercial concerns contributed only about one quarter of the final private sector total. There was a response from Cornish businesses, although as time passed, the recession sweeping the country made it increasingly difficult for local companies, often branches of national concerns, to pledge more than a token amount. Nevertheless, the many small donations added up to a magnificent sum.

A key figure in obtaining a number of these donations was (Sir) Geoffrey Holland, who was at that time Permanent Secretary at the Department of Employment. He recalls:

I wrote a personal letter to the Chairman or Chief Executive of some forty major companies to tell them about the project and ask for their support. Not everyone responded, of course, but those who did, contributed a total in excess of £100,000. Perhaps more important even than this was that, in this way, awareness of, and interest in, the St Ives project was extended to a further influential group of people.

Geoffrey Holland ensured that many in senior positions in Whitehall knew what was happening, and he also used his good offices to pave the way for approaches to particular Departments, notably the Department of the Environment and the Office of Arts and Libraries, by Richard Carew Pole, Richard Lester and others.

For a while it was hoped that one major donor might come forward who would give its name to the gallery as a whole, or to one particular room. With this in mind, Ian Martin and his staff at County Hall prepared a series of brochures outlining the project, and indicating the prestigious advantages that would accrue

3 A list of the companies and trusts who donated more than £1,000 to Tate Gallery St. Ives appears at the end of the book under 'Major Funding'.

to major fund raisers should they make a contribution. Containing reproductions of some of the St Ives works owned by the Tate Gallery, one of these publications was translated into both Japanese and German in an attempt to interest a wider, overseas audience. In the event, no major donor appeared. However, this was seen, in retrospect, to be an advantage; the gallery never found itself becoming dominated by one powerful body wishing to put its overall corporate stamp on management policy.

The gallery had to be operated somehow. Richard Lester and his department began work on setting up a local trust. There was some urgency in this, as the charitable company proposed to manage and run the operation would shortly be required to accept the donations and covenants that were being promised. The plan was for the prospective organisation, provisionally named 'The Cornwall Arts Foundation', to take a lease of the building from the County Council. Early in 1990 the Steering Group discussed the Foundation's rather complicated organisational structure which consisted of: founder members of the company - the three relevant local authorities and the Tate Gallery; a Council of Management, with approximately fifteen members from public and private bodies, who would meet perhaps twice a year, and who would be expected to appoint an Executive Committee 'to carry out the duties of the Board'; and finally a mangement group, headed by a Managing Director responsible for the day-to-day running of the gallery.[4]

Meanwhile, the Tate Trustees were still unwilling for the word 'Tate' to be used in the title for the gallery as they wanted to keep a firm hold on their 'brand-name', and Peter Wilson remembers that the issue was discussed on many occasions in London. The Steering Group, nevertheless, insisted use of that nomenclature was the only way the gallery could achieve national recognition. At the same time the fund raising group in St Ive was frustrated at the lack of a proper name, and probably embarrassed the Tate Trustees by calling itself the St Ives *Tate* Action Group.[5] Through all this, however, the newspapers continued to call the gallery 'The Tate of the West' until its doors opened.

To overcome the problem, and at the suggestion of STAG, Richard Lester asked Nicholas Serota whether the Trustees would accept the words 'The Tate collection of St Ives painting and sculpture' when describing the gallery publicly? After some consideration this was finally agreed by the Trustees in March 1990.

A sea-change was taking place in London, however. At the beginning of 1988 there had been serious concern that Sir Alan Bowness' unknown successor might have little interest in a St Ives outpost of any kind. In the event, from the beginning of his directorship in the autumn of that year, Nicholas Serota showed his total commitment to the project. As soon as he was appointed he sought the Trustees' continuing support, and that winter he personally involved himself in the siting of the proposed gallery, putting his 'seal of approval' on the derelict gasworks.

The subject of the gallery was regularly brought up at Trustees' meetings, but there is no doubt that, during 1989, an 'arms length' attitude was adopted in case the whole idea proved to be beyond the capability of the County Council. At that time, of course, no financial expenditure had been approved by the councillors, and despite assistance on individual matters by the Tate's Director, such as approving the wording of the fund raising brochures, the Trustees remained committed only to loaning the works.

With the promise of a quarter of a million pounds from the Henry Moore Foundation, however, and the planning of the architectural competition well under way, slowly the project became a more serious proposition. Tate Gallery Liverpool was successfully up and running, and the idea for a 'Tate in the East' at Norwich was being considered. By the time Evans and Shalev had been selected as

4 The main object of 'The Cornwall Arts Foundation' as set out in the draft Memorandum and Articles of Association of April 1990 was: 'To advance the education of the public including visitors to the County in the appreciation and enjoyment of works of art of any kind...'

5 The name St Ives Tate Action Group was chosen partly because its initial letters - STAG - rolled off the tongue so easily.

architects, in early 1990, a positive regional policy was being debated by the Trustees, which gave the Director the opportunity to hint that a possible option might be for the Tate Gallery to take a lease on the building.

From then on, Nicholas Serota involved himself in all the major decisions being taken. By May 1990, he was only too aware of the commitment to the gallery, not only through substantial promises of private financing and the possibility of substantial public funding, but also by the resolve of the county councillors themselves. The success of STAG's early fund raising, too, played a part. For the first time the Director conceded openly that the Tate Gallery might be actively involved in the day-to-day running of the gallery. The Tate's presence 'would ensure high standards and bring prestige...[and] there were obvious savings to be made if the new gallery's administration were linked to that of the Barbara Hepworth Museum.' He put his proposals to the next Trustees' meeting, and they were agreed in principle.

That June, the Director visited Cornwall and attended a meeting of the Steering Committee at Truro, as well as travelling to St Ives, where he met members of STAG and many of the local artists.[6] He particularly pleased his Truro audience when he told them: 'I recognise the crucial importance of maintaining and developing links with the local community'.

The Director now assigned members of his staff to look at various aspects of the project, and a coordinating group was set up in London, under his chairmanship. It met formally for the first time on 11 June 1990. Those attending included Peter Wilson, responsible for the building project from London; Catherine Kinley, a Curator in the Modern Collection who had a particular interest in the work of the St Ives artists and whose responsibility it was to look at both the paintings and sculpture that could be loaned; Teresa Gleadowe, to deal with press inquiries and Sarah Fox Pitt, responsible for the Tate's archival records.

A few weeks later, on 17 July, the first of a series of meetings took place in London between Tate Gallery staff, Richard Carew Pole and Richard Lester, which were again chaired by Nicholas Serota. Later Carol Holland joined the group.

That summer final decisions were made on the overall design of the building, and certain items were omitted to reduce costs, including the air conditioning. It was at that period that the cautious assertion was made that 75,000 visitors were likely to come to the building each year. The figure was never deviated from.[7]

Discussions took place on long-term financing of the gallery. Cornwall County Council did not want to take on such a responsibility and Richard Lester, for his part, was adamant that the County 'was not going to carry any deficits'. As a result, the July meeting in London agreed to approach the problem by seriously considering the advantages of the Tate Gallery managing the new gallery in consultation with an advisory body.[8]

In fact strong pressure was already being put on the County Council to make a decision whether or not it should continue to set up its charitable company. At the same time Richard Lester feared that a tripartite structure, involving the County Council, the Tate Gallery and local management, was unwieldy and might lead to serious differences of opinion on major policy. More immediately and practically, there was still no mechanism in place for accepting promised donations, and the Department of the Environment was anxious to know who would be operating the gallery for the purposes of approving a European Regional Development Fund grant. The decisions taken at the London meeting helped to solve all these problems, and serious negotiations soon got underway between Richard Lester and Francis Carnwath, the Tate's Deputy Director, to agree the terms of a lease between the County Council and the Tate Gallery.

6 For a full account of Nicholas Serota's visit to St Ives, see Chapter 13 - The Local Campaign : St Ives Tate Action Group.

7 It is interesting to see from the files that no-one ever calculated what might happen if the gallery proved to be a success, let alone an overwhelming one.

8 The Director of the Tate Gallery always hoped that the Office of Arts and Libraries might be able to match local revenue funding. But Richard Lester heard later in July that because the scheme was for a new gallery, no monies would be available from the Museums and Galleries Improvement Fund.

Matters were now proceeding at a rapid pace. The full Council meeting to review whether or not to proceed with the construction of the gallery was finally scheduled for February 1991.[9] The Councillors were also to be asked to approve a total County expenditure of £595,000.

The County Council was informed that Francis Carnwath had opened a bank account in London to receive donations, both in the form of one-off payments and four-year covenants.[10] Arrangements for the appointment of a curator were being made, and negotiations for the lease were well in hand. Even the Office of Arts and Libraries, alerted to the fact that staff would need to be hired prior to the gallery's opening, when there would be no revenue available to cover their salaries, agreed to give the Tate Gallery an extra £100,000 for this purpose.[11]

Although the Office of Arts and Libraries announced their extra funding with quite a fanfare, that sum was the only direct financial assistance the Government provided. Timothy Renton, who was Richard Luce's successor as Arts Minister, made it clear that there could be no increase to the Tate's grant-in-aid before March 1993. It was to the Trustees' credit therefore, that, despite this rebuff, they were prepared to make a long-term commitment to the gallery

The County Council was prepared to proceed with the lease on the basis of a strong partnership, sharing the financial responsibility for operating the gallery. With the exact number of expected visitors an unknown quantity, both sides went into negotiations with the assumption that, based on an annual attendance figure of 75,000, the gallery at best would break even.

By the time the Council meeting took place, on 26 February, 1991, everyone involved had done their work. The Councillors had been lobbied by the project's supporters to make sure they were fully aware of the efforts that had been made locally, and the positive impact the gallery would make on the county. By the end of the debate, it was overwhelmingly agreed (by 57 votes to 9) that, amongst other things: total capital costs of the scheme amounting to £2.755 million should be approved; a contract for the construction of the gallery in the sum of £2.015 million should be entered into with the Plymouth-based firm of Dudley Coles Ltd; the Chief Executive and Clerk would be authorised to settle the terms of, and to enter into, a lease with the Trustees of the Tate Gallery; and the Steering Group would continue to monitor the project, in consultation with the Tate Gallery.

Credit for the success of the enterprise was laid squarely at the door of the Steering Group's Chairman. Summing up the debate, Councillor John Hurst said: 'Thank you Mr Carew Pole for the immense knowledge and skill you have brought to this project; no-one in the County Council could have brought it to this point.' In reply, the Chairman warmly thanked everyone for their support, but said that the Council 'still had a long way to go. It is like coming across a rough sea in a small boat'.

A month later, the Chairman of the Tate Trustees, in his turn, confirmed that the Trustees had formally agreed to enter into a lease agreement with the County Council, giving them a twenty-one year lease of the building, at a peppercorn rent, with an option to renew. The Tate was responsible for all running costs and the employment of staff. The County Council was responsible for the structure of the building and its external maintenance. An Advisory Council would be set up, after the gallery had opened, that would meet four times a year to discuss major issues affecting its management. The level of admission charges would be proposed by the Tate Gallery and approved by the County Council. Finally, apart from managing the gallery, the Tate had, as a main aim, the promotion of community and educational interests and would develop links and collaborate with other galleries in the area.

9 Originally this important meeting had been planned to take place in November 1990, but it was agreed to defer the final decision for three months, partly because of the delay in sending out tender documents. (See Chapter 15 - Building Construction.)

10 The Tate Gallery operates as a charitable company and is therefore able to take advantage of tax incentives.

11 It is likely that the offer of £100,000 from the Office of Arts and Libraries was made as a result of the earlier support for the project which had been given by the then Arts Minister, Richard Luce.

By February 1991 the Councillors learned, too, that a major grant was available from the European Regional Development Fund. It was this vital contribution that made the project possible. The grant had taken many months to negotiate but, even at this late stage, it was discovered that not all the hurdles had been overcome.

A view of the Council Chamber at County Hall, Truro, where the councillors voted to support the gallery in St Ives. In the seats below the County's coat of arms sit the Chairman, Vice Chairman and Chief Executive of the Council; in front of them sit the Clerks. The Chief Officers and their Deputies sit in the two blocks on either side. In the main area of seating, the county councillors sit in their political groupings, with the chairmen of the various committees in the front row. Labour are to the left of the Chairman; Conservatives to the right; the Liberal Democrats (the largest grouping) predominate to the right of the Labour group, while the Independents are positioned adjacent to the Conservatives.

12 European And Other Public Funding

By far the largest single donation towards the construction of the gallery, over £800,000, came neither from a private individual, charitable organisation or company, but from Europe. The County Council had been aware from the earliest days, that a European Regional Development Fund grant was vital to the success of the project. But at that stage no one could have known just how much the grant system itself was being put to the test, nor, because of an administrative upset, how close the gallery came to being abandoned just before building work was due to begin.

On Friday 4 March 1994, nine months after Tate Gallery St Ives opened to the public, Bruce Millan, one of the United Kingdom's two European Commissioners,[1] who was responsible for Regional Policy, visited Cornwall at the invitation of the County Council. He had come to see for himself a number of projects that had been brought to fruition with the assistance of money from the European Regional Development Fund. One of the destinations on Bruce Millan's itinerary was Tate Gallery St Ives.

The Commissioner's visit gave public recognition to the many years' efforts made by County Council officers and staff from the very inception of the project. For in the summer of 1986, when the idea of having a gallery in St Ives to accommodate the Tate's collection of paintings and sculpture was first discussed, a grant application to Europe was thought to be an essential source of funding.

Two years later, the newly formed Steering Group proposed that the project be financed equally from both private and public sources, in line with current government thinking. The planned £2 million gallery therefore sought £1 million from the public sector.

Cornwall County Council was perfectly placed to make the best use of any European funds available, as St Ives was designated by the Government as having 'Assisted Area' status,[2] that is, eligible for grants from the European Regional Development Fund. Such a designation applied because the region, along with many others across Europe, had problems creating sufficient wealth from agriculture. Economic diversity was therefore seen to be essential.

Cornwall's particular economic problems stemmed from the fact that, in the early 1980s, many traditional industries such as fishing, agriculture and tin mining, were in decline. The peninsula was remote from the industrial heartlands of Britain and Europe, and certain major facilities, for example trunk roads, water and sewage disposal and industrial estates, were inadequate. These factors resulted in high unemployment and low incomes compared with the rest of England. The county's scattered and sparse population compounded the problems.

The region was seen to be unique, however. The high quality of its environment had led to many areas, especially around its coast, being designated 'Areas of Outstanding Natural Beauty'. Cornwall's charm and comparative remoteness had led to tourism becoming a vital part of its economy after the end of the Second World War. Nevertheless, before too long, easier continental travel to guaranteed sunny destinations began to have a detrimental effect on this unpredictable industry.

European funding was introduced in 1975. From that date a number of schemes in Cornwall had been identified as eligible for receiving grants. These had originally been dealt with on a 'project by project' basis; but, as time passed, it was

1 In early 1994, the other European Commissioner was Sir Leon Brittan.

2 The rest of Penwith as well as Kerrier district and the area around Newquay, all in west Cornwall, were also designated as having 'Assisted Area' status in the late 1980s.

realised that European funding merited a more co-ordinated approach. In 1988, therefore, after a year's careful preparation, 'The National Programme of Community Interest' (NPCI) was submitted by the Department of the Environment to the European Commission on behalf of the County and District Councils in Cornwall. The NPCI made a bid for funds totalling £16.311 million. It identified a variety of projects requiring funding over a four-year period, from 1988 to 1991, grouped under five categories: industrial land and buildings; tourism; communications; water and sewerage; business support and promotion.

The category which had been budgeted to receive the largest share - amounting to £6,349,000 - was tourism. Projects listed under this classification had to be seen to contribute towards four objectives:

1 To increase the annual number of holiday visitors in the Assisted Areas by up to half a million people,

2 To increase the number of overseas visitors by up to fifty thousand persons per annum,

3 To generate up to an additional fifty million pounds per annum in the local economy, and

4 To develop tourism growth sectors and extend the tourist season by developing specialist 'out of season' holidays and 'short break' holidays.

The Programme was soon approved, and the Tourism Sub-Programme, as accepted, listed a number of leisure and heritage centres. By far the most ambitious project earmarked for funds, in the four year period ending 1991, was the Penzance Harbourside Development Scheme.[3]

In July 1988, when the gallery's Steering Group was in a position to seriously recommend to the County Council that an ERDF grant *should* be applied for, the project was too late to be incorporated into the County's NPCI submission.

At the same time, the rules for claiming money were very clearly defined, none of which appeared to be particularly applicable to the gallery project. An ERDF grant could be awarded only to a local authority, and for an approved project, over which that authority would have to retain ownership. Funds could not be given specifically for artistic purposes, and because of the timing of the NPCI submission, any project receiving grant aid from that programme had to be 'substantially completed' by the end of 1991.

Nevertheless there was a particular 'route' through which projects progressed. Application was made first to a local Working Group administered by the Department of the Environment in Bristol, and consisting of representatives of bodies eligible to receive grants and the West Country Tourist Board. The Group met four times a year and discussed in detail the projects that had been submitted. At this stage proposed schemes were screened to determine whether or not they were likely to be eligible for funding. Ill-conceived ideas were thrown out and alterations made to good submissions that might not have sold themselves sufficiently, but which, the Group decided, needed supporting.

Approved projects passed to the next stage: submission to the Co-ordinating Committee, a formal decision-making group, meeting twice a year, chaired by the Regional Director of the Department of Environment and Transport, and comprised of Chief Executives of the relevant interested organisations.

The gallery was to be a unique project as far as European funding was concerned. According to the rules, in order to be incorporated into the current NPCI submission, the project would normally have been in its final planning stages. However, in 1988, it was nowhere near obtaining formal approval from the County Council, which was one of the basic conditions for making a claim. There was no site identified, no money pledged, no architect appointed, and its original

3 The Penzance Harbourside Development Scheme proposed linking a leisure centre with improved industrial facilities, a new road layout and adjacent car parking on the southern side of the Penwith peninsula.

124

impetus had largely stemmed from needing to find a building to house a specialist group of works of art that were not easily 'accessible' to the general public. The County Council, moreover, because it was not in a position to manage such an undertaking, planned to create a charitable organisation to operate the gallery. Such a body, according to the rules, was eligible for only a small grant.

A further complication was that in order to receive funding, the gallery had to be 'substantially completed' in a mere three and a half years!

To the newly created Steering Group it must have seemed an impossible task. However, Richard Carew Pole recognised that a substantial ERDF grant was essential if the gallery was to become a reality. The Planning Department, therefore, was formally asked by the Group to investigate this potential source of funding.

The County was particularly fortunate to have David Pattison on its Planning staff. He had worked for the County Council since the late 1970s, and knew everything about the workings of the ERDF. Not only had he been responsible for preparing the NPCI document itself, he was a member of the Working Group and, as a special concession, of the Coordinating Committee also. He was in constant touch with the DoE staff in Bristol, whose sympathetic and supportive Regional Director, Miss Hopkins, had always interested herself in Cornwall and its projects.

Another important contact for David Pattison was the County's recently-opened Brussels office, whose staff were later to become responsible for projects in Devon. They were 'on the spot', and therefore able to give advice and information not only to the two County Councils but to all the area's District Councils. They were on hand to smooth out current applications, and occasionally by-pass central government when it became bogged down in bureaucracy. The Brussels office had been set up during the 1980s on the instigation of Geoffrey Burgess, Cornwall County Council's Chief Executive.[4]

David Pattison recalls that the gallery project tested the ERDF grant system to its fullest extent. Rather than the County Council bringing an approved project to the ERDF in an attempt to obtain additional funding - which was the normal procedure - approval of ERDF funding was vital if the project was to get financial approval from the County Council!

Nowadays, *private* sponsorship can be set against ERDF grants. But, in 1988, for every one pound of grant, one pound had to be raised from local authorities and other public sources only. Such a policy put an onus on the County Council to raise as much public money as possible, without spending too much of its own capital.

Once the site for the gallery was identified at the end of 1988, it was clear that the agreed purchase price of £200,000 from British Gas had to be raised from the County's own budget, for which internal approval needed to be obtained. The County Treasurer attempted to obtain a special additional capital allocation (a licence to spend money) from the DoE to cover the £200,000, but his request was turned down. Nevertheless this initial expenditure was eligible to be set against the European grant.

During the first part of 1989, general discussions took place with Guido Bernadini, the Commission official in Brussels responsible for Regional Policy (and therefore the person making the decisions on the gallery project). As a result of these conversations, the County Council was heartened to learn that, in principle, ERDF funds would be available. The County learnt, too, that any contributions from Penwith District Council and St Ives Town Council would also be eligible for matching against funds. Thankfully, at this stage, the DoE let it be known that it did not think that the establishment of a charitable company to manage and operate the gallery, would make the County Council ineligible for a grant.

By July 1989, the NPCI Working Group announced formally that it would

4 Sandra Penning, a Belgian national, was appointed as the County's first European Liaison Officer. In 1991 she was succeeded by Suzanne Bond. Both had served as trainees with the Commission.

support the project. They recommended that: 'Grant aid of £0.4 million be accepted as the minimum necessary to enable the project to go ahead. Requests for further amounts of ERDF grant aid should be considered by the Coordinating Committee'. They also suggested that a formal grant application be made by the County Council 'When the project cost details are fully known following the private sponsorship campaign and identification of other sources of finance'.

It was decided that an application should be made under the 'Tourism Sub-Programme' although, on paper, these funds had already been fully committed in the NPCI submission. The gallery, in fact, met five of the six 'Criteria for Selection of Projects' under the 'Tourism' heading. These were:

1 The provision of visitor attractions which project the character of the area and the uniqueness of Cornwall as a holiday destination, i.e. local history, culture, art, economic heritage and uniqueness of landscape,

2 The provision of all-weather facilities especially if related to existing centres for tourism and attracting visitors over a long season,

3 The provision of information and interpretation facilities,

5 Projects which improve the attractiveness of town centres and other tourist locations to visitors,

6 Projects aimed at increasing the range of choice and achieving higher standards in accommodation.[5]

The clear stipulation that funds would only be available if the building was 'substantially complete' by 1991, put intense pressure on the county councillors to approve capital spending on the project when they set the County's annual budget at County Hall in February 1990. The gallery had to compete with other capital projects in the county, especially those put forward by the Education Committee.[6] After a lively debate, during which some of the councillors complained that the scheme was being rushed through and should therefore be delayed a year, an initial sum of £410,000 for the gallery was approved.

The tight timescale forced the Commission, also, to approve the necessary funding in record time.

At the six-monthly meeting of the Co-ordinating Committee at the Caradon District Council offices, Liskeard, on 22 March 1990, the decision was taken as to how much ERDF funding might be allocated for the gallery project. Geoffrey Burgess recalls that he attended a pre-meeting with the District Chief Executives to agree the allocations of the different projects:

The sub-programme that seemed to take most of the grant and the attention was the Tourism Sub-Programme, which looked as if it might be oversubscribed. My brief was to get £400,000 for the Tate project because that was the figure we had to match against public spending. But I would try to secure £600,000 at that stage in order to provide some leeway. During the negotiatons I found that if I pressed hard I could get £800,000, and I got it. It was always possible to come down, but if, unexpectedly, we later found we needed more grant, it would have been very difficult to increase the amount. These were early days and we were dealing with estimates...In the main Coordinating Committee meeting £800,000 was agreed for the Tate project.

By July 1990 David Pattison had drawn up a formal application on behalf of the County Council. He applied for a total grant of £715,000, and hoped that this amount would finally be matched by public funds. The project itself looked more promising. The gallery's unusual and much acclaimed design had been given planning permission, and the County Planning Department had carried out an economic and employment appraisal of the proposals which would be of assistance to those assessing the grant application. The appraisal concluded that between thirty to sixty new jobs would be created.[7] It was now possible to show that the five criteria of the Tourism Sub-Programme were likely to be met.

5 Point 4 provided for extra car parking facilities, a criteria which the gallery was not able to fulfil.

6 The subject of school buildings was usually an emotive one at annual budget meetings of the County Council.

7 The calculation was made by adding the number of construction workers and full-time gallery personnel required, to the number of extra jobs the project would be likely to create in the local service industries due, hopefully, to the holiday season being extended in St Ives.

The Department of Environment was now made aware that the Tate Gallery was seriously considering taking over responsibility for the management and staffing of the gallery. This was seen to strengthen the grant application, and David Pattison hoped that the project could be placed on the agenda of the next Co-ordinating Committee meeting, due to be held in September 1990, a mere two months away.

The DoE in Bristol, however, did not wish to be hurried, and it informed the County Council that its application could not go forward without certain important documents being produced. The DoE asked for a report from the West Country Tourist Board endorsing the project, a copy of the agreement and lease between the County Council and the Tate Gallery, and the County Council's business plan, which was expected to show that the gallery would be financially viable when it opened to the public. The DoE also made it known that even if this information was received within the next few weeks, it could give no guarantee that the application would be dealt with at the September meeting.

Richard Lester was particularly concerned by this delay. He hoped to receive tenders by January 1991, which would allow the County Council to give its final agreement to the building contract on 26 February. Approval would then allow work to commence on site by March. However, if the Co-ordinating Committee was not able to give assurance that the money was forthcoming at its meeting in September 1990, Richard Lester knew that the Councillors would never approve the project the following February.

On the positive side, it was discovered that fees and salaries for the design and supervision of the project, including consultants' fees, were allowable against grant money. And not long after, *all* money spent by the officers and staff working on the project was found to be eligible.

It transpired that the Co-ordinating Committee was more supportive than offical correspondence might have indicated. At its September meeting, unusually held at Falmouth Town Hall, in the presence of both Richard Lester and David Pattison (Geoffrey Burgess was visiting Brussels) the exceptional decision was made to approve the bid *in principle*, subject to the DoE being satisfied on certain points of detail. But another problem had arisen.

While the ERDF application was being prepared, Richard Carew Pole was attempting to obtain a Rural Development Grant. Set up by the Rural Development Commission and also funded by the Department of the Environment, the Rural Development Programme had come into existence, in Cornwall, as recently as 1984. Aimed at a broad spectrum of rural development work, its role was to help finance two kinds of projects - social and community, and economic and tourism - in areas of the country where unemployment was high and there was a lack of public facilities, such as transport. 85% of Cornwall was acknowledged to come into this category.

Each year the County was provided with a relatively small allocation from the Commission of around £300,000, a sum sufficient to finance between a quarter and a half of the cost of about sixty projects. The grant was created particularly to fund small community-based projects, usually local amenities, such as refurbishing village halls and providing ramps for the disabled in public places.

Applications for a grant from this programme were normally channelled through Jim Cooper in the County Council's Planning Department. He vetted each project before passing them on to the Rural Development Programme Committee for Cornwall, where they were sent to its Exeter office for final approval.

The gallery, however, could not be dealt with through the usual channels. Firstly, a major project such as this was too large to be funded from the County's annual allocation. The money needed to be found from elsewhere, and required approval from a higher level. Secondly, the Rural Development Commission felt that the gallery, with its strong artistic bias, did not come high on its list of priorities.

Nevertheless the status of the project was growing. The Commission, therefore, did not wish to appear unsupportive. But realistically it recognised that, with a limited budget, any help was likely to be no more than a 'top up' in public funding.

Despite the lack of a positive decision, by April 1990 it was important for the County Council to find out just how much the Commission might contribute. Two months later an offer was made which was less than hoped for, although its Director acknowledged that 'this initiative...is just the kind of innovative project that Cornwall needs'. He did agree, however, to give the matter further consideration.

Richard Lester was counting on the fact that any Rural Development Grant would generate extra ERDF monies. Unfortunately there was no hard and fast policy on this, so he was disappointed when the DoE made it clear that any RDC contribution would be excluded from the ERDF grant's calculation.

Richard Carew Pole, in the meantime, kept in touch with the Commission's Chairman, Lord Vinson, over the size of the proposed grant. His persistence paid off. Lord Vinson announced in December 1990 that the RDC would offer £40,000; a figure that, for them, was substantial, and indicated the value the Commission attached to the project.

In the summer of 1990 pressure was put on the County Council officers and staff to provide the documents for the ERDF submission as rapidly as possible. As far as the legalities were concerned, Richard Lester and Francis Carnwath worked together for many months agreeing the terms of a lease which would be acceptable to both the County Council and the Tate Gallery. The West Country Tourist Board, for its part, very willingly endorsed the project, saying that 'it recognises the particular strength and appeal of such an important and unique new cultural attraction in this area'. The Board believed that the figure of 75,000 tourists calculated to visit the gallery each year was achievable. And the Planning Department ascertained that entrance charges from this number of visitors would allow the gallery to break even.

By December 1990, the application was still being considered by the DoE, both in Bristol and London. Time was running out. The lease with the Tate Gallery was still being negotiated, the DoE in London was seeking the Commission's approval, and the County Council meeting was only two months away.

A breakthrough came in the following January. The Rural Development Commission, on the advice of the DoE, advised the County Council that, in this instance, its grant could be used by the County to attract additional ERDF money. It only asked that when the galley opened some physical recognition could be made of its contribution.

By 26 February 1991 everything was at such an advanced stage of planning that the County Councillors voted overwhelmingly for the gallery to go ahead. A few days later it was learnt that the European Commission had approved the County Council's bid in full; a sum of £877,500, in fact, would be forthcoming.

The only hurdle now was to decide where the money should physically come from. Neither the ERDF's tourism or industrial sub-programmes had sufficient spare cash to meet this sum in full. The additional allocation of funds required virement from other parts of the programme where funding was not totally committed.

But this was not quite the end of the story. During March Geoffrey Burgess and Colin Griffin, the County Planning Officer, were in Brussels on one of their routine visits.[8] Geoffrey Burgess remembers that he and Colin Griffin were horrified to learn from Tim Foley, Guido Bernadini's assistant, 'that there were no funds for the Tate project that year' because an additional £400,000 had been allocated to another Cornish project from the Tourism Sub-Programme with Guido Bernadini's approval. There followed some furious activity. Geoffrey Burgess recalls:

When we saw Mr Bernadini he told us that nothing could be done. The project would have to be deferred until the following year. We explained why that would not be possible and that it was crucial to have an immediate approval of funding because the building contract was due to be let the following week. We suggested virement from the Industrial Sub-Programme which was underspent, but Mr Bernadini said that was not possible because the Industrial Sub-Programme had a higher priority rating than the Tourism Sub-Programme. After lengthy discussions, when we stressed the importance of such a prestige project for Cornwall, he managed to find a way forward and arranged for Richard Lester to fax from County Hall that day the information that Mr Bernadini required. The funding was eventually secured, but I dread to think what might have happened if Colin Griffin and I had not happened to be in Brussels that week.

And so the money was found. During building work a large sign on the site, twelve gold stars on a blue background, indicated that the construction of the gallery was partly financed with the assistance of an ERDF grant. And a permanent sign, just inside the main door of the finished building, unveiled by Commissioner Bruce Millan when he toured the gallery in the spring of 1994, publicly acknowledges this fact.

It can now be seen, with hindsight, how the European grant system, as set up and modified over the years, used a wide range of resources to their best advantage. David Pattison and his colleagues, preparing to raise grants for new projects to help regenerate other parts of Cornwall, under rules that have already changed since the gallery was funded, can feel well pleased with the way the scheme operated to secure 1,000,000 ecus for Tate Gallery St Ives.

While grants were being negotiated in Bristol and beyond, nearer home there was a group working independently to raise money for the gallery. But they found they had a second equally important task on their hands; to give the gallery a high local profile.

8 Geoffrey Burgess found that personal contacts between Chief Executives and Senior Commission officials were vital for the smooth running of projects.

1 An early meeting of members of the St Ives Tate Action Group (STAG) planning their fund raising campaign launch at the Tregenna Castle Hotel, in February 1990. Seated around the table (from left to right): Steve Herbert, John Kilby, Toni Carver, Jeremy Knights, Carol Holland, Henry Gilbert, Janet Axten, Ian Martin (Cornwall County Council), Roy Ray, Gareth Saunders and Leon Suddaby.

Dr Roger Slack

2 The first event STAG organised was an artist's lunch at the St Ives School of Painting in March 1990. This was held in order for Richard Carew Pole to tell the artists in the town of the plans for the new gallery before it was made public to anyone else in the area. The School of Painting was opened in 1938 by the portrait painter Leonard J Fuller and his wife Marjorie Mostyn. Its current Principal is the painter Roy Ray.

13   The Local Campaign : St Ives Tate Action Group

County Councillors have said that they often receive letters of complaint, but they rarely learn of the positive results that come from the decisions they make. It was of immense importance for many Councillors, therefore, to discover that there were a large number of people in St Ives who actively backed the gallery. They say that this constant support helped give them confidence to vote for the necessary funds when the project came up at budget meetings.

Spearheading this support was the St Ives Tate Action Group. From early 1990 until the gallery opened in the summer of 1993, its members worked ceaselessly to raise a large amount of money towards the building costs. But perhaps more importantly, they raised people's awareness of what a gallery of this stature in St Ives would mean, both to the local community and the arts in the region.

'I am here to get your support for the project. We are trying to show the County Council that there will be a local commitment', is how Councillor Richard Carew Pole summed up his presentation to twenty-one representatives of the St Ives business and artists' community on 30 November 1989, at the town's Pedn Olva Hotel. In his continuing search for £1 million from the private sector, he had asked Derek White, Chairman of the St Ives Chamber of Trade, to assemble a group who might take an interest in the gallery. Although not immediately connected with the arts himself, Derek White had chosen his audience well.

By the end of the meeting, such was their enthusiasm that seven people immediately got together to plan a campaign that would lead to more than three years' hard work. The small committee was named the St Ives Tate Action Group (STAG) by Steve Herbert, Chairman of the St Ives Hoteliers and Guest House Association.[1] Without Chairman or formal officers, and without previous fund raising experience, but with professional expertise in printing, design, accountancy, the arts, tourism, local business and administration, and working for a common purpose, STAG became responsible for :

- raising £100,000 towards the building costs (and later a further £35,000 for equipping the Education Room) as well as setting up the necessary procedures to receive pledges, donations and covenants,
- raising awareness of the project both locally and nationally,
- convincing the County Council of continuing local support, and making the local community's views known to the Council's Steering Group through its two representatives, Carol Holland and Toni Carver,
- taking a special interest in the educational potential of the gallery and forging early links with Cornish schools and colleges,
- forming close ties with the Tate Gallery, especially during the period when the Tate Trustees were maintaining a careful arms-length attitude, even stating they 'did not want to give the appearance that the gallery was a branch of the Tate',
- making contact with local artists, galleries and art organisations in the county, and
- sustaining local support by working regularly with the media and by other means of communication, such as setting up public meetings and displays.

Many people were called upon or volunteered at different times to help achieve these aims; all gave their services freely. Carol Holland, who had been a member of

1 Over the three years the core group expanded. But there was never a formal committee. Some people joined STAG for a short period of time to lend professional expertise for a particular event; others were involved over the entire period.

1

2

ST·IVES TATE
Action Group

PLEASE SUPPORT THE NEW

MAJOR ST·IVES GALLERY
TO BE BUILT ON THIS SITE ·

FOR CORNWALL COUNTY COUNCIL

TO HOUSE THE TATE
COLLECTION OF ST·IVES
PAINTINGS AND SCULPTURE

Further information from:
St Ives Tourist Information Office,
The Guildhall, Street-an-Pol, St Ives
or from local galleries

3

1 The ballroom of the Tregenna Castle Hotel was used as the venue for STAG to launch its fund raising campaign on 30 March 1990. The photograph shows guests waiting to hear a presentation of the new gallery by officers from the County Council. In the background, to the left, is part of the Cornwall Education Committee's Collection of St Ives works of art; to the right an archive exhibition of the St Ives artists. Seated in the front row are Brian Bearne, Chairman 'Business Partners in the Arts' (left) and Alan Groves, County Architect.

2 Richard Carew Pole speaking to the assembled guests at the Tregenna Castle Hotel. Behind him sits (from left to right): Derek White, Chairman St Ives Chamber of Trade, Councillor Mike Peters, Mayor of St Ives and Richard Lester, Deputy Chief Executive, Cornwall County Council. Behind are three greatly enlarged reproductions of the architects' impression of the gallery.

3 Roy Ray and Janet Axten proudly show off the sign STAG had erected on the wall of the derelict gasworks site in April 1990 to indicate where the gallery was proposed to be built. The sign remained in place until the gallery was completed more than three years later.

the Steering Group since its inception, was invited to join STAG early in 1990. Roy Ray recalls:

Her experience in communicating and public relations, allied to Janet Axten's ability to co-ordinate the expertise of other members, particularly in the writing, design and printing of the group's publicity material, gave STAG an immediate credibility.

As the project progressed from idea to reality, the role of STAG inevitably changed. It passed through three distinct phases.

The first phase formally began when STAG, working closely with officers from the County Council, officially launched their campaign at the end of March 1990 at the Tregenna Castle Hotel, to around three hundred people and the press.

However, a more *informal* event had taken place a few days earlier, when many of the artists in the town were specially briefed about the proposed gallery at a lunch at the St Ives School of Painting by Richard Carew Pole. Also attending was John Farmer, Library and Arts Officer of Cornwall County Council, who emphasised the unique nature of the project, and explained the positive impact it would have on the marketing of other galleries in the area.

The main public launch, in the ballroom of the Tregenna Castle Hotel, was the culmination of four months meticulous planning. STAG had no money, so all expenses and services were either given free or sponsored by local businesses.

At 12.30 on 31 March, on a brilliantly warm and sunny spring day, the invited guests drove up to the hotel entrance to be greeted by members of STAG.

Displayed in the hotel's ballroom were paintings, sculpture and ceramics from the County Council Education Committee's own collection of St Ives works as a backdrop to the proceedings,[2] complemented by boards displaying photographs and press cuttings of the history of the St Ives artists, compiled by Roy Ray, Principal of the St Ives School of Painting.[3] Along one side of the room the Hoteliers had laid out a spectacular buffet, while Shirley Beck and Chris Cocklin of Kenegie Manor Ltd supplied drinks.

For the formal presentation, guests seated themselves in front of a large STAG logo, designed by Colin Orchard, whose shape and colour echoed the bay at Porthmeor, with its sand, sea and buildings. Adjacent to the logo were displayed greatly enlarged copies of the architects' impression of the gallery.

Derek White was STAG's spokesman. The introduction he gave was followed by an account of the background to the project and its future timetable by Richard Carew Pole. Alan Groves, the County Architect, described the way in which the architects had been selected and gave brief details of the building itself, the contract and construction schedule, after which Brian Bearne, Senior Partner of Bearne's Fine Art Auctioneers and Chairman of a group of companies called 'Business Partners in the Arts' presented an award to Eldred Evans and David Shalev (a sculpture by Denis Mitchell) for their architectural achievements in Truro. The 'Business Partners' also used the opportunity to hand over a cheque to STAG.[4] The Mayor of St Ives, Councillor Mike Peters, on behalf of the town formally thanked the Tate Gallery and the County Council for making the project possible. Finally Richard Carew Pole explained to his listeners how they could support the project; by pledging or donating money, and encouraging others to do so.

As a result, over £22,000 was donated or pledged on that day, almost one quarter of STAG's target.[5] The event was a promising beginning to the local campaign, and gave STAG vital credibility to play a major role in the development of the project.

To raise the gallery's public profile further, a week after the launch, STAG organised a large sign to be made and erected in front of the site above Porthmeor

2 The County Council Education Committee's collection was originally assembled in 1962 under the auspices of J G Harris, CBE, Secretary for Education in Cornwall, and added to later. Works were circulated around the county's schools during term time and shown in the libraries in the holiday periods.

3 The 'collage' was first put together in 1985 for an exhibition in the Crypt of the Mariner's Church to coincide with the Tate Gallery's 'St Ives' exhibition in London.

4 The Partners had recently been formed to fund particular arts projects in the region. Brian Bearne described the scheme as businesses putting something back into the community 'as well as taking things from the community'. In 1990 the group consisted of TSW (Television South West); Bearne's Fine Art Auctioneers; J T Group, Bristol; Hewlett Packard; Praxis plc and British Telecom.

5 The promises of money were recorded on attractive and informative leaflets, written by Roy Ray and Janet Axten, designed by Colin Orchard and printed by St Ives Printing and Publishing.

Andrew Besley

Colin Ross

1

2

Andrew Besley

ST·IVES TATE   ACTION GROUP

Please mind steps

1 The first formal visit to the site was made by Maxwell Hutchinson, President of the Royal Institute of British Architects (right) in April 1990. He is shown admiring the architects' impression of the new gallery with Alan Groves, the County Architect (left), and Mike Bradbury, Chairman of the Cornwall Branch of the RIBA.

2 The Minister for the Arts, The Rt. Hon. Timothy Renton, MP (centre left) looks at the plans of the new gallery on the gasworks site in April 1991. With him are (from left to right): Janet Axten, Richard Carew Pole, Malcolm Henderson, Deputy County Architect, Carol Holland and Mrs Renton.

3 Richard Carew Pole addresses a large audience at The Guildhall in St Ives in July 1990 about the detailed plans for the proposed gallery. Sitting at the table (from left to right): Alan Groves, Councillor Brian Portman, Mayor of St Ives, Patrick Heron, Carol Holland, Richard Carew Pole and Catherine Kinley, Curator, Tate Gallery Modern Collection.

3

Beach, so that for the first time it was possible to see where the building would be located. Although it was only expected to last for about a year, despite the gales and construction work, the white sign with its prominent logo and black lettering was still standing, almost unscathed, when the building was completed more than three years later; a poignant reminder of the early exciting planning days.

STAG's great advantage was being 'on the spot'. As the prime movers of the project were based in Truro, STAG members were asked to assist with hosting important visitors who visited the site. The first of these was the President of the Royal Institute of British Architects, Maxwell Hutchinson, who chose St Ives as part of a whirlwind tour of the whole country. It was a perfect sunny April day on which to show off the plans and the location of the gallery. For members of STAG it was the first time they had passed through the great wire gates that, for so long, had guarded the derelict site. Maxwell Hutchinson was shown around by Alan Groves and Mike Bradbury (Chairman of the Cornwall Branch of the RIBA). A 'modernist' in his views the President, with a calm deep blue and purple sea acting as his backdrop, praised Cornwall County Council for 'continuing to support contemporary architecture' and went on to say:

We should be creating buildings that people will look back on as being contemporary with our present time...I believe that significant buildings become social and historical markers and this building will conform to that, not just for St Ives and Cornwall but for the country as a whole.

By contrast, exactly one year later, the Minister for the Arts, Timothy Renton and his wife, made a quick visit to the Barbara Hepworth Museum and the gasworks site, on a cold, grey, blustery afternoon. No public comments by the Minister were recorded of *that* tour; but later, after the gallery had been open for a few months, he wrote of a recent visit he had made to the town in *The Independent* of 21 April 1994:

It's a marvellous example...of a beautiful little gallery that in its first year has brought new life and business and excitement to St Ives.

STAG next presented the detailed plans of the gallery to the public, not only to keep people informed of progress, but hopefully to raise more money.[6] On 24 July 1990, at The Guildhall, a large invited audience assembled in the presence of the town's Mayor, Brian Portman. At the back of the hall a small exhibition was set up by Mike Bradbury and Colin Orchard to display the architects' plans, sections and elevations, and to give information about the progress of STAG's fund raising.

Carol Holland, who had now been appointed the Group's President and spokesperson, chaired the event. Richard Carew Pole updated his audience on the project, Alan Groves talked about the building in detail, and Patrick Heron recalled amusing anecdotes about the earlier artists in St Ives. Provocative questions were then directed to the speakers on such aspects as the ratio of gallery space to the size of the building as a whole; the choice and number of works to be hung, and the problems of car parking, especially in the summer months.

Not to waste an opportunity, members of STAG presented their current and future fund raising activities. Details were displayed of a portfolio of etchings being produced, and Eric Williams had a 'stall' selling tickets for the various variety shows he was organising.

One of the most significant events for the fund raisers led STAG's operations into its second phase. Nicholas Serota, Director of the Tate Gallery, visited St Ives on 15 June 1990. He had come to talk to the members of STAG after meeting the Steering Group in Truro. The venue chosen was the Penwith Gallery, not far from the gasworks site. Richard Carew Pole chaired the session and John Farmer, Ian

6 The formal invitations were produced free of charge by Tim Guthrie of Design & Print Services, Hayle.

1 In June 1991 the County Council hosted a small group from Japan, who visited the site of the new gallery. Pictured is the Mayor of St Ives, Councillor Beryl James, receiving a glass vase from Professor Seiji Oshima, Director of the Setagaya Art Museum, Tokyo, in the grounds of the Tregenna Castle Hotel. They are accompanied by (from left to right): Carol Holland, Mr Haruo Suzuki, President of the Association for Corporate Support of the Arts, Mr Yoshio Tsuboushi, Chairman of the Setagaya Foundation for the Arts and Sachiko Quayle, who acted as interpreter.

2 The first cheque for £25,000 from STAG's fund raising campaign is formally handed over to the Tate Gallery at the derelict gasworks in June 1991 just after site clearance had begun. From left to right: Tony Luke, Project Manager for Dudley Coles Ltd., Denis Stevenson, Chairman of the Tate Trustees, Richard Carew Pole, Danny Wilson, STAG Treasurer, Alan Groves, Carol Holland and Councillor Beryl James, Mayor of St Ives.

3 Nicholas Serota, Director of the Tate Gallery, standing in front of STAG's sign on the wall of the gasworks site on 30 June 1990. The Director had just met members of STAG and local artists at the Penwith Gallery.

Martin and Malcolm Henderson, from the County Council, were there also. After members of STAG had individually reported to the Director on their progress and outlined their plans for the future, Nicholas Serota revealed:

After initial scepticism by the Trustees, they are now very impressed by what Cornwall County Council has achieved towards making this project come to fruition, as well as by what is happening in St Ives itself. In May the Trustees promised their fullest support for the project.

He went on to stress, particularly, the educational dimension of the gallery, which would be of benefit to both local schools and adult education.

One of STAG's chief concerns, Nicholas Serota was told, was that there was no one in London to contact about the project. As a direct result of his visit, the Director asked three of his staff to involve themselves with St Ives: Catherine Kinley, on curatorial matters, Peter Wilson on the building project, and Teresa Gleadowe, Head of Information Services, to assist with press and other queries. From that time on, STAG no longer felt that it was working in a vacuum.

Nicholas Serota had asked to meet with the artists who lived locally, and so immediately after the meeting with STAG, he spoke to a large gathering in the Penwith Gallery. With his surroundings in mind, he observed:

Although many constructive meetings have taken place in this building, some of them with previous Directors of the Tate Gallery, I am the first Director to offer something.

He described Evans and Shalev's building as a 'grand palazzo', which would have a domestic feel to it; a building that would feel right whether there were ten or a hundred people in it. And faced with an audience whose work would be unlikely to be part of the public collection, the Director particularly hoped that the gallery's success would secure the future of the other galleries in the area, and that local artists could become involved in its education programme.

Despite the outward enthusiasm of everyone involved, for some time there was uncertainty about the future of the project, which did not entirely disappear until the County Councillors gave it their final approval in February 1991. STAG played an important role in this decision-making process. Councillors were approached personally to encourage them to give their approval. And to reinforce these contacts, STAG helped to mobilize the national press.

As a result, Kenneth Powell, the architectural correspondent of *The Sunday Telegraph*, wrote a very supportive and timely article on 3 February that was handed to each of the councillors at the start of their deliberations. Under the headline 'High noon for the Tate's western union' he wrote that the sense of community in St Ives 'underlies the Tate of the West project and makes it all the more imperative that the new gallery is built.'

STAG took no chances on the day of the meeting. A visual display outside the Council Chamber was set up, showing the local support and its achievements over the previous twelve months. At the end of the session there were an overwhelming 57 votes to release the funds and 9 against. Nevertheless, STAG had been prepared for every eventuality, producing an angry press statement which would have been released in the unlikely event that the voting had gone the other way.

With activity now focussed on St Ives itself, the building contract signed, and work starting on site, STAG acquired a new role alongside its continuing fund raising actvities; meeting many of the individuals and groups who showed interest in the emerging building.

On 12 and 13 June 1991, the County Council hosted a visit by a small group of Japanese business people, led by Professor Seiji Oshima. As Director of the Setagaya Art Museum in Tokyo the Professor, in 1989, had organised a St Ives exhibition of painting, sculpture and ceramics which had toured to three Japanese cities, curated by Dr David Brown. Now the Professor was visiting St Ives for the first time. The group was met at the station by Carol Holland, Toni Carver and other members of the Steering Group, as well as by the Mayor, Councillor Beryl James. With Sachiko Quayle, a local Japanese lady acting as interpreter, they visited the Hepworth Museum and the building site. Professor Oshima thought that it must be one of the finest sites for a gallery anywhere.

Then a few days later, on 21 June, the Chairman of the Tate's Trustees, Denis Stevenson, visited St Ives and was formally presented with STAG's first cheque for £25,000 from the group's Treasurer, Danny Wilson. (Site clearance had recently commenced so, from now on, visitors allowed inside the perimeter fence were required to wear hard hats.) Denis Stevenson praised the 'bedrock' of support from the local community. He went on:

In particular I cannot speak too highly of STAG. They are a group of people who have got off their backsides to get this incredibly exciting project off the ground.

A lunch followed at the Pedn Olva hotel where the Tate's Chairman and members of STAG were joined by Eldred Evans, Richard Carew Pole, Patrick Heron, Teresa Gleadowe from the Tate Gallery, and the Mayor of St Ives, Councillor Beryl James and her consort, Father William Leah. Many questions were posed to the Chairman, as there was now a real need to understand exactly how the gallery would operate in the areas of running costs, publicity, education and the kind of curator being sought.

1992 saw an even closer relationship develop with the Tate Gallery, following the appointment of Michael Tooby as Curator of what was now to be called 'Tate Gallery St Ives'. For the fundraisers the project went into its third and final phase. STAG immediately organised for Mike Tooby to meet, formally and informally, people from the town. First, he and his wife met members of STAG at a supper at the St Ives School of Painting. The newly appointed Curator showed slides of the exhibitions he had mounted at the previous galleries in which he had worked, particularly the Mappin Art Gallery in Sheffield. He greatly impressed his audience, some of whom felt that Sheffield must be unhappy to lose such an energetic and imaginative curator.

Shortly afterwards, with the permission of the town's doctors, local artists and gallery owners met Mike Tooby at the conference room of the recently opened Stennack Surgery, the old school building that in 1986 had been considered for the proposed gallery. Finally, a cross-section of the St Ives and district community, including school teachers, talked to the Curator-elect at The Guildhall.

At the end of that year, STAG hosted another 'get-together' at the St Ives School of Painting. A Christmas party was held for the newly appointed full-time gallery staff so that they would have a chance to meet each other before starting work at the beginning of 1993. One of the team present was the Education Officer.

Education had been one of the key areas defined by STAG at the outset of its campaign. It was recognised that such a facility in the new gallery would be of immense benefit to the local children. In May 1990, at STAG's instigation, a working group was set up of school teachers from St Ives Comprehensive School, St Ives Junior School, St Ives Infants School, St Uny School, Lelant and Nance-alverne Special School, Penzance, under the leadership of a local schoolteacher, David Beer, whose brainchild it was. They set themselves a number of aims:

- to create from the start an awareness of the gallery among local schools, the culmination of which was an information package sent to all the schools in the county, in the late spring of 1992,
- to make recommendations to the County Council on educational facilities in the gallery, after having sought information on this subject from the

Whitechapel Art Gallery, Tate Gallery Liverpool and the Glyn Vivian Gallery in Swansea,

- to assist in identifying the responsibilities of an education officer, after talking to one of the Tate Gallery's Education Officers, Polly Penrose,[7]
- to ensure that the gallery fulfilled the needs of the schools with respect to the requirements of the forthcoming National Curriculum,
- to assist with fundraising at a later stage in the campaign.

As a result of the working group's initiatives, and after the County Council had appointed its own Education Advisor, Peter Kendall, a special meeting took place at County Hall on 21 November 1990 to discuss these issues with a wider group.

None of STAG's efforts, however, would have had the impact they did if there had not been a concerted publicity campaign. Every opportunity was taken to promote the gallery project in the media. Regular press releases were produced and circulated throughout the county and beyond, which resulted in a steady stream of news items appearing in the newspapers. Toni Carver ensured that stories regularly appeared on the front pages of *The St Ives Times & Echo*. There was cooperation, too, from Douglas Williams of *The Western Morning News*, who wrote a number of special articles. Local radio was covered: Stephen Strong and Tim Hubbard of Radio Cornwall ran items of news, or organised live interviews for insertion into regular programmes.

As well as news stories, special features were recorded. 'Coast to Coast' and 'Seen and Heard' on Radio Cornwall covered the gallery during 1990. Radio 4, too, brought their microphones to St Ives: Robert Robinson recorded a programme in his series 'Ad Lib' from the St Ives Arts Club; and the School of Painting featured in 'Goodbye to all that' in February 1993, a series on colonies of famous people.

Television was much in evidence. Television South West and BBC South West were often to be seen at STAG functions. A particularly long news item was put together by TSW at the time of the art auction held at David Lay's Auction House in Penzance, in the autumn of 1991.

Occasionally there was unexpected publicity. At the sign of any local controversy, Stephen Strong would appear unannounced to record an interview with the protagonists on behalf of Radio Cornwall. Although this could be slightly unnerving, with a little practice several STAG members became quite adept at having a microphone thrust at them! But more importantly, it allowed further opportunities to put forward the positive reasons for having the gallery in the town. They were always reminded that 'there is no such thing as bad publicity'.[8]

It had been hoped that the entire project could be filmed for a major television programme. Tony Mangion and his locally based film company attempted, for at least a year, to gain funding from any number of sources, in order to finance the making of such a documentary. His crew, with their cameras and sound equipment, became a regular feature at the early public meetings, where he interviewed many of those taking part. Unfortunately, despite a good deal of canvassing, no money was forthcoming and the project had to be abandoned before construction of the gallery started.

But it was to raise money that STAG had originally been set up. To the amazement of many St Ives residents, the £100,000 target they had set for themselves on the first day of their campaign, was reached after only two years. Of this, £44,000 was raised through individuals taking out covenants.[9] STAG had deliberately decided not to become registered as a charity, and it was therefore unable to accept covenants on its own behalf. Initially it took the risk of asking for

7 It had been made known that a suggestion was put forward by the County Council for the newly appointed Art Advisor for schools in Cornwall to divide his or her time equally between advisory responsibilities and organising the Education Department at the new Tate. This idea was rejected by the Working Group on the basis that there might have been a feeling that the new position would have been a token gesture to both jobs. Another money saving proposal was also criticised: that of combining the positions of Education Officer at the Tate Gallery with that at Newlyn Orion.

8 For the reasons for many of the controversies see Chapter 14 - Public Concerns.

9 Covenanting enables financial gifts to be increased by taking advantage of tax benefits.

Andrew Besley

1 The STAG Education Working Group who met on a number of occasions to make suggestions concerning the role of education in the new gallery. From left to right: David Beer, who led the group, Mary Henderson, Stuart Peters, Hugh John, John McWilliams and Terry Lister.

2 A major fund raising project was the creation of a portfolio of ten etchings, in the autumn of 1990, which raised £12,500. The portfolio was launched at the Wills Lane Gallery. From left to right: (front) Carol Holland, Chris Maunder, Hawthorn Prints, Naomi Frears, Sheila Oliner, Bryan Pearce, Roy Ray; (rear) Stephen Dove, Professor Alan Livingston, Principal of Falmouth School of Art and Design, (who spoke at the launch), Michael Foreman, John Emanuel, Roy Walker and Henry Gilbert, owner of the Wills Lane Gallery.

3 David Lay, the Penzance auctioneer, during the STAG auction of fine and applied art which was held in October 1991. The auction raised £27,500. David Lay opened his auction house in Morrab Road in 1979. It was transferred to its present spacious location in Alverton ten years later.

4 Nicholas Serota discusses one of the lots for the STAG auction with David Lay: a painting by Rose Hilton which was used to advertise the auction in the art magazine *Modern Painters*.

Brian Atkinson

Andrew Besley

140

pledges; but it was not until June 1991, fifteen months after the first pledges had been made, that the Tate Gallery (which has charitable status) agreed to take a lease of the building, and arranged for these pledges to be converted into covenants. Despite the passage of time and a deepening economic recession, most people who had promised money honoured their pledges and took out four-year covenants.[10]

A considerable number of people made single donations towards the building fund during the course of the campaign. Facilities for receiving and recording each direct payment were provided by Barclays Bank in St Ives, through the generous assistance of Mr Triniman, its Manager, and his staff. He arranged that no charges would be made to the various accounts held by STAG. The donations went into a savings account which, in the early days of the campaign, accrued very high interest rates, adding to the group's steadily rising total.

Money also came in through collecting boxes. These were distributed around the town, especially in the local galleries. A box was put in the foyer of County Hall in Truro next to one of a series of posters specially designed by local artists, which advertised the project.[11] All donations and covenants were recorded and banked by STAG's first treasurer, Gareth Saunders and his staff. He was replaced by another St Ives accountant, Danny Wilson, whose efficient assistant Dawn Clayton, paid the bills, looked after the collection boxes, took over the banking and was able to provide, often at very short notice, detailed records of the group's latest financial position.

To most people, however, STAG will best be remembered for its wide variety of fund raising events organised between 1990 and 1992. The informality of STAG's basic structure was clearly noticeable here. Anyone could suggest an idea for raising funds, whether or not they lived in St Ives. After initial discussions, a working party would be set up consisting of volunteers who had the expertise to plan an event in detail and make it a success.

The most important money raising ventures involved the artists themselves, reflecting their enormous commitment to the gallery, despite the fact that their work was unlikely to be shown there. In 1990, ten local artists produced a portfolio of etchings, of which there were seventy-five copies available. The artists were: Stephen Dove, John Emanuel, Michael Foreman, Naomi Frears, Rose Hilton, Sheila Oliner (whose idea it was), Bryan Pearce, Roy Ray, Maurice Sumray and Roy Walker. The portfolio was printed by Chris Maunder of Hawthorn Prints at Newbridge near Penzance, at a nominal cost, and a number of sponsors helped to keep the expenses down.[12]

There was considerable uncertainty at first as to whether the portfolio would prove to be popular. The artists however need not have worried. It was such a success that the complete edition sold out before editioning took place. Prospective buyers had not even seen the images! Henry Gilbert hosted the portfolio's launch at the Wills Lane Gallery on 27 October 1990 at which the Principal of Falmouth School of Art and Design, Professor Alan Livingston, a keen supporter of the new gallery, gave an introductory talk. £12,500 was raised from this venture.

The most ambitious project that STAG undertook was an auction of paintings, sculpture, ceramics and other donated works of art, in the autumn of 1991. Held at David Lay's Auction House in Penzance, a total of two hundred and sixty nine lots realised £27,500 from buyers throughout the country, at the most well attended event ever seen there. The crush on the day of the auction was so great that closed-circuit television was set up in the hallway to let prospective buyers know when to force their way into the auction room to make their bids.

The project involved many months of planning by a hard-working team. David and Sarah Lay, well known for their support of charitable causes, with the

10 Many donors actually covenanted more money than they had originally promised.

11 Artists contributing to this advertising campaign by providing a painting that was photographed on the County Planning Department's laser colour copier were: Richard Ayling, Max Barrett, Bob Crossley, John Clark, Bob Devereux, Stephen Dove, John Emanuel, Robert Floyd, Donald Grant, Jeremy King, Kathie Lancaster, Louise McClary, Bryan Pearce, Ponckle, Roy Ray, Morwenna Thistlethwaite, Nigel Trezise, Maurice Sumray, Peter Ward and Terry Whybrow.

12 The sponsors of the portfolio were: Gillian Jason Gallery, Cornwall Paper Company, Spectrum Design & Print, The Framing Studio in Penzance, Beric Tempest, Colin Orchard and Dr Roger Slack.

1 Maestri from the International Musicians Seminar (IMS) after a chamber concert they gave in aid of STAG funds at St Ives Parish Church in April 1991. Pictured at the reception at the Pedn Olva Hotel (from left to right): Peter Evans, Lorand Fenyvez, Hilary Tunstall-Behrens, IMS founder and organiser, Sir Alan Bowness, Director of the Henry Moore Foundation, Steven Isserlis, (seated): Carol Holland and Tabea Zimmerman.

2 Pictured at the Westgate Patchworks gallery in the spring of 1991, a group pose in front of the quilt they made which was raffled as part of STAG's fund raising campaign. From left to right (standing): Lesley Ward, Valerie Barnes, Eleanor Beard, Ann Atkinson, Freda Harper, Gillian Farrell; (sitting): Celia Orchard, Daphne Turner; (kneeling): Pepe Turner, Maeve Spencer, Annie Smith, Sarah Watson, Joyce Hayward. The quilt was won by Edith Franklin from Helston.

3 A few of the performers meet the cameras after the gala performance of the review 'Cream of Cornish' at The Guildhall in St Ives in October 1990. Left to right: Councillor and Mrs Brian Portman, Mayor and Mayoress of St Ives, Eric Williams, producer and creator of the review, Michelle Sharkey, Derrick Phoenix, Carol Holland, (on right) Councillor John Jago, Chairman of Penwith District Council and Mrs Jago.

4 Gerry Phillips playing the part of the painter Alfred Wallis in the one-man play 'Back Road West' by Marion Whybrow, which was performed during the Alfred Wallis fortnight in September 1992. 'Alfred Wallis' is reading from the bible, while his strangely shaped 'paintings' hang on the wall of his room.

assistance of all their staff, ensured its success. The STAG working group, with whom they collaborated, consisted of Ann Atkinson and Janet Axten, who between them wrote the ambitious catalogue, and artists Stephen Dove, Theresa Gilder and Sheelagh O'Donnell. Barry Mills and Jonathan Statham of the County Council's Planning Department helped design the catalogue and set it up on their computer ready for printing. A lengthy introductory essay was specially written by Dr David Brown, who had organised the Tate Gallery's 'St Ives 1939-64' exhibition. The paper for the catalogue was donated by Arjo Wiggins Appleton plc, Business and Fine Papers Division of Basingstoke, Hampshire.

The names of possible participating artists were suggested by local galleries and Cornwall Crafts Association. Each artist who chose to donate a work was identified in the catalogue by a brief biography and a black and white photograph of their donation.

The working group realised that the auction's success depended upon a build-up of press publicity over the summer months. The local arts' journalist, Frank Ruhrmund, assisted in this by writing a succession of articles about the auction that appeared in a variety of newspapers and magazines. Alongside this, Mike Barlow, of Alan Leather Associates, architects in St Austell, designed, produced and sponsored a widely distributed poster using computer aided design techniques.

The auction made the pages of *Art Monthly*. The August 1991 issue in its 'Salerooms' column, under the heading 'when kindness is not enough', asked whether Nicholas 'Serota can do for the Tate in St Ives later this year what he did for the Whitechapel [auction in 1987]'.[13] The article generated a special item on the back page of the following issue, written by Frank Ruhrmund, who explained that it was the local effort, not the Tate Gallery's Director, that was responsible for the auction. Nicholas Serota took a special interest in the venture, however. He personally attended the auction as well as two previews: the first for potential buyers, the second for the artists who had donated works and all the helpers.

Many of STAG's events had the support of well established organisations. In the spring of 1991 the International Musicians Seminar, who visit West Cornwall twice a year, gave a chamber concert to a capacity audience in the Parish Church in St Ives, with kind permision of the Vicar, Father William Leah. Organised by Janet Slack, Jackie Ball and Caroline White, who were Friends of IMS, and Janet Axten of STAG, the concert was followed by a buffet supper at the Pedn Olva Hotel. Some of the world's finest soloists took part: Steven Isserlis, cello, Tabea Zimmerman, viola, Paul Coker and Peter Evans, piano and Lorand Fenyvez, violin. Hilary Tunstall-Behrens, co-founder and organiser of IMS was particularly anxious to see a special relationship develop between the musicians and Tate Gallery St Ives, a relationship that he referred to as 'a meeting of art and music at the highest level'.

During the gallery's planning, the Royal Cornwall Museum in Truro was seeking funds to refurbish their own galleries on River Street. Thanks to the sympathetic and supportive attitude of their Council and Director, Caroline Dudley, on several occasions they joined forces with STAG to share the proceeds from a series of functions: two antiques road shows; a baroque music concert given by the Belerion Consort, and a lecture by Nicholas Serota entitled 'The Tate Gallery - a national collection in the making'.

The St Ives Arts Club worked with STAG also. A one-day literary festival was held in the Club and, more ambitiously, a two-week celebration of the life and work of the painter Alfred Wallis was organised to commemorate the fiftieth anniversary of his death. Taking place in the first two weeks of September 1992, Michael Tooby assisted with its planning. Events included: walking tours of the town that highlighted places associated with the artist and his paintings, lectures, Marion

13 The Whitechapel auction in the summer of 1987 had been a spectacular success.

1

2

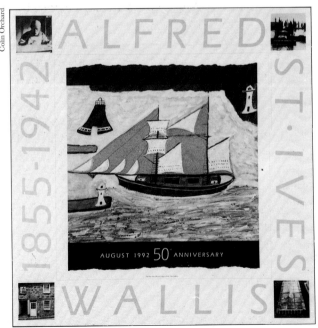

3

1 STAG's first poster, sold to raise funds for the gallery, was painted by Martin Leman from an original idea by nine-year old Bridget Trezise. Launching the poster at the Pedn Olva Hotel are (from left to right): Declan Trezise, Carol Trezise, Martin Leman, Nigel Trezise, Carol Holland, Bridget Trezise holding her original poster containing the words 'Kits, cats, sacks and wives, bring the Tate to St Ives', and Janet Axten.

2 Winners of the STAG Childrens Painting Competition received their prizes at a ceremony at the Penwith Gallery in January 1993. Pictured with the winners is David Beer, Coordinator of the STAG Education Working Party and Michael Tooby, Curator Tate Gallery St Ives (far right). Sponsors of the competition were: Bill and Joan Armstrong; Arts and Graphics, Redruth; Peter Barnes; James McNaughton Paper; Spectrum Colour Printers; St Ives School of Painting and the Wills Lane Gallery. The paintings and drawings were on show that day at the Penwith Gallery. They were exhibited again in the Tate St Ives Education Room after the new gallery opened in June 1993.

3 An Alfred Wallis poster was designed by Colin Orchard. It uses a square format, and the painting 'The Blue Ship' c.1934 by Wallis (owned by the Tate Gallery and reproduced with their permission) served as the centrepiece, with a black border added top and bottom. In the four corners are photographs of: Alfred Wallis' house in Back Road West, Aldred Wallis at his table, fishing boats in St Ives Harbour, and Wallis' grave at Porthmeor cemetery of tiles made and decorated by Bernard Leach.

Whybrow's play 'Back Road West' starring Gerry Phillips in the part of Alfred Wallis, films about the painter and a display of memorabilia and videos at the St Ives Library. Dr Roger Slack gave two showings of his popular tape recordings of local people who remembered Wallis, and a highlight of the festival was a talk given by Edwin Mullins who, in 1967, had written an important but rare book about the artist.[14] Many of the lectures took place in the Stennack School Surgery Conference Room. The Doctor's Management Committee allowed STAG to use the room free of charge.

As the festival gained momentum tickets to events became scarce. Its obvious success led to the feeling in certain quarters that the painter himself might not have been very happy with all the fuss being made. However, much to everyone's pleasure, the festival involved more local residents than any other STAG event had achieved, and it brought home the realisation that the new gallery was likely to have a much greater impact on the town than many might first have realised. It also gave the new Curator his first opportunity to work on an art project with the local community.

Another fund raising event was the raffle of a quilt designed by Daphne Turner of Westgate Patchworks, St Ives, and made by twenty-five quilters from St Ives and Launceston.[15] This, a simple, random-patterned quilt, based on an Amish design, was exhibited in galleries throughout the county in the summer of 1991.

Other events included: a charity showing of a David Puttnam Second World War film 'Memphis Belle', organised in Plymouth by the *Western Morning News*; a Fifties and Sixties disco at Mr Peggottys in St Ives with the support of Roger Symonds, at which not-so-young dancers sported the appropriate fancy dress; a lavish variety show organised by Eric Williams at The Guildhall with a special supper served on the Gala Night; a concert given by the Marazion Appollo Male Choir with the St Dennis Band and guest stars from the Duchy Opera; a concert and buffet supper at Trevethoe House, Lelant, with generous permission of Rose Tempest; lectures by the writer Tom Cross and the musician David Allan; dinners at the Hoi Tin and Russets restaurants, and a children's painting competition organised by Colin Orchard, for which there were three hundred and sixty contestants in five categories between the ages of four and eighteen.[16]

A particularly successful way of raising funds was through the sale of specially produced items. In 1990 a limited edition print, together with a poster and Christmas card, of an image of a cat among St Ives paintings, was commissioned by Henry Gilbert. It was created by the artist Martin Leman from an original idea by nine-year old Bridget Trezise. In 1992 an Alfred Wallis commemorative poster showing one of the artist's paintings in the Tate Gallery's collection, and two greetings cards were designed by Colin Orchard. Also that year Janet and Roger Slack organised the production of an Alfred Wallis sweatshirt. These were all sold in a number of galleries in St Ives.

With the £100,000 target achieved in only two years, it was decided, at the end of 1991, that any further money raised should be used for equipping the Education Room at the gallery. Town Councillors had been particularly concerned by the deferment of work to this important amenity, due to a lack of funds, and were therefore particularly pleased by this decision.[17] STAG made contact with every school in the county informing them of the plans for the gallery and the education facilities that would be provided, eliciting their support. Schools and individuals were able to donate money for particular pieces of furniture if they wished; the largest donation, video equipment, being given by Falmouth School of Art and Design.

Throughout the entire three years of the campaign, a complete record was

14 Edwin Mullins' book had become unavailable soon after it was published.

15 Daphne Turner and her husband Pepe had previously lived in Launceston, where they had run a successful shop, Windmill Patchworks, and taught patchwork and quilting.

16 The winners of the children's painting competition were taken by train to London to see behind the scenes of the Tate Gallery. Their entries were then displayed in the Education Room of the newly opened gallery in St Ives.

17 The circumstances surrounding the deferment of the fitting out of the gallery's Education Room are outlined in Chapter 15 - Building Construction.

1

1 During 1990 a working group was set up to organise a number of fund raising events. From left to right: Geoffrey Knights, Janet Slack, Carol Holland, Bret Guthrie (who, in 1986 was Chairman of the Cyril Noall Community Group, which aimed to preserve the Stennack School as a community centre) and Eric Williams.

2 Members of STAG on the stairs of Tate Gallery St Ives before it opened. From the top: Colin Orchard, Roy Ray, John Kilby, Henry Gilbert, David Beer, Toni Carver, Mike Bradbury, Dawn Clayton, Carol Holland and Janet Axten.

2

made of all that had taken place. Dr Roger Slack took photographs of the events and made tape recordings of important speeches, while Ann Atkinson tirelessly compiled a full set of press cuttings from local and national newspapers and journals which filled three volumes.

After all these efforts, it was a poignant day when everyone involved with STAG was invited to meet together in the empty gallery in April 1993, to watch with pride the final cheque being presented to Sir Richard Carew Pole. After a memorable tour of the building (which included a display showing the history of the project put together by Colin Orchard, Mike Bradbury, Roger Slack and Janet Axten) and a farewell party at the Penwith Gallery, the supporters disbanded to make way for a new era in the story of Tate St Ives.

Behind the desk, at the entrance to the gallery, there are several display boards. One contains a list of contributors of £100,000 or more. Along with 'The Henry Moore Foundation' and 'European Regional Development Fund', the words 'The St Ives Tate Action Group and its Supporters' are there for all to see. They are a permanent reminder of the significant role played by that group of enthusiasts.

Despite everyone's best efforts, however, the project did not receive universal approval. One of STAG's regular tasks was to listen and comment on the, often constructive, criticisms that were levelled.

1

2

3

4

There were people who did not want a new gallery to be built in St Ives. They felt that the Tate's collection of paintings and sculpture could well be accommodated in one of four other buildings in the area.

1 Trinity House National Lighthouse Centre in Penzance, formally opened in April 1990 by HRH Prince Andrew, Duke of York.

2 Penzance Museum and Art Gallery, located in Morrab Gardens. It houses many of the Newlyn School paintings as well as a collection of Newlyn copper.

3 Newlyn Gallery, a building designed by J Passmore Edwards and completed in 1895. Home of the Newlyn Society of Artists for a century, it has recently been renovated and redesigned.

4 Royal Cornwall Museum, River Street, Truro, home of the Royal Institution. The building was extended in 1990 into the chapel to the right of the photograph, in order to provide extra exhibition space and a restaurant. (See the 1919 engraving of the Museum on page 4.)

14   Public Concerns

While I was outside the Gallery with Mike Tooby two elderly St Ives women came by; one defiantly hissed - bloody disgrace. I was left reflecting on how a visitor is to perceive the relationships between all these different versions of art: the avant garde art...and the mass of fishing boat and seagull paintings. (Simon Morley *Art Monthly*, July-August 1993)

No project comes to fruition without its critics. The high profile gallery was no exception. It was important, therefore, for those working closely with the venture in Truro, St Ives and London, to listen and respond to such criticism. Some adverse comments could be refuted immediately; others could be satisfactorily dealt with only after the gallery finally opened.

An early complaint was that it was difficult to understand why substantial public funds should be used to build another gallery in a town which already appeared to have more than its fair share. Various suggestions were put forward for housing the collection elsewhere in West Cornwall. Penwith District Council thought it might be appropriate for the work to be incorporated in its Trinity House National Lighthouse Museum, a project already underway in Penzance. The local Member of Parliament, on the other hand, thought an enlarged Penlee Gallery, also in Penzance (now known as Penzance Museum and Art Gallery) was a more appropriate location.[1] A third proposal was for it to be included in the Royal Cornwall Museum, Truro, where County Council money was currently helping to finance its expansion.

In May 1988 Alan Bowness made it clear that the collection must be housed in a building in or close to St Ives, where the work had originally been produced.[2] There was, nevertheless, nowhere suitable in the town for exhibiting a permanent historical collection of art, despite the proliferation of commercial galleries. It was also important that St Ives paintings should be displayed separately from the Newlyn School. However many of the County Councillors were probably unaware of the difference between the two 'schools', and it was expected that they would be surprised when the mostly abstract works were finally exhibited! To compound this confusion, the two major TV channels often muddled the paintings in their local programmes. While the gallery was under construction they sometimes illustrated their news reports by showing photographs of the paintings of Stanhope Forbes. The other suggested location, Truro, was never a serious possibility; when the gallery was planned, that part of Cornwall was not eligible for a European grant.

There was a more complex issue aired in the early days. It was felt that the County was making no attempt to develop an overall 'arts policy' that included Newlyn Orion Gallery, Royal Cornwall Museum at Truro and the new gallery in St Ives, yet all three would be requiring both public and private funding. In 1989, both Newlyn and the Royal Cornwall Museum already had expansion and refurbishment programmes planned. John Halkes, then Director of Newlyn Orion, feared that major funding for St Ives would be at the expense of the other two venues. Moreover, the lack of a county-wide arts policy, he believed, would prevent grants being channelled to where they were most needed. Additionally, the recently appointed Director of the Royal Cornwall Museum, Caroline Dudley, feared, not without reason, that once the gallery in St Ives was up and running, the County might find itself having to finance its maintenance programme, possibly at the expense of other local arts organisations.

Both Martin Rewcastle and John Farmer spent much energy assuring both

1 Penlee House, now owned by Penzance Town Council, was built in 1865 and purchased, together with fifteen acres of parkland, by the former Penzance Borough Council in 1946 as a war memorial for the town. Set now in public gardens, it serves as a Museum for the area, covering the history of West Cornwall from 4,000 BC to the present day, and houses a permanent art collection from the Newlyn School, including paintings by Stanhope Forbes, Walter Langley, Norman Garstin and Harold Harvey.

2 Alan Bowness put forward this stipulation at a meeting at the Tate Gallery with Officers from the County Council, Martin Rewcastle from South West Arts and the local M.P. for St Ives, David Harris.

Newlyn Orion and the Royal Cornwall Museum that it was only possible to raise money for specific projects, especially when large sums were involved. The County Council confirmed that it had no intention of cutting grants to other galleries; the new proposed gallery's maintenance programme would be financed by admission charges. John Farmer pointed out that, in the long run, the facility would be of benefit to everyone. If this particular scheme was abandoned, the money already promised from both public and private sectors would be lost. Also, as the gallery in St Ives was likely to be a catalyst for the area, he explained, to oppose the project would only be to the detriment of other arts organisations in the long run.

There were other constructive criticisms voiced, especially when plans were far from finalised. The Penzance-based monthly satirical magazine *Peninsula Voice* canvassed the views of local artists and gallery owners in the spring of 1990. Some of the concerns levelled were: that an admission charge was not a good idea; that more contemporary work ought to be shown; and that there was a likelihood of 'cultural elitism' - only showing works of art, on yet more gallery walls, when they should be available to the community at large.

Perhaps a more serious charge came from some of the artists and their families whose work was likely to be exhibited. They feared that bringing the works back to St Ives was a retrograde step. Public recognition had finally come about through their work being acquired by the Tate Gallery in London. The capital was chauvenistically believed to be the 'centre of the art world'. St Ives was certainly not seen in this light; indeed it appeared to some people to be a far-flung outpost. There was also a suspicion that the Tate was trying to 'off load' some of the works they had no room for, in order to return them to the 'provinces'.

In the area of education, too, there were concerns. A number of teachers around the county, even from St Ives itself, could not believe that the gallery could be of any benefit to them, and that the journey would be beyond many of the schools' resources when so many other activities competed for scarce funds. Furthermore, it was believed that the abstract nature of the works shown would be of no interest to the children.

It is true that admission charges would always be a bone of contention. The Tate Gallery had a policy not to charge for entrance in London and Liverpool, except to specialist exhibitions. But it was known that if the new gallery was not to be a burden on the ratepayers, somehow it would have to support itself. When plans were initially made for a charitable company to run the gallery, various financial calculations undertaken by the County Planning Department showed that if annual attendance reached 75,000, entrance charges would allow the enterprise to pay its way. When, later, the Tate Gallery agreed to manage the gallery, they too reluctantly agreed to make a charge. They had learned that the Office of Arts and Libraries would allow them no extra annual grant to assist with their new outpost's operation.[3]

The other worries could only be laid to rest once the gallery had opened. The Curator, from the beginning, made it a policy to commission and show specific works from contemporary artists, both living in the area and from further afield, who would complement the displays and be involved in other gallery projects, such as educational workshops. The gallery immediately became part of the local community, being particularly welcoming to young people, both through schools' visits and children's painting classes, thereby breaking down the charges of 'elitism'. In the first months of 1993, both the Curator and Education Coordinator made a point of visiting a large number of schools around the county, at which they sought to pursuade teachers that the gallery was going to be of real benefit to them, as well as to the children. For example, they discussed how it would help them to reach the Attainment Targets that the Department of Education was setting as part of the

3 The Tate Gallery made it plain, however, that their policy of charging entry to the gallery in St Ives would not extend to Millbank or Liverpool. (Although at both locations entry is charged to see loan exhibitions.)

new National Curriculum. The schoolchildren, in fact, once they came to the gallery, were far more responsive to the abstract art than their elders, and parties soon began arriving in large numbers.

Finally, once the scaffolding had been removed, the building's architecture was seen to be spectacular. Together with the strength of the Tate name, it became clear that here was a space in which it was a privilege to be exhibited, rather than a place to be 'banished' to. Its immediate popularity with visitors from all over the world brought the works of art to a much wider public than ever before, while the Tate Trustees guaranteed that works from St Ives would continue to be shown in both London and Liverpool, as well as toured to other venues in Great Britain and abroad.

But what of the residents of St Ives; what did they think about all the fuss? With the town seemingly full to overflowing with galleries, it was difficult for those who knew little of contemporary art to understand why a 'minority' audience should have the benefit of yet another place to look at paintings. There was a lengthy campaign waged by a few shopkeepers, who tried to persuade local people that the whole scheme was 'a waste of public money'. They accused the County Council of allowing the building to breach the town's sewage embargo. Sewage had, for many years, been a problem in the area, which a succession of ambitious schemes put forward since the mid-1970s, but not executed, had tried to eradicate. The idea of many extra visitors coming to St Ives, therefore, only appeared to exacerbate the matter. Some residents took a different point of view, arguing that the site could be put to better use. More housing for elderly people was suggested,[4] as was a leisure centre or a town swimming pool. And what about the thorny problem of car parking which was known to be notoriously difficult in the summer months? No-one was likely to visit the gallery if there was nowhere to park nearby, it was believed.

The sewage issue was seen, in the lively correspondence columns of the local newspapers, to be 'personal ambition' on the part of the complainants. This major problem would be solved only at government and European level; no advantage would be served by bringing such a complex issue into discussion of the gallery. In any event, it was expected that most of the extra visitors would come to St Ives outside the peak holiday season of June to September, putting few extra pressures on the town's infrastructure. If this occurred, the gallery would benefit from having two currently underused car parks relatively close by.[5] The shopkeepers, in fact, benefitted considerably from visitors having to park at a distance from their destination in the summer months. They saw far more of St Ives than the Porthmeor area, visiting shops and restaurants on their way to the gallery, and were easily distinguishable as visitors because of the coloured Tate St Ives stickers they proudly wore.

For many years St Ives had wanted an indoor swimming pool which would be especially popular with holidaymakers on wet days. A local action group had been established, which no doubt felt unhappy at the energy and public money being put towards another gallery, while the pool remained only an idea. But as the Education Coordinator, Lizzie Barker, said when she discovered this controversy on her first visit to the town: 'If you have a Tate Gallery, you will probably be able to organise a swimming pool later. Having a swimming pool first is no guarantee of having a Tate Gallery.'

All these criticisms were, in fact, helpful. The local press was particularly interested in any controversy that might make a good news story. And as far as the gallery's supporters were concerned, regular interviews of the protagonists, for both local radio and newspapers, allowed opportunities for publicly expressing their

4 Housing for elderly people had been the original plan for the derelict gasworks site; the Meadow Flats development had been phases one and two of this plan, but once British Gas decided to retain ownership of the land, the idea of elderly people's housing had to be abandoned. (See Chapter 9 - Porthmeor and its Gasworks.)

5 The two nearest car parks to Tate St Ives are Barnoon above the gallery and Porthmeor to the west, at the bottom of Porthmeor Hill.

aspirations: that the gallery, as Richard Carew Pole regularly pointed out, would be a 'project of excellence' and bring 'considerable cultural and economic benefits to St Ives and focus national and international artistic attention on the town'. It would also bring a more cosmopolitan visitor to the area.

The spending of tax payers' money was put into perspective when *The St Ives Times & Echo* of 20 April, 1990 reported that:

The funding from County was a one-off capital amount that should be measured against only £25,000 spent on museums and galleries out of a capital allocation on education, roads, social services and other items of £156 million in the past 10 years.

For those well acquainted with the works of art coming to St Ives, there were two main concerns: that the gallery would be 'a mausoleum to dead artists', and that the work of artists in the town, created before 1930, would not be represented, despite being bought by the Chantrey Bequest, a collection owned by the Tate Gallery for many years.[6] The new museum would therefore not be showing what was believed to be important work created prior to the 'modernist' period. In response to these accusations it was pointed out, firstly, that a number of the artists whose work was to be shown were still very much alive. With changing exhibitions and a lively education programme, the Curator believed he would be able to create a 'living' place. Secondly, no-one was ruling out the possibility that earlier works would *not* be shown as an introduction to the main display, but the rationale behind the gallery was to exhibit the works of those artists who, especially in the 1940s and 50s, had been at the forefront of British avant-garde art.

Des Hannigan, a local freelance journalist, following the ebbs and flows of opinion, wrote a perceptive article in *The St Ives Times & Echo* on 27 April 1990, under the title 'Storm in a paint pot'. He quietly rebuked those who criticised the gallery, although he said: 'It would have been disappointing in fact, in a community where there is a unique mix of interests and passions' if there had not been such comments. But then he asked:

Will there be fun and laughter and free movement throughout St Ives' own gallery, for local people as a reflection of their history and tradition and beautiful surroundings rather than just sterile art appreciation in hushed tones, from the trans-European connoisseur of the picture frame with the cucumber sandwiches in the shoulder bag? St Ives made the artists in the first place, not vice versa...When the pilchard was King in St Ives, the streets ran with blood and stank to high heaven. Art, culture, politics and money all rolled down the gutters with not an artist or a leisure businessman in sight, to exploit - upmarket or down market - the image of the town.

Time would tell.

Finally, there were criticisms from some of the County Councillors. The small Labour group on the Council decided to make a political stand and vote 'en bloc' against allocating public funds to the gallery, on the basis that the money should be put towards much needed improvements to the county's schools. In response it was recognised that the comparatively small funding allocated to the gallery, if spread around the county's educational establishments, would hardly have paid for many new books, let alone more major facilities.[7]

Then there was one particular councillor, Mrs Pat Rowe, who, throughout the project never wavered in her negative feelings for the gallery. At the full council meeting held on 26 February 1991, she summed these up: she didn't like the look of the building, it reminded her of an Odeon cinema; she felt that there were far more important charitable causes for people to spend their money on; she was unhappy that the building was going to cost more to build than had been estimated and she could not justify the spending of Council money on what she felt was a luxury

6 Ten artists have been identified by Marion Whybrow from the *Dictionary of British Artists* as having their paintings bought for the Tate Gallery by the Chantrey Bequest between 1888 and 1940.

7 One councillor had a longer term view: 'We build schools for children to learn to read and write and to stretch their imaginations. If we bring back into Cornwall something of our heritage we will be doing something for our children in the future.'

project during a recession.

Richard Carew Pole was, in fact, not at all disturbed by the criticisms levelled at the gallery. He felt 'it kept our performance sharp'. Most councillors had been persuaded by the Steering Group Chairman's conviction for the gallery, and were very enthusiastic about having the opportunity to vote for such a prestigious project in Cornwall. They saw how the 'Tate in the North' had benefitted Liverpool since its opening in 1988, in the same way as the arrival of the Burrell Collection had improved the cultural image of Glasgow. The councillors were aware, too, that they would have been thought of as 'failures' if they had turned their backs on this once-in-a-lifetime opportunity. They knew that if the gallery did not go ahead, the large amount of money promised from Europe and major private sponsors would be lost to the county for ever. Some councillors even saw the gallery as a 'bargain'. And for those who believed it was never the right time to do anything out of the ordinary, the answer was that 'now is the time to have the vision and the "guts" to get on with it'.

Having made the commitment, everyone optimistically looked forward to the climax of the scheme, the building of the gallery itself.

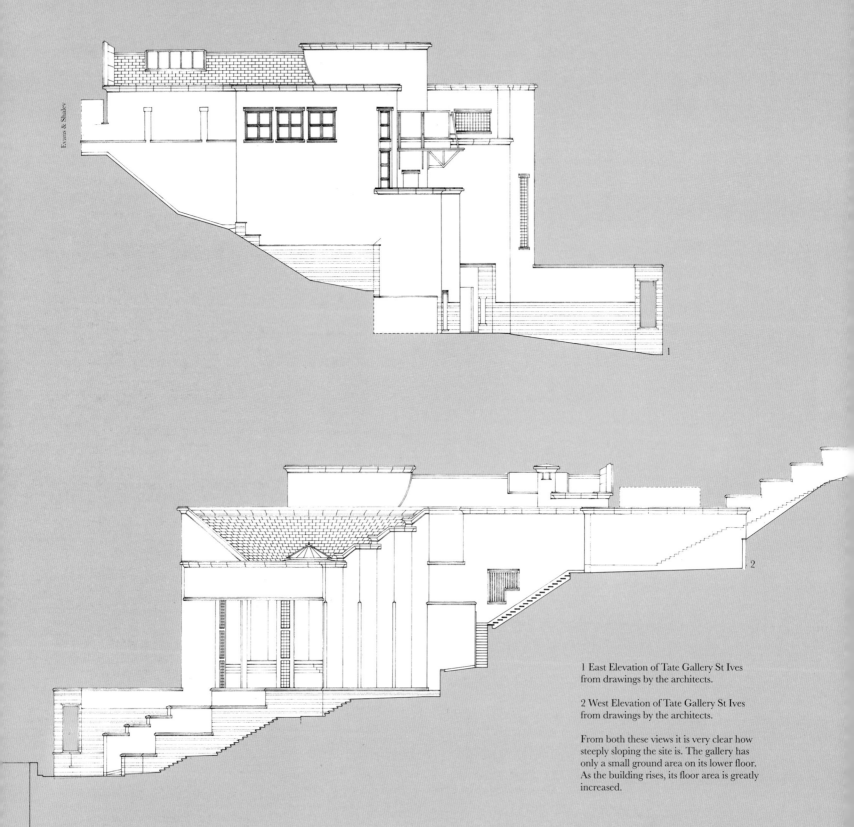

Evans & Shalev

1

2

1 East Elevation of Tate Gallery St Ives
from drawings by the architects.

2 West Elevation of Tate Gallery St Ives
from drawings by the architects.

From both these views it is very clear how
steeply sloping the site is. The gallery has
only a small ground area on its lower floor.
As the building rises, its floor area is greatly
increased.

15   Building Construction

The summer of 1991 saw the focus of attention transfer to St Ives itself. But if the Steering Group believed their troubles were over, they soon discovered new problems confronting them, both financial as well as actually above and below ground. From the moment tenders were received, through the construction work itself, until the day the gallery opened, the Group battled to ensure that the project was kept to its tight budget. But alongside this, a unique building slowly and spectacularly emerged sideways across the derelict ground at Porthmeor.

The Council meeting on 26 February 1991 was the culmination of all the planning that had taken place since that summer of 1986. The Councillors were asked to vote on the financial implications of the project and to give the final go-ahead to the gallery so that construction could begin, hopefully, within a few weeks. They were informed that the site had been purchased; detailed plans had been prepared; £820,000 had been promised from the private sector towards the Steering Group's target of £1 million; funding of £877,500 from the ERDF would shortly be cleared by the Commission; a Rural Development Grant of £40,000 had been agreed; Penwith District Council had pledged £75,000 and St Ives Town Council £15,000; a Derelict Land Grant in the region of £300,000 would be forthcoming from the DoE to clear contamination from the site; STAG was well on its way towards reaching its £100,000 target, and finally the management arrangements with the Tate Gallery had been agreed and negotiations for a draft lease were nearing completion.

Costs associated with the employment of staff and day-to-day operation of the gallery would be the responsibility of the Tate Gallery, while debt charges, education provision, external maintenance and replacement of major equipment the province of the County Council. A proportion of the gallery's admission charges would be taken up by the County to finance these latter costs.

The next stage was for the County formally to accept the lowest tender and sign the building contract.

In the previous November, the County Architect's Department put the gallery out to tender. At 10.15am on 17 January 1991, in the Clerk's Department, seven bids were opened,[1] and the difficulties started.

The Brief sent to prospective architects two years previously, clearly stipulated that the building should cost only £1.5 million to construct. Because of the unusual design chosen, it soon became clear that this was an unrealistic figure. The Steering Group agreed therefore that the ceiling would have to be raised to £2 million.

On that January morning, the lowest tender received - from Dudley Coles - was £421,000 *above* this second figure. Richard Carew Pole recalls:

There was a meeting just afterwards with Doris Ansari, John Hurst, Alan Groves, Richard Lester and myself. We told the architects in no uncertain terms that if a tender for this amount went before the Council it would be turned down.

It was an anxious time. Members of the Steering Group feared that, even at this eleventh hour, the project might have to be abandoned if the figure could not be reduced. They knew that putting the gallery out to tender again would only delay the project to an unacceptable degree, and there was little chance that a further attempt would produce a lower figure; probably the opposite would be the case.

[1] Tenders were received from Dudley Coles, Alfred MacAlpine, Midas Construction of St Austell, Costain Construction, F R Bartlett Ltd., Dean and Dyball Construction Ltd. and E Thomas Construction Ltd.

1

1 An artificially posed photograph of Richard Carew Pole signing the building contract on behalf of the County Council at County Hall, Truro, in the spring of 1991. In fact by this time the contract was not ready to be signed because a number of problems had arisen. Uncertainty seems to be reflected in some of the faces of the participants. Left to right with Richard Carew Pole: David Roberts, Chairman, Cornwall County Council, Peter Wilson, Head of Gallery Services, Tate Gallery, and Councillor John Hurst.

2 Bryan Hammond and Tony Luke from Dudley Coles, the contractors for Tate Gallery St Ives, pictured in front of the Truro Crown Courts (for which they had also been the contractors) at the time it opened in 1988. Bryan Hammond had been Project Manager and Tony Luke his deputy.

2

Peter Wilson spent a lot of time with Eldred Evans and David Shalev to see what could be omitted from the contract. Monk Dunstan, the Quantity Surveyors, went through the Bill of Quantities with Alan Groves and Peter Fazakerley for the same purpose. The decision was taken that nothing should be removed that could not be reinstated at a later date, if and when more money became available from the fund raising campaign. The external appearance of the gallery, therefore, was not altered other than to take out some of the granite from the sides of the building. The internal layout also remained the same. Omitted at this stage was the fitting out of the kitchen, restaurant, shop and education room.

The temporary removal of the education facility upset some members of the St Ives Town Council, who felt that this was one area of the project that would definitely be of benefit to the residents of the town. Always a champion of the under-privileged, Councillor Alan Harvey was so angry about the decision that he was reported to have said that the Town Council should withhold its contribution of £15,000 until this element of the building contract had been reinstated. 'We supported the Tate because the educational facilities were in the contract', he complained at a Council meeting. 'Now we're being told they have to be sponsored'. Councillor Betty Berriman was more relaxed about the whole affair. 'Rome was not built in a day' she was quoted as saying in *The St Ives Times & Echo* of 3 May 1991, 'Let's get the walls up. As money becomes available the education fac-ilities will come'.[2]

A major expense was the air conditioning equipment. It was believed that the tender figure could be brought down to a more acceptable level if it was omitted. However, the decision was taken to install the necessary pipe work and ducts from the start, so that the system could be incorporated at a later date.[3] As the project progressed, extra money *was* raised from a special grant of £150,000 from the Sport and Arts Foundation, which surprised and delighted the Steering Group. As a result the gallery opened with a computer controlled system that has kept the galleries perfectly heated or cooled, and makes a visit, at any time of the year, a comfortable experience.

The delicate decision as to what would finally be omitted was taken with the Tate Gallery's agreement and with the assistance of Richard Carew Pole, John Hurst and Doris Ansari. The building contract, worth £2,014,000, was finally signed on 20 May, with little public ceremony, after the rather frustrating delays.

Dudley Coles was the ideal company to build the gallery. It brought together again a team of men who had recently worked on two major projects in Truro: Evans and Shalev's Crown Courts and the Phase IV major extension at Treliske Hospital. The company which, in 1994, had celebrated its sixtieth anniversary, was founded by 24-year old Mr Dudley Coles of Plymouth. The company quickly grew in size, and played a large part in the immediate post-war housing and rec-onstruction programme throughout Devon and Cornwall, in particular helping to rebuild much of Plymouth city centre after it had been severely bombed.

In 1963 an area office was opened in Truro which undertook major work in the High Cross area of the city, following which the company began a long association with Treliske Hospital. Dudley Coles was acquired by a number of different firms over the years. During construction of Tate Gallery St Ives, in July 1992, it was bought by the Kier Group following its successful 'management and employee buy-out'. Operating within the Regional structure of Kier, it continues to provide a service to clients in both Devon and Cornwall. Other major projects have been the Fine Art Block at Falmouth School of Art and Design, and the Grange Restaurant and Tea Rooms at Buckfast Abbey for which it won a Civic Trust Award.

Dudley Coles' Area Manager, Bryan Hammond, had worked for the company for thirty-two years by the time the gallery was completed. In 1986 he was

2 As already described, it was in response to this outcry that STAG decided, a few months after its £100,000 target had been reached, that any extra funds raised by them should be put towards equipping the Education Room.

3 With the gallery right beside the sea, correct temperature and humidity control were seen to be essential if all the St Ives works from London were to be brought to the town, especially those made of wood or on paper.

Andrew Besley

A general view of the derelict gasworks site taken from the west, in winter, looking towards The Island. The different 'tiers' are clearly visible, as are the large concrete plinths on which the high pressure gas holder stood for many years.

Malcolm Henderson

1

2

Two views of the derelict gasworks site:
1 From the entrance gates on Beach Road,
2 From one of the upper tiers of the site.
The colourful flowers contrast, yet merge
with the man-made rubbish that covers the
area.

appointed Project Manager for the Crown Courts in Truro, for which he received the MBE. Working with Eldred Evans and David Shalev for the first time he realised: 'Every aspect of the architects' designs had a reason, right down to the final finishes'. He found them one of the best and most sympathetic architectural partnerships he had ever worked with. Hammond's deputy on the Truro job, Tony Luke, who had worked for Dudley Coles for twenty-five years, was appointed Project Manager for Tate Gallery St Ives, and Bryan Hammond took on a managerial role behind the scenes.

The entire construction team moved across the county to St Ives to officially begin work on 11 June 1991, three weeks after signing the building contract and start of site clearance.

The 0.13 hectare site was a very complex one for the contractors, from all points of view. Access was extremely difficult. Tate Gallery St Ives, like the Crown Courts, does not have a conventional front entrance where traffic drives up and discharges both people and materials. These two public buildings can only be approached by foot, up a large number of steps or a ramp.[4] In St Ives there is only one access to the site - at the end of the town's one-way system.[5]

The stipulation was made that no building materials or equipment should come through the centre of town. Instead everything had to be brought into St Ives from the west; down the Stennack, turning left at the corner of Bullans Lane. There the Old Stennack School was being converted into a Medical Centre for the town, coincidentally by a team from the same contractors. To make sure that deliveries for the gallery were not muddled with deliveries to the School, a bright yellow sign with the words 'Dudley Coles Gallery' pointing up Bullans Lane was attached to the School's railing.[6] Loaded lorries then went up the hill to Ayr, and down the steep gradient of Porthmeor Hill (with its panoramic view of the bay below) to the gates of the site located just past the turning circle at the beginning of the one-way system. This method of delivery proved very successful, and brought the least amount of disruption to the town.

The site itself was terraced down the precipitous hillside, and fell approximately fourteen metres between the street level of Godrevy Terrace and Beach Road below. Hemmed in between the four blocks of Meadow Flats, it was recognised that everyone nearby was to be subject to a great deal of noise, dust and disruption from early morning to late afternoon, Monday to Friday, and on Saturday mornings.

Parking was a problem for the contractors. In order for their vehicles to be as close to the site as possible, negotiations took take place with the owner of the guest house above the retaining wall so that he could have spaces allocated to him in the adjacent District-owned Barnoon Car Park.

As far as the derelict site itself was concerned, it still contained the concrete slabs on which the cylindrical gas holder had stood, together with other concrete structures that seemed to grow out of the grassy tiers at the back of the site. Rusty barbed wire, bright blue plastic flapping in the wind, the remains of a brick wall with an arched window - its glass long gone - and ancient scaffolding, competed with a profusion of wild flowers for much of the year. Despite these patches of bright colour, the overall feel of the place was one of forlorn desolation.

But below the ground there lurked an even greater menace. It had always been known that the area was polluted because of the presence of the gasworks. As early as December 1989, three companies tendered for a derelict land site investigation, looking particularly at the nature and extent of contamination and other dereliction, and making proposals for dealing with it. In January 1990 the firm of Kenchington Little plc was appointed to undertake this work.[7] Boreholes were dug in various parts of the site. The report, completed in early June, confirmed that the

4 Prisoners, of course, do not arrive at the County Courts by the front entrance, they are brought by bus to the back of the building.

5 The town's one-way system was introduced in 1962 in order to relieve the chronic traffic congestion that built up each holiday season.

6 The 'Dudley Coles Gallery' sign on the School's railings caused surprise from some residents who had thought that the building at Porthmeor was a 'Tate Gallery'!

7 In fact, the site investigation was not begun until the land had finally been bought from British Gas, three months after Kenchington Little's appointment.

Bryan Hardman

1

1 The old coking ovens/furnaces revealed, in August 1991, during early construction work on the site. The measuring stick shows that the ovens reached a depth of about 2.4 metres below ground level.

2 Bryan Hardman, Clerk of the Works, in his distinctive hard hat, pictured with the architects David Shalev and Eldred Evans on completion of the gallery in June 1993. Bryan Hardman said that Tate Gallery St Ives was the finest job he had ever worked on. A number of unusual photographs of the construction work in this chapter were taken by him. He was able to record those parts of the project not seen by other photographers.

Bryan Hardman

2

Bryan Hardman

3

3 July 1991 - In the background can be seen the first stages of blockwork to the gallery to be constructed on the site; the bin store, located at its far eastern end. The fence on the left is the boundary line between the gallery and Meadow Flats.

ground was, indeed, contaminated, which would affect not only the safety of the construction workers but also attack any new building materials. At this stage removal of the contamination from the site was only one option for dealing with the matter.

The cost of removal might have proved to be an insurmountable burden on the County Council's already stretched budget. However, Chris Trevan, working in the Planning Department, one day overheard a conversation to the effect that the cost of the project was giving concern. He was aware that Cornwall, along with the other local authorities, had access to one hundred per cent funding from the Department of the Environment 'towards the cost of works to reclaim land which has been so damaged by previous development that it is incapable of further use without treatment.'[8] Trevan queried whether the idea of a Derelict Land Grant had been pursued by the County Council? The DoE office in Bristol, already dealing with the ERDF grant, could not have been more helpful. After agreeing to assist, Peter Fazakerley, the Chief Quantity Surveyor in the Architect's Department, conducted the lengthy negotiations and a figure of £279,417 was arrived at.

As soon as the contractors started to dig, however, they realised that the exploratory holes had not been bored in the most revealing places. The extent of the pollution was much greater than anyone had anticipated. Everything under the ground had to be removed, including the original coking ovens, before any foundations could be dug. As the extent of the additional costs emerged, Peter Fazakerley, over a period of several months, continued his negotiations with the DoE in Bristol. He remembers:

[I was] eventually able to report to the Steering Group that, although the agreement broke new ground for the DoE, the Derelict Land Grant was increased to cover all the additional removal costs, including the cost of disruption and prolongation of the contract, as well as other costs associated with the delay that inevitably resulted.

Under the close supervision of the County Surveyor's Chemist, over the next few weeks 1,436 tons of contaminated material was taken away from the site in 102 ten-ton lorries, to a specially approved site in Cornwall. Overseeing this complex operation, and all future site activities, was the Clerk of the Works.

One of eight Clerks in the County Council's Architect's Department, Bryan Hardman had been an apprentice joiner in Lancashire, and then moved to Cornwall where he had lived for twenty years. After two years with Penwith District Council, responsible for council house maintenance, he moved to the County Council, where he was involved in projects all over the county, including the construction of several schools.[9]

Bryan Hardman, who was the link person on site between the client (Cornwall County Council) and Dudley Coles, has said that: 'this was the most difficult and challenging job I had ever worked on...we had to throw away the book'. The original Architects' Brief had asked for a gallery of 743m[2] that included circulation, storage and services. The gallery, as finally designed and built, had a much greater total floor area - 1,728m[2], which included the entrance Loggia and Mall areas.

The finished building occupied the entire site. There was nowhere to store the materials when they arrived, and it was necessary, therefore, to order and receive only those items that could be used immediately. Tony Luke was responsible for this vital aspect of the work.

When Tony Luke and the Clerk of the Works were not actually in the building itself, they spent their time in one of the two small site offices - two Portacabins, one perched on top of the other - erected just inside the gate. These temporary premises were dismantled when the Loggia was built because of the lack of space, and Bryan

8 Directions for the application of Derelict Land Grants were outlined in the National Programme of Community Interest (NPCI) 1988-1991. (See Chapter 12 - European and Other Public Funding.)

9 By the time the gallery opened, in the summer of 1993, Bryan Hardman had been promoted to Chief Clerk of the Works.

A view of the derelict site as seen from the
entrance looking upwards to the tiers of
concrete.

Andrew Besley

164

Andrew Besley

The same view of the site seen from the entrance gate, in the autumn of 1991. The gallery is beginning to emerge on the left-hand side of the photograph. The concrete has been removed from the upper tier, and work is just beginning to underpin the south boundary wall at the rear of the site.

Andrew Besley

1

1 The two Portacabins, which served as offices and meeting room for the Clerk of the Works and the general contractor, stacked one on top of the other at the entrance to the building site. The shed, on the other side of the gate was the workmen's canteen.

2 Preparing for that part of the gallery that would house the shop photographed in July 1991. It was necessary to drill into blue elvan rock (the hardest rock on earth) for several weeks (on the left) with the green 'pecker' (seen at the rear of the photograph).

3 The small circular Rotunda seen from the inside of the building looking west towards the area that will become the Loggia. The interior is now being used for storing materials that will shortly be required, including the air conditioning extract ducts for the kitchen.

Bryan Hardman

2

Bryan Hardman

3

166

Hardman and Tony Luke had to find alternative accommodation in the unfinished gallery.

It was in these cramped Portacabins that the regular site meetings were held, chaired by David Shalev and attended by, amongst others, Bryan Hardman, Alan Groves, who managed the construction process from the County Council end and Peter Wilson from London. Later Mike Tooby joined the sessions.

Unusually, building work commenced before the entire site could be cleared. The gallery was constructed in sections, starting at the four-storey east end[10] and working westwards across the site, rather than upwards in the conventional way. The entrance to the one-storey Loggia was completed only on the morning of the day the Prince of Wales opened the building, exactly two years after construction began.

Further complications arose when work on the north boundary foundations revealed the brick-built gasworks furnace/coking ovens from the old site. Bryan Hardman recalls:

removal of these took the levels down a further two metres, and the specifications of the reinforcement columns in the Mall area had to be revised. Neil Tutt of Jenkins and Potter, Consulting Engineers for the contract, sorted this out, the revised details being passed to the contractor via the Clerk of the Works, in order to minimise any delay.

Neil Tutt and Bryan Hardman worked in close collaboration throughout the contract to overcome the many structural difficulties. Blue elvan rock, too, was discovered, where the shop was to be sited. This, the hardest rock on earth, nearly broke the machine that had been brought in to break it up.

The huge south retaining wall also gave problems; the entire cliff face behind it was liable to collapse. Over the years the wall had been patched up in places to prevent pieces falling off. Bryan Hardman remembers:

the ground above the old wall was systematically underpinned by excavating and casting, in situ, strips of concrete, approximately one metre wide.[11] As the underpinning of the south boundary progressed, it was followed by the construction of the reinforced concrete retaining wall with damp proof membrane, and drainage cavity behind. Ducts were also installed to allow for escape of any radon gas that might accumulate beneath the building.

Everything was unstable. Work had to be undertaken very carefully to ensure that no mishaps occurred to the houses and car park above the site. The Clerk of the Works believed that this whole delicate operation was crucial to the progress of the building. As the gallery grew sideways, and the remaining land excavated, the materials being delivered had to be stored *inside* the building. The restaurant area was a particularly useful place for this purpose. However, the floors could only cope with certain loads, and so it was vital that these were never exceeded. The correct placing of stored materials was an important part of Bryan Hardman's responsibilities to prevent overloading of the suspended floor slabs.

The original circular retaining wall from the gas holder was never removed. When excavation began in this area, many months into the project, a large amount of water was found at the bottom of the wall,[12] and had to be removed, together with decades of accumulated sludge. This, too, was taken away to the tip. The resulting hole was then filled with sulphate resistant concrete before the foundations could be put in.

[It is interesting to note here that the architects had another reason for incorporating a circular area into their design. Eldred Evans remembered and liked the curved wall in one of the galleries at the National Museum of Wales in Cardiff. She had become familiar with the Museum when her father, Merlyn Evans, had exhibited there in 1962.[13]]

The Loggia section of the new gallery was another complexity. Its stepped roof

10 The first 'room' to be constructed was the bin store.

11 The Derelict Land Grant helped to pay for some of the underpinning work on the retaining wall.

12 It is not surprising that water was found at the bottom of the wall. Gas holders had to sit in water to aid their movement up and down, as the gas inside them filled or emptied.

13 The imposing building in Cathays Park, designed by A Dunbar Smith and C C Brewer, was formally opened in 1927 by H M King George V. Its design was thought to be influenced by both Grecian and Neo-Classical styles. Its top lit semi-circular gallery, projecting out from the eastern wall of the museum, and containing British painting and sculpture from the late 19th and early 20th centuries is, in fact, the upper floor of a large lecture theatre.

1

1 The high voltage electric cable that connected the two sets of Meadow Flats ran across the site and was covered in yellow warning tape, as seen in October 1991. Throughout the entire contract the builders worked perilously close to it. (The photograph shows the underpinning of the south wall taking place). A new cable was laid in a specially created duct.

2 A view looking east in February 1992. The workmen stand on the stairs leading from the internal garden to the roof terrace. Above them the skeleton roof of Gallery Five is put in position.

2

beam had to be constructed entirely on site during the winter of 1992/93 which, unlike the first, was wet and extremely windy. The work to the Loggia took three months to complete. Nevertheless, while external work was still in its early stages on this section of the gallery, internal finishes were well underway in the building's eastern end.

To the many visitors who came to look through the wire gates at the construction work, it was difficult to visualise how the building would actually look when it was completed. In the concrete block stage, with its rooms seemingly hanging out into space, and with fifty to sixty workmen dispersed throughout different parts of the structure - many perched precariously above a vast hole in the ground - the whole project seemed a mystery.

A prominent landmark was the huge MacSalvors red mobile crane that towered above the site on the many days it was required. In order to reduce costs, Dudley Coles ruled out the use of a tower crane which would have given extra problems to the contractors. Such an edifice would have trespassed over the Meadow Flats' air space and would have been unstable in high winds. Also it might not have been easy to remove once most of the gallery had been completed.

Visitors entitled to see the inside of the building at various periods of its construction, including members of STAG, could not fail to notice a bulky cable running the entire length of the building at the galleries level. This high voltage cable was the main electricity supply to Meadow Flats! It had to be very carefully watched during the whole period of construction, while heavy machinery was continually being moved around it. When work finally came to an end, a new cable was put into a specially created duct passing close to the Curator's office. Then the day arrived when the changeover occurred, and the redundant lifeline was finally removed.

Gradually the gallery emerged like a swan from an ugly duckling. In place of the dark, rather forbidding concrete, looming large from behind its fencing, there appeared a white structure whose external surface was covered with marble chippings.[14] The sweeping curves of what would become Gallery Two began to take shape, and within its shadows a vast concave glass wall was put in place to allow visitors inside a spectacular view of the whole of Porthmeor Beach. The roof of the Loggia projecting out from the glass, reduced the amount of daylight into the gallery. Until almost opening day, this area was filled with scaffolding from top to bottom, making it impossible to understand how the final section would look, even from inside.

Because of bad weather that winter, and the complications of constructing both the substructure and superstructure of the Loggia, the project was delayed by several months. It was essential for the gallery to open to the public for the summer of 1993, and time was getting short. Pressure was put on the contractors by Alan Groves to complete, and in the first week of May that part of the structure which was finished, but lacking in certain amenities, was formally handed over to the County Council for occupation by the Tate staff.

The Mall became the final storage and rest area for the builders. From the end of March 1993, this space was dominated by the very large coloured glass window, designed by Patrick Heron, and manufactured by Studio Derix in Tannhausen, near Wiesbaden, Germany. The cost of its construction was additional to the main contract price, and was met by the Friends of the Tate Gallery. It was the architects who approached the artist about designing a window for this aperture. The great window-space they were looking to fill was 4.6m x 4.2m, and it backed immediately on to one of the blocks of flats. Patrick Heron, after many months of deliberation,

14 Marble chippings were also used on the external surface of the Truro Crown Courts.

Bryan Hardman

1

2

1 and 2 Remnants of the old gasholder exposed by excavations. It is being cut into manageable sections. It was then taken to Falmouth School of Art and Design where it was made into a sculpture by Trevor Vance, one of the students, and briefly installed on the roof of Tate Gallery St Ives in the summer of 1993.

3 Sculpture for Tate Gallery St Ives by Trevor Vance as it appeared in situ on the gallery roof. Three and a half metres in length (the work projected down into the garden area below) the sculpture only remained in place for two weeks, because the gap behind the slate bench on which it was placed was seen as a danger to children. Trevor Vance is from Enniskillen, Northern Ireland. After taking a foundation course at Falmouth School of Art and Design in 1991, he chose to work in metal in the first year of his degree course. His tutor, Andrew Stonier, knew of the fragment of gasholder taken from the site of the gallery, and suggested that Vance was the appropriate student to make good use of the material. As a result of a visit to the incomplete gallery, Vance decided to design the work with the architecture particularly in mind. He wished to link two floors in a way that the Loggia area (from where the fragment had come) connects the different floors. He cut the metal with an oxyacetaline torch in the college workshops, and removed the surface rust. The final sculpture, however, was not polished, as it would in any case have rusted in the sea air. After the work was removed from the gallery it was returned to Falmouth and dismantled.

Bob Berry

3

accepted the invitation and painted a small gouache, measuring only 184mm x 165mm, which consisted of eight colour areas, in a style reminiscent of his paintings of the 1960s and 70s. He made the design as a gift to the gallery.

The artist had very positive requirements about the way his window was to be made. He said to *The Cornishman* on 1 April, 1993:

The last thing I wanted was a stained glass window with leading, medieval like a cathedral. I wanted the colour areas to abut direct upon each other along the lines of my drawing.

A different method of constructing the window had therefore to be found. After a long search, the name of Wilhelm Derix was brought to the architects' attention by Katharine Heron. A long established family business, Studio Derix had recently perfected a process for laminating large areas of hand-made antique glass onto clear thick float glass from Pilkingtons. The company's owner, Wilhelm Derix, was so enthusiastic about the proposed commission, that the moment he was approached by the architects, he and his wife jumped into their Mercedes, drove to the offices of Evans and Shalev in London, and then direct to Eagles Nest at Zennor to meet Patrick Heron. Derix offered to make the window to Heron's main requirements.

Patrick Heron visited Germany twice. The first time he matched the colours of the glass to approximate the colours of the original gouache, without literally imitating them. With the assistance of the architect Julian Feary, who accompanied him to Wiesbaden on both occasions, the design was carefully divided into a grid pattern, as there was no way that each colour area could be made from a single piece of glass.

On the second visit Patrick Heron was presented with a full scale cartoon the actual size of the window itself. Heron recalls:

this cartoon took the form of pencil lines traced on white paper by Derix's team. Although these lines were a faithful transcription on to the white cartoon of the actual positions of the 'frontiers' dividing the colour areas, they nevertheless had no expressive quality, as lines. I therefore redrew them direct with a black Pentel pen, crawling about on the huge paper cartoon which was on tables, in order to do so. This bestowed my own lines to the drawing on the cartoon.

After Heron and Feary's departure, the antique coloured glass was sawn into shapes, which virtually reproduced the linear character of the lines that Heron had drawn on the cartoon.

Towards the end of March 1993, a green lorry, owned by the Frankfurt firm of Glazbau Hahn, arrived outside the gallery. It was at Frankfurt that the pieces of coloured glass, supplied and cut by Derix, were put into position onto two unequal pieces of thick transparent float glass which constituted the window. One section was clamped to the outside of one side of the vehicle and the second section clamped to the other. Two young men from Hahn helped swing the two sections from the lorry, which was parked just off the road.

In a high wind the two segments were individually brought around the corner of the building and then eased between the gallery and the back of the flats on a mobile crane. Great suction pads, brought by Hahn, enabled the crane to lift the glass and swing it through the opening in the Mall, where it was carefully lowered into position through a hole in the metal scaffolding that still covered much of the outside of the building. After five or six hours it was finally slotted into place. As the installation of the window was outside the building contract, supervision for it became the responsibility of the Clerk of the Works under the watchful eyes of Julian Feary and Patrick Heron.

At this moment Patrick Heron remembers a special problem presented itself:

Since the head of the crane could not be positioned immediately over the window aperture,

1

1 A view looking towards the south retaining wall showing the water in the hole that surrounded Number One gasholder. The water originally aided its movement when it filled or emptied, according to how much gas the holder contained.

2 Excavation of the gas holder looking down into the 'pit' February/March 1992. The workman is supervising the water being pumped out by the pipe on the left.

2

Tony Luke, the Project Manager, in white hat, inspects the clearance of the sludge from the base of the old gasholder in May 1992, while the gallery grows ever westwards. The curved wall at the rear of the photograph was never removed.

1

1 Work progressing along the south boundary wall (the photograph was taken looking west) in November 1991. The poor state of the wall can be clearly seen as workmen underpin the area.

2 Work progressing along the south boundary wall a month later (the photograph was taken looking east). Reinforced concrete is being poured into moulds, and a damp proof membrane is inserted between the concrete and the wall, allowing for a drainage cavity behind.

2

due to an overlap in the exterior of the building, the immensely heavy window, swinging on its suction pads, had to be manhandled through a ninety-degree rotation. Several hours seemed to elapse while the two young Germans calculated the possibility of making this rotation without opposite corners of the window striking either the concrete sill or lintel of the window.

It was not, of course, until Patrick Heron entered the building, a few minutes after this manoeuvre had been completed, that he was able to see, for the first time, what his window looked like with the light coming through.

The result was even more spectacular than could have been imagined. Wilhelm Derix, when he finally saw it in place a few months later, was pleased by the fact that he had manufactured a window which, he said, clocked up 'two firsts', namely that it was the largest coloured glass window in the world which was totally devoid of leading, and it was the largest single unit of design which his firm had ever made in the one hundred and twenty years of its existence.

Three months after the window was installed, and the night before the Prince of Wales arrived for the opening ceremony, all the builders were still completing the final section of the gallery; the steps leading up from the pavement on Beach Road to the Loggia, and the capping of the top of the walls beside the stairway. It was an extremely noisy and dusty operation to cut the concrete slabs to size there on site. Fascinated onlookers walked up and down Beach Road at all hours of that final night and early morning to watch and photograph and even video the builders (accompanied by their constant companion, Molly the dog) hard at work under powerful arc lights. The waiting crowd even applauded when the men returned to their tasks after taking a meal break!

The ugly derelict site, so quickly a distant memory, was transformed into a beautiful white gallery, unique in its design, which nestled comfortably between the neighbouring flats and beside one of the loveliest beaches in the country. The builders, who had for two years worked as a dedicated team, were especially proud of all they had achieved. They were not alone. Sir Richard Carew Pole recalls asking David Shalev, on the evening of the opening, what he thought of the building? The architect said he felt it was their finest design.

A gallery, of course, does not function without staff. While construction was taking place, a team was being assembled to transform the building into the purpose for which it was first conceived, a fine art gallery rooted in its context, and an integral part of the life of St Ives.

Andrew Besley

1

2

1 A view of the site during May 1992 from the upper level looking towards The Island (compare with the photograph on pages 160-61). The main entrance door can be seen in the bottom left-hand corner, and the curved floor of Gallery Two is beginning to take shape. Nearing completion in the background is the pitched roof of Gallery Five, adjacent to the restaurant.

2 The unusual circular gallery at the National Museum of Wales in Cardiff with its top windows. Opened in 1927 the Museum housed an auditorium, and this gallery was its upper floor. The space partly inspired Eldred Evans to design the curved Gallery Two at Tate St Ives.

1 The internal end wall of Gallery Five as it looked in September 1992, with its circular window above the door. Behind the medium density fibreboard that lines the walls, can be seen blue polythene and timber battens. At the top left, the added insulation indicates that this corner of the room is an outside wall.

2 A visitor's eye-view of the site from the main gate, shows the complexities of the building as it appeared in the summer of 1992. The Upper Terrace of Gallery Two, that will contain the ceramics display, is taking shape, while on the far right is the space that will become the Curator's office.

1

2

Andrew Besley

1 Another glimpse of the hole in the ground below the Loggia in July 1992. (Compare with the photograph on page 98 of the men looking into the bomb crater.) In the centre a workman sweeps the floor at what will be the main doorway into Tate Gallery St Ives. Because of the gallery's sideways progress, a toothing effect was used in the concrete blocks to aid the building's onward construction.

2 The building during construction, taken in the autumn of 1992. In the centre is the floor of the Loggia with the newly created undercroft from the space once occupied by the foundations of Number One gasholder. Above can be seen the floor of Gallery Two, and the bottom beam to support the curved window. Above again is the ceramics display area and roof above. Overhead the red MacSalvors crane brings materials to where they are needed.

1

Roger Harvey ABIPP

2

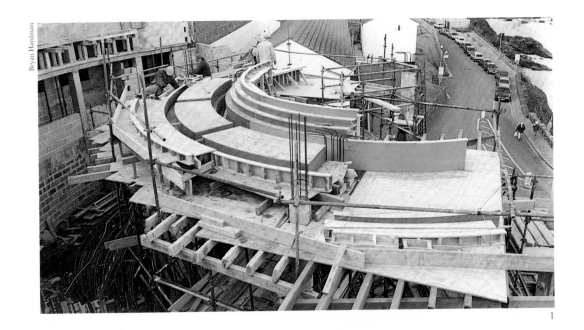

Bryan Hardman

1

Bryan Hardman

2

The Loggia roof begins to take shape. All views are seen looking west.

1 October/November 1992. The timber form works for the concrete beams were constructed on site. To the left the balcony of Gallery Two can be seen.

2 November/December 1992. The metal roof light centre to the Loggia (right of the photograph) is put in place to support the radial steel lattice beams on which the timber roof is constructed.

3 March 1992. The roof tiles are being put into position on Gallery Two. In the centre is the roof of the Loggia.

4 A fish-eye close-up view of the Loggia roof from the air. To the left of the photograph the roof terrace can clearly be seen, which in the summer acts as an extension to the restaurant. The Loggia roof was covered with a durable flexible membrane. In the front is a flat area covered with gravel.

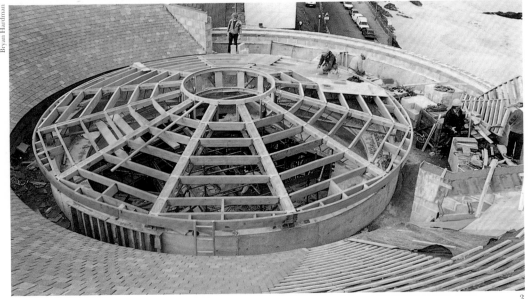

Bryan Hardman

3

180

4

A view of the rusting gasworks seen from Beach Road, taken in the 1970s.

Andrew Besley

1

Three views of the site to show its development from the same position as the photograph on page 182.

1 The gallery in June 1992. Prominent at the upper level is the restaurant behind its scaffolding, with the pitched roof of Gallery Five almost completed.

2 The front elevation of the roof beam of the Loggia is being rendered prior to being spa dashed in April 1993. The restaurant area on the left has already been finished in this manner.

3 The gallery nearing completion in June 1993. The scaffolding has been taken down from inside the Loggia to reveal, in its darkened depths, the curved glass wall. The Portacabins and the old wall around the gasworks have finally been removed.

Andrew Besley

2

Roger Harvey ABIPP

3

1

2

3

5

4

A succession of photographs showing the installation of Patrick Heron's coloured glass window which was delivered to the site in March 1993.

1 The green lorry from Glasbau Hahn, Frankfurt, is driven into the space between the incomplete gallery and the block of Meadow flats.

2 One of the two sheets of coloured glass is revealed for the first time as its protective covering is removed by the two young Germans from Hahn.

3 The glass is carefully swung from the side of the lorry and guided towards the large aperture in the gallery by means of four suction pads provided by Hahn, and held by the MacSalvors crane. The colours of the window appear muted due to the fact that the glass was covered with a fine layer of plastic.

4 The glass is turned from the horizontal to the upright position with the help of seven men. The operation was made more complex by the scaffolding being in place on either side of the window frame. The head of the crane can be seen almost touching the roof of the aperture.

5 The glass swung into place, as seen from inside the gallery. With the light behind, the window's design can now be seen in its true colours.

184

Patrick Heron looks at his finished window soon after it had been installed. Outside is silhouetted a workman on a ladder, cleaning the window's outer surface. The coloured glass was cut and laminated onto Pilkington's 'float' glass by Studio Derix of Wiesbaden, Germany, and it is the largest coloured glass window in the world without leading.

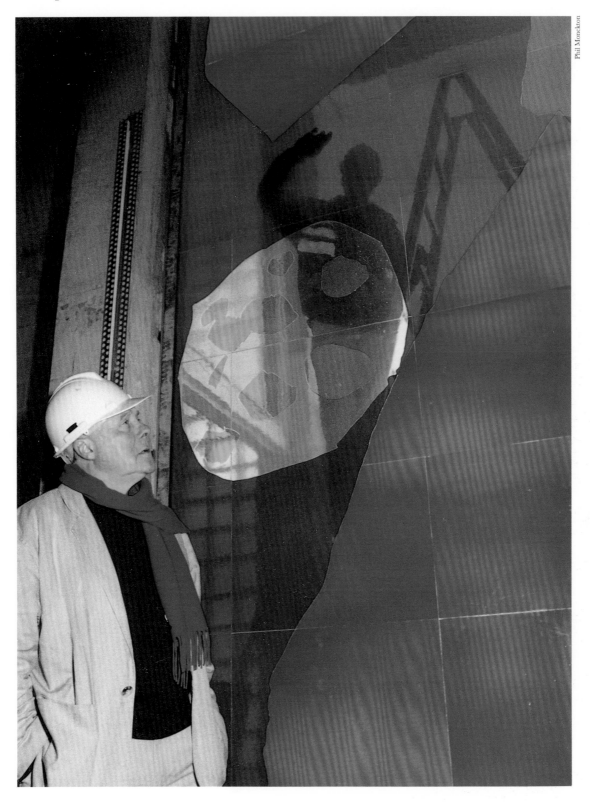

Roger Harvey ABIPP

1

Colin Orchard

2

Colin Orchard

3

Bob Berry

4

1 The stone blocks being laid in the floor of the Loggia. Many members of the construction team had their own radios, and each seemed to be tuned into different stations.

2 Molly the dog, who has been on site every day, supervises the last minute work on the entrance steps leading to the Loggia.

3 The evening before the gallery is due to be opened by Prince Charles. In bright sunshine the entire team of workmen are struggling against the clock to finish the steps leading into the gallery. A member of the public thought he was witnessing a project organised by Anneka Rice for television.

4 Part of the restaurant counter being lowered into the building, under watchful eyes, by way of the roof terrace, using the large MacSalvors crane. Bob Berry just happened to be passing the gallery at that moment with his camera, and witnessed the scene.

186

Roger Harvey ABIPP

At 4.00 on the afternoon before the gallery opened, all those who had worked on the gallery (except Bob, the Senior Foreman) assembled in the Loggia for this group photograph. On the far left is David Shalev and Eldred Evans; far right is Bryan Hardman. Tony Luke can be seen fourth from the left at the back, while Molly the dog takes pride of place.

Overleaf. The finished building, photographed on the path to Man's Head by Bob Berry, in August 1994, shows how well the gallery blends into the bay as a whole. On a sunny day, such as this, the link between gallery, town and beach, with all its facilities, is especially marked. The full impact of the building can be obtained from this particular vantage point.

John Lyne, Western Morning News Company Limited

1

1 Prince Charles enters Gallery Four of Tate Gallery St Ives on his tour of the building on 23 June 1993. To his right the Director of the Tate Gallery, Nicholas Serota, appears to be explaining the paintings the Prince is about to see, while on his left, the Curator, Michael Tooby watches attentively.

2 Morley Easthorne carves the wording into the stone that will be unveiled in the Loggia by the Prince of Wales. The marble had to be cut in such a way that it fitted perfectly into the slight curvature of the Loggia wall.

3 Michael Tooby, Tate Gallery St Ives' first Curator. The photograph was taken on the day Prince Charles opened the gallery.

Roger Harvey ABIPP

2

Barry Swaebe

3

16   Dream Finally Becomes Reality

'Royal approval for art gallery' was the headline on the front page of *The Western Morning News* on Thursday 24 June 1993. The colour photograph which accompanied this pronouncement showed a tanned Prince of Wales wearing a beige suit, blue shirt and striped red tie entering one of the galleries, flanked by Nicholas Serota and Michael Tooby, both conventionally dressed in dark suits and ties and white shirts. Following behind was a posse of dignitaries who also appeared to be attired in dark colours.

Prince Charles made a leisurely tour of the gallery where he was introduced to many of the people who had helped bring the project to fruition, as well as to the living artists whose work he had just seen. Then after unveiling a slightly curved marble plaque in the Loggia, its fine letters carved by the monumental sculptor, Morley Easthorne, the Prince spoke of the 'special atmosphere' he had encountered within the building. 'One of the great skills of architecture is to enclose a space' he told his audience. 'In this case the achievement has been remarkable, particularly on such a difficult site.' There were quiet sighs of relief when those listening realised that the speech was not going to be used as another condemnation of modern architecture.

The glittering three days of social events that followed the ceremony, celebrating the gallery's opening, was in fact the culmination of several months intense effort from planners in St Ives, London and Truro.

Heading the St Ives team was the indefatigable Michael Tooby, whose appointment as Curator, fifteen months earlier, had brought him and his family from a long established, generally publicly funded institution in one of England's industrial heartlands - the Mappin Art Gallery in Sheffield - to a brand new gallery in a remote part of the country. He chose the once-in-a-lifetime opportunity to create a small specialist gallery from scratch. As a result, not only was he subject to great pressures to achieve this challenge under the watchful eye of both the Tate Gallery and Cornwall County Council, but he became subject to intense public scrutiny from St Ives itself.

Mike Tooby's background: Assistant Curator at Kettle's Yard in Cambridge; Exhibitions Organiser at the Third Eye Centre in Glasgow; and finally, since 1984, Keeper of the Mappin Art Gallery, had brought him into contact, at various times, with the work of the St Ives artists. He says he has always believed that 'art is explained by stories of a sense of place'. Such a response to his new environment would be one of the keys to his curatorship.

He began his new job not in a void, however, where he could create a role entirely of his own making. He found himself at the centre of a large group of people who had pursued the gallery project with enormous dedication for over two years, and who had formed definite ideas about what it might mean to themselves and the town. Mike Tooby was also surrounded by many of the artists whose work would hang in the gallery, each of whom had their own ideas as to what local public exposure would mean for them individually.

The supporters were relieved to learn that the Curator-elect was aware of this unusual background to the project. Mike Tooby told *The St Ives Times & Echo* on 13 March 1992, soon after his appointment:

I know I will benefit from the evident commitment and enthusiasm of the many people already involved in getting the project to the present state, and look forward to becoming part of the wider community who will share in the gallery's work.

When he formally took up the position, on 25 May of that year, more than twelve months before the gallery eventually opened, Mike Tooby had certain key tasks: to take over the running of the Barbara Hepworth Museum and to integrate it into the overall plan without losing its unique identity; to get to know intimately the hollow structure growing rapidly on its windswept site beside Porthmeor Beach, and learn to understand how he and his staff could transform it into a working space in a way that would fulfil his criteria of it being 'about people and people's experiences'; to recruit a small team who would work together, under intense pressure, to ensure that the gallery was planned, opened and operated successfully; to become acquainted with the local and wider community, in order to show how the gallery could play a vital part in the lives of the populace; to work with the Tate Gallery in London to select the initial works to be exhibited, and prepare a twelve-month exhibition programme; and finally, to organise the opening events, which would include a Royal visit, at an unspecified date.

For some time it had been planned that the Barbara Hepworth Museum and garden should be run in conjunction with the new gallery, thus giving it much greater exposure. The number of visitors seeking peace and tranquility within its high walls reached about 20,000 a year in 1992, and it was believed that the house and garden would benefit from being linked to the Tate's education programme, encouraging a new, younger generation of visitors to appreciate Hepworth's life and work. It was, for Mike Tooby, fortuitous that Brian Smith's curatorship at the Museum was due to end in the middle of August of that year due to his retirement, allowing a smooth natural transition to take place.

The new Curator spent his first two months learning how the Tate Gallery in London operated, and becoming better acquainted with the works of art that would be brought to St Ives. Then on Brian Smith's departure he, and shortly afterwards, his temporary secretary, Kerry Olkes, moved into what had once been the gentlemen's lavatory in the Palais de Danse. With the aid of little more than a mobile telephone they began to tackle the correspondence that was already starting to pour in.

The Museum had two permanent members of staff. Since April 1986 Dell Castagli had manned the desk located just inside the front door; and Norman Pollard, recruited in September 1985, had been responsible for looking after the garden, made small repairs and kept the sculptures clean. When Mike Tooby moved in, Norman Pollard's job changed; he took over much of Brian Smith's administrative work, while both he and Dell Castagli helped Kerry Olkes to understand the close-knit community of which she had become a part. She remembers:

At the Barbara Hepworth Museum it felt like it had been there for years, and the people there were very apprehensive about what was going to happen...George [Wilkinson, who had been Norman Pollard's predecessor] would chat to me for hours about his time with Barbara Hepworth, and took me around the Palais, and that really got me going. I had never really been interested in art before. Being with people who were excited about it was very important.

The Museum ran happily under its new regime. Over the next twelve months it received a record number of visitors due to the publicity St Ives and the gallery were beginning to generate in the media.

At the heart of this growing activity was the grey empty building, rising sideways out of its muddy site. In the April before Mike Tooby officially took up his job, he attended a high powered, three-day working session for Tate Gallery staff at the Tregenna Castle Hotel in St Ives. Under the leadership of Nicholas Serota, those most intimately associated with the project were able to start planning the gallery's future and the Curator-elect outlined his initial plans.[1]

Mike Tooby felt, in those early days, that the gallery could have been any building. But aware of just how dramatic it would become, and the nature of the works that would be shown inside, he attempted from the outset to enthuse everyone he met by saying to them: 'Just think of all the things it could be.' His permanent secretary, Carolyn Trevivian, remembers being shown the site in November 1992.

The week I joined, Mike stopped the car as we drove past and pointed out my office which was just a hole in the blocks! He always gave us a sense of the gallery's reality. It was going to be much more than a place where I was to work.

The Curator regularly attended site meetings as an observer in the cramped Portacabin. From these sessions he was able to get a feel of the building's progress or lack of it. Originally anticipated to open to the public in the Easter of 1993, Mike Tooby, as the weeks passed, realised that the gallery would never by ready by then. He quietly began to adjust his plans.

Major unseen changes were being made to the building in its final year of construction. The Mall area, which had been planned as an open, empty space, was instead enclosed at the Loggia. At the same time, due to the fact that a great deal of contaminated earth had been excavated from under the Loggia, it was now possible to create a lower level in the soft earth known as the 'undercroft'. Mike Tooby watched the gallery expand in this way, and played a part in choosing how to make good use of the unexpected extra space that had been created: a long narrow corridor behind the Mall for storage of coats and surfboards; an additional space in the Education Room; and a large area under the Loggia itself which could be used for painting plinths, maintenance work and storing work created by the Education programme.

The core group of staff was required before the end of 1992 if, as was then anticipated, the gallery was to open the following spring. The first position to be advertised was that of Education Coordinator. Financed by the Tate for the first three months, and then by Cornwall County Council, this post was seen to be a key resource for the entire county. Five other positions were advertised a few weeks later: secretary, two information officers, gallery coordinator and a technician, while Norman Pollard at the Hepworth Museum was given a wider role, as technician responsible for sculpture.

There were 1,300 applications! Mike Tooby remembers taking three days to read the forms. The interviews took place in an upstairs room at The Palais (with kind permission of the Hepworth Estate) under the guidance of the Personnel Manager from Millbank. After three weeks the decisions were made. Kerry Olkes, who had worked temporarily with Mike Tooby since the end of August, became one of the Information Officers. She soon found herself working with the Education Co-ordinator, Lizzie Barker, whose previous position had been in the Education Department at the National Gallery in London. The other Information Officer, responsible for all contacts with the press, was Ina Cole. She had formerly lived and worked in Brighton.

The remaining staff were already living locally: Carolyn Trevivian joined as the Curator's Secretary, and played a major administrative role in setting up the Tate Friends St Ives group, under the chairmanship of Carol Holland; Dick Perkins became Gallery Coordinator, and immediately set up vital telephone and computer systems. Finally, Andy Dalton became the second Technician, responsible for the paintings.

The staff met together for the first time just before Christmas. Wondering what kind of adventure they were embarking upon, they were invited to join members of

1 Mike Tooby remembers that it was at the session at the Tregenna Castle Hotel that he learnt of the idea, put forward by Catherine Kinley, that as well as changing the collection annually, one gallery would be set aside for a succession of varied study displays.

1 In late April 1992, just after Michael Tooby had been appointed Curator, a group of Tate staff from London visited St Ives for several days to plan the gallery's future. It was an unseasonably cold spring day when they went to look at the building's progress. From left to right: Katharine Lomas, Press Officer, Teresa Gleadowe, Head of Information, Peter Wilson, Head of Gallery Services, Michael Tooby, Nicholas Serota, Rosemary Harris, Curator, Modern Collection, Simon Wilson, Education and Catherine Kinley, Curator, Modern Collection.

2 The Tate Gallery St Ives team pose for a photograph on the stairs by the Information desk. From the top: Kerry Olkes, Information Officer, Norman Pollard, Technician, Lizzie Barker, Education Co-ordinator, Dick Perkins, Gallery Coordinator, Michael Tooby, Curator. From left to right, Andy Dalton, Technician, Ina Cole, Information Officer and Carolyn Trevivian, Secretary.

1

2

STAG at a Christmas party at the St Ives School of Painting. Ina Cole thought the School 'a weird and wonderful place smelling of paint'. Like St Ives itself, it seemed to her to have 'a timeless quality.' The staff dispersed. By the end of February they had all taken up their posts.

Michael Tooby was anxious that his team should have an opportunity to get to know each other as a group. He was conscious of the fact that few of his staff had previously worked in an art gallery. He therefore organised for them to spend a week together, visiting the Tate Gallery in London, Tate Gallery Liverpool and Kettle's Yard in Cambridge. Andy Dalton remembers the week well:

It was then that we learnt first about Mike's energy. He runs around eveywhere. He actually put his back out with his rushing. Then we all came together as a team. Tate Gallery Liverpool felt a little more like it would be in St Ives - it was not on such a huge scale as London...in Liverpool people actually communicate face to face.

The continuing delay in the completion of the building now posed serious accommodation problems for the staff. The only space available for the eight of them was one small office at the Hepworth Museum. The gallery itself still had no glass in the windows. This hardly catered for their growing needs. They hunted for temporary quarters. Their first find was a cottage used for summer holiday lets, located not far from the Penwith Gallery. As well as providing office accommodation and a venue for meetings for the three months leading up to Easter, Ina Cole lived there while searching for somewhere to rent. Kerry Olkes, who also made use of the space in the cottage, recalls:

I had the spare bedroom upstairs; my bed was the desk and I sat on the floor with a lap-top on the bed...We had meetings around the dining room table.

Carolyn Trevivian, meanwhile, was sharing the cramped Palais space and struggling against an ever-mounting tide of paperwork, much of it general enquiries. To find peace and quiet she, Mike Tooby and Dick Perkins moved into two offices in the Stennack Surgery - a fitting place! However, at first no connecting telephones linked the three locations, and Kerry Olkes remembers:

There were members of staff running around the three sites with bundles of papers and typewriters.

Visitors to the Curator would be asked to come to the Surgery. Carolyn Trevivian, entering the large reception area remembers:

I searched for people who looked healthy, which meant they were not coming to see a doctor.

The staff were introduced to the gallery. At the beginning of the year, wearing hard hats, and surrounded by sand and cement, they began to explore their future workspace. It was, as yet, only possible to enter the building by climbing a ladder at the point where the ramp for disabled visitors now winds its way up from the pavement level.[2] Once inside the building they were confronted by a maze of grey rooms. They wondered if the gallery would be finished in time, and whether they would ever be able to find their way about? Those were exhilerating days, with a shared goal. Mike Tooby remembers:

For everyone involved, it was a first-in-a-life-time thing...you had that incredible sense of the importance of the project.

By late April the building was finally ready for occupancy, although it was by no means complete. There was no furniture, no telephones or computer system. Also

2 Later, entrance to the gallery was via the door at the eastern end of the building behind the flats, next to the bin store and kitchens. However, for some time it was necessary to climb along planks over muddy ground to enter by this route.

1

1 A view of the Loggia from the Upper Terrace of Gallery Two soon after the staff had moved in. The forest of scaffolding outside the curved glass window remained in place for some time, making it very difficult to comprehend how the finished entrance way would look.

2 A view of the gallery from The Island. To the right hand side at the bottom of the picture can be seen the Porthmeor Café, perched above the beach huts, where Tate St Ives staff regularly met and ate before the gallery's facilities were in place. The workmen used the café too, during the winter of 1992.

3 The Launch of Tate Friends St Ives at The Guildhall in December 1992. Pictured from left to right: Michael Tooby, Councillor William Thomas, Mayor of St Ives (signing up to be the first Friend), Carol Holland, Chairman of Tate Friends St Ives and Wilf Weeks, Chairman, Friends of the Tate. The Mayor felt sure that when the gallery opened it would be 'A Mecca for art lovers all over the world'.

2

3

to complicate matters further, the air conditioning was not operating, because the gallery was not yet sealed from the elements at its far western end. This meant that the works of art could not be brought from London until 10 June, less than two weeks before the Royal opening.

From the start of 1993 a multi-layered press campaign began to gain momentum. Spearheaded by the London-based press agency, Bolton & Quinn, a very effective collaboration took place between Ina Cole in St Ives, the press office at the Tate Gallery and Mark Nicholson at Cornwall County Council. They worked in conjunction with the Tourist Board and the Central Office of Information; the latter being responsible for the foreign press. As a result of these efforts, journalists from all over the world began to arrive to view the empty building.[3]

Ina Cole showed many of the groups around, providing them with hard hats from Bryan Hardman's office. Later she supervised cameramen filming among the technicians, two of whom had arrived from Millbank to hang the displays. On one occasion, despite everyone's best efforts, three film crews arrived on the same day! Andy Dalton, assisting with the hanging of the works, felt that sometimes things seemed to take an age.

Each time a different camera crew arrived they wanted to think they were attending the first hanging, so we had to keep taking things down only to put back them back up again.

Ina Cole introduced a number of journalists to the artists: Patrick Heron, Terry Frost and Wilhelmina Barns-Graham regularly entertained members of the press at their homes or at the gallery. For a time St Ives seemed to take on a 'cult status', much to the concern of Mike Tooby, who recalled having to struggle hard to get any interest from the press at his previous job in Sheffield. But the town remained sanguine. Intense publicity and being parodied in the press, in cartoons, was nothing new.[4] As Toni Carver wrote in *The St Ives Times & Echo* of 25 September 1992: 'When all is said and done the artists have been the town's chief publicity agents for 75 years.' It was exciting to be under the spotlight. Journalists clutching microphones could regularly be found on street corners, in pubs and galleries, asking unsuspecting shopkeepers, residents and visitors alike whether the Tate Gallery was going to be 'a good thing' for the town.[5]

In the gallery itself, one major task for the technicians was making plinths. Norman Pollard had this responsibility thrust upon him when Andy Dalton suddenly became very ill.

We had to make about sixty [especially for the ceramics]. All the plinths had to be made the right size, but I knew a few carpenters around St Ives who made them for us...When we started we didn't have any transport, and we had an old carpenter's four-wheel truck for picking up plinths from the different workshops all around the town - we looked like rag and bone men...When the Tate technicians came from London first they couldn't believe it when they saw our truck!

Meanwhile, with a lack of furniture and nowhere to eat in the building, the staff found a quiet place for meetings and meals, the Porthmeor Café on the beach in front of the gallery. Many planning discussions took place there, out of reach of telephones, but with the Atlantic rollers pounding over the sand only a few yards away.

Because of a shortage of funds at the time the building contract was signed, the fitting out of the restaurant and shop had been delayed. In fact by the time the gallery opened to the public, neither was operating the way it it was planned. Janet Bennette was appointed to manage the shop. In the days leading up to the Royal opening she could be seen surrounded by packing cases, and when she finally managed to organise herself a telephone to place orders, she had to perch it on top

3 Some of the observations and photographs of these journalists are included in Chapter 17 - A Tour of the Building.

4 Both serious articles and cartoons appeared in the press in the 1960s, especially when the 'beatniks' and the artists became particularly newsworthy.

5 Some responses were very negative, although soon after the gallery opened the most outspoken critics publicly apologised for having underestimated the building's positive contribution to St Ives.

Roger Harvey ABIPP

Gallery Four, with some of the paintings
waiting to be hung. Each work arrived in its
individual packing case (see right of the
picture) and was then unpacked and put
into its approximate place, facing the wall,
but kept off the floor.

of a pile of books while she waited for the specially designed shelves to arrive. Suzanne Small and Ronald Webb, running the restaurant on a franchise basis, had similar problems. There were initially very few facilities installed in their roof-top eyrie.

Extra help was found to be essential. Mark Ley and his dog (inherited from Dudley Coles) and Wally Thomas were responsible for security. Wally Thomas handed out passes to the growing number of visitors who found their way into the gallery via the back door. Meanwhile, Dave Davis and Sue Dalton were given the unenviable but vital task of vacuuming the galleries from morning until night, keeping the dust at bay, while the workmen were finishing the internal fixtures.

Getting to know the local community was an enormous task, not only for Mike Tooby, but for those staff who were not familiar with St Ives. One of Carolyn Trevivian's first responsibilities was to arrange for the Curator to meet and speak to many local groups. At the same time he attended both the regular meetings held in London to discuss the artistic arrangements for the gallery, as well as the Steering Group meetings in Truro. Inter-City became an important part of the Tate Gallery staff's life.

The education programme began to take shape well before the building opened to the public, and Kerry Olkes was very much at the centre of this initiative. She organised and accompanied the young prizewinners of the STAG painting competition on a trip by train to the Tate Gallery, where they toured behind the scenes. At Easter she and Lizzie Barker ran a 'First Impressions' workshop at the School of Painting, assisted by local artists. Children were invited from three nearby schools, and students from Falmouth School of Art and Design made a video of the results. Kerry Olkes remembers nostalgically how, in those early days: 'We didn't have to worry about paperwork and administration.'

Tate Friends St Ives was set up. After carefully planning how it should be administered, the Friends was formally launched in December 1992 at a ceremony at The Guildhall, during which the Mayor of St Ives, Councillor William Thomas, headed the list of members. It was decided that the St Ives group should be managed by the Friends office in London, to ease the amount of local administration work that was likely to accumulate. Carolyn Trevivian worked alongside Carol Holland to organise some early events for the growing membership; first in the Stennack Surgery, the Barbara Hepworth Museum and the Tregenna Castle Hotel, and then in the gallery itself. Pre-booked groups, who toured through the empty white building with members of staff, had to negotiate a path around the workmen and their materials, as the race against time to complete the building became ever more urgent.

There was no shortage of recruits. Becoming a Friend gave members and a friend free unlimited access to the gallery for a year. More immediately, Friends were automatically invited to one of two special evening receptions after the Royal opening. To the surprise of the London office, membership reached 1,000 in a very short time.

Special contact was made with another group of local people, the long-suffering residents of Meadow Flats who had endured noise, dust and vibration for many months, as well as a power cut. As completion of the building grew nearer, the residents seemed to become more querulous. Bad-tempered letters appeared in the local newspaper asking whether the inconvenience was going to be worthwhile? Mike Tooby kept in touch with these elderly people, meeting with them and trying to solve particular difficulties, such as their future privacy. He made sure they were first to be formally entertained in the empty gallery, where they were all given a Cornish cream tea. They were reassured to see local residents, like Norman

Colin Orchard

1

Colin Orchard

2

Barry Swaebe

3

1 Early morning of 23 June 1993 and the workmen are still at the site painting panels that will obscure the incomplete frontage of the Gallery.

2 Policemen arrive early to prepare for the Prince of Wales' visit, while contractors, after a full night's work, lay the last of the stone steps. When Prince Charles entered the building a few hours later, some of the stones were still loose.

3 Inside the Mall, waiting for the visit of the Prince of Wales. From left to right: Malcolm Veal, Town Clerk, St Ives Town Council, Councillor Shirley Beck, Mayor of St Ives, Malcolm Furneaux, Director of Central Services, Penwith District Council and Alan Harvey, Chairman of Penwith District Council, a Town Councillor and member of the Gallery Steering Group.

Pollard, among the staff. Three of them attended the Royal opening, while the others were provided with seats outside the building to meet and speak to Prince Charles before he began his tour of the gallery on 23 June.

Long term involvement with the wider community was established through the setting up of an Advisory Council. Such a body had been a condition of the lease between the Tate Gallery and the County Council. Chaired by Sir Richard Carew Pole it would meet four times a year. Consisting of County, District and Town Councillors, art experts from other parts of the country, local residents and Tate staff, the Council was there to ensure that the Curator had a level of support and advice from a diverse group with a wider range of points of view than he would normally have access to.

The works of art began to arrive. They were slowly and carefully put into position under the watchful direction of Nicholas Serota who played a leading part in the gallery's first 'hang'.

Alongside all these activities, complex arrangements were underway to prepare not only for Prince Charles' visit, but for a large number of events that would cater, in total, for three thousand people by the time the gallery opened to the public. The staff found it extremely difficult to maintain the continuing process of working on the project alongside planning of the opening ceremonies. Mike Tooby and Dick Perkins spent many hours making sure that all the security arrangements were in place and that, with the help of Tate staff in London, the correct people had been invited to the various events.

Wednesday 23 June arrived. The steps up into the gallery were finally constructed, (although they were not quite secure, as the Prince of Wales was to discover). The sun was shining. Everyone was in place. The town seemed to hold its breath. Inside the building Carolyn Trevivian remembers:

On the morning of the Royal opening we were working away and then we were asked to get into position, but we really wanted to go on working.

While she had been spending long hours helping with the complex arrangements for something that still seemed, to her, an abstract concept, she recalls that she had been encouraged by the enthusiasm of many local people. At times of stress this had given her strength to keep going. She summed up the feeling of all the staff, when she said that she hoped they:

could pull it off for them. We wanted to bring to fruition what everyone had been working on for so long.

Colin Orchard

1

Colin Orchard

2

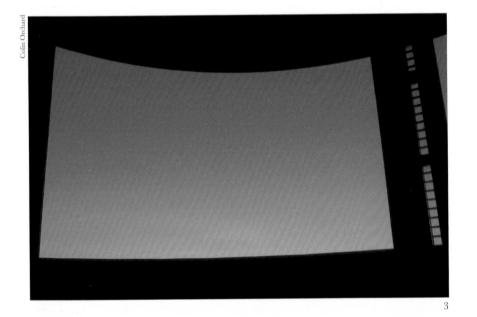

Colin Orchard

3

1 A view of the entrance steps. A long queue of visitors quickly formed on the day the gallery first opened to the public, 26 June 1993.

2 The Loggia with curved seats; the area is a perfect meeting place.

3 A morning shot of an almost clear blue sky seen between two of the pillars in the Loggia.

4 A night shot taken from the same position.

Colin Orchard

4

17   A Tour Of The Building

Evans and Shalev's airy white spiral of a building reminded me of a lighthouse perched on a hillside, but of a lighthouse in which it is the visitor who rotates almost 360 degrees to take in the surrounding view. (Richard Dorment *Daily Telegraph*).

No-one who has journeyed to Tate Gallery St Ives can fail to marvel at the unique and friendly building they have visited. It is hoped that the following detailed tour, with the added assistance of contemporary responses of a number of journalists, will allow visitors to appreciate, more fully, what the architects set out to achieve.

Arriving at the building from Back Road West visitors will find the gallery rises up on their left-hand side; to the right is the beach and sea. The Loggia is entered by means of four short flights of sand-coloured steps. Through their colour and texture these reflect the beach below, and are an important link between the sea-side, town and gallery. Entering a building by means of steps gives the visitor the awareness of its presence. In the case of Tate St Ives it also gives it a tranquility, a contrast to the bustle of the holiday resort so quickly left behind.

Roman in design and feel, the Loggia conceals a curved ramp that winds its way around the central amphitheatre.[1] The architects hoped that the Loggia might become not only a quiet meeting place, but also an area for live music and other public events.

Sitting on one of the two tiers of sand-coloured curved 'seats' in the Loggia, looking towards Porthmeor Beach, it is easy to be overwhelmed by the surroundings, even though there is nothing to be seen but the sky. On a sunny day, the huge curved rectangle of blue below the over-hanging roof, contrasts strikingly with the white columns on either side, the curved white ceiling above and the white wall below. On a day when clouds scurry across the sky, one is reminded of a Magritte painting. At night, however, with the lights in the gallery behind switched on, that rectangle is the densest black imaginable. 'Views' such as these help to keep spectators constantly in touch with the outside elements.

With lights at the top of each of their three sides, the four slim white triangular columns in the Loggia are one of the architects' trademarks.[2] These columns join the curved edge of the stepped roof beam above, and appear to be reflected on the other side of the great curved glass wall that is the window of Gallery Two. High above, in the centre of the ceiling, a circular glass apse throws a soft light down onto the area below.

Visitors now begin a journey which will take them backwards and forwards throughout the entire site, at the same time spiralling upwards to an exhilarating climax.

There is only a short distance from the top of the entrance steps to the main gallery entrance. Before the door is reached, on the left, a curved marble plaque almost merges with the white wall, behind a small 'dais' on which H R H Prince Charles, Duke of Cornwall stood to open the gallery on 23 June 1993. And from this position a gaze upwards reveals visitors walking about inside the gallery or leaning over balconies on an upper level; while at ground level a fairly discreet glass door comes into view, flanked by two sculpture niches.

Once inside, the visitor is confronted by a narrow rectangular area housing a large table at which gallery staff sell entrance tickets and hand out coloured stickers to aid identification.[3] Behind the desk, where helpful security guards are also

1 The ramp is for use by those who find the steps awkward to negotiate.

2 There are similar white columns in the main public concourse of the Crown Courts at Truro in the heart of that building; an internal meeting place. (See photograph on page 110)

3 The stickers also serve the purpose of revealing to the town's shopkeepers exactly how many of their customers have come to St Ives to visit the Tate.

A night view of the roof of the Loggia with
its central apse, taken from the top of the
entrance steps, in the autumn of 1993.
Ahead can be seen part of the Upper
Terrace of Gallery Two, and the glass brick
windows high above.

seated, a hidden storage area houses coats, rucksacks and the occasional surfboard.

Even here, inside the building, there is a continuing reminder of the dominance of the external features. The walls in this area and the Mall beyond are covered in marble chippings, while the floor continues the sand-coloured reconstructed stone slabs. On the walls are information boards; their black lettering briefly describing the details of gallery opening times, and major donors who financed the building. There is also a plaque commemorating the fact that the gallery was built with a contribution from the European Regional Development Fund. Passing this point, voices seem to lower; the visitor has entered a very special place.

In an otherwise empty chamber, saturated with a strange violet light, Patrick Heron's colossal glass window stages an ambush on the left wall. (Richard Cork *The Times*)

The Mall, an empty room save for a few white chairs, is dominated on the left-hand side by the window. The density of its reflected colour appears especially noticeable when leaving the whiteness of the gallery spaces on the way out of the building. Four information boards, on one wall, supply an introduction to the building and its collection, while a discreet glass case, containing an open book, records the names of those who generously donated money.

High above, over the entrance way, is a square window belonging to the Education Room. Through it the visitor can often observe colourful paintings on its walls and lively mobiles hanging from its ceiling. The sight is unexpected. It is impossible to tell, from this vantage point, how one can gain access into the room.

A second set of glass doors takes visitors from the Mall into what the architects consider to be the gallery's first 'internal space', the Rotunda. This is a small circular area with slate floor and plain smooth white walls, which is in marked contrast to the tactile materials used on the outside of the building and in the Mall. On the left-hand side, a large curved window of glass blocks radiates a pure white light into the space; another distinctive feature often used by the architects.[4] Like the coloured glass window, the opaque panes conceal the back of one of the blocks of flats, and both have been used to great effect.

High in the Rotunda are three circular windows, like giant portholes. Through two of these, visitors to the gallery pass backwards and forwards, as in some distant world. On the floor the slate tiles are laid diagonally, accentuating the very different kind of space to that of the Mall, whose sand-coloured floor slabs are laid parallel with its walls. Opposite the window of glass blocks, a small entrance way conceals a lift to the building's upper floors, while beside this alcove the first of a number of perspex triangular signs points the visitor upwards to the galleries.

Ahead rises the staircase; its destination hidden from view. It turns through one hundred and eighty degrees within another small circular area. The stairs and bannisters are made of ash, lime-washed, sanded and lightly varnished.[5]

The balustrades make the staircases very distinct, with their baluster poles formed like miniature ladders. Still more unusual are the flat-topped handrails, which curiously have the same profile as the treads below. (Marcus Binney *The Times Magazine*)

The hard-wearing grey rubber flooring on the stairs has also been laid in most of the rooms, its neutral colour preventing any distraction from the works of art on the gallery walls.

At the end of the second flight of stairs is the mezzanine level, containing the gallery shop. From this vantage point the visitor can look through one of the circular 'portholes', onto the people walking in and out of the Rotunda. The whiteness of the wall in that small circular space compares strikingly with the purple-lit floor that lies below on the other side of the glass doors. Ahead lies the square window of the Education Room.

A glass door on the left of the 'porthole' leads into the shop, naturally lit by three

4 Glass bricks are also used in the Crown Courts at Truro.

5 The stairs and bannisters were constructed by joiners at E Thomas Construction of Ponsanooth, near Truro.

A view of the Mall looking towards the front entrance of the gallery. Above the doorway is the window of the Education Room. Four information boards are attached to the wall, while the coloured glass window dominates the entire area.

narrow windows, above the shelves high on its south side. No views can be glimpsed through their apertures, only the grass and rock of the steeply sloping hill outside. The shop is a quiet and popular place to browse through the wide selection of books, magazines and cards that fill the lime-washed ash shelves that cover the walls, and always provides items of interest for the whole family. Children, singly and in groups, are made to feel welcome in Tate St Ives. ·

Continuing upwards through the building, at the top of the third flight of stairs, there is a semi-circular balcony lit by a long narrow window. A fourth flight of stairs leads to a cloakroom for the disabled on the left while, straight ahead, a door consisting of small square glass panes brings the visitor to the main information area. A double set of stairs dominates the space, curving round and out of sight towards the restaurant above. On the right-hand side is the Information desk, a large counter, designed by the architects and decorated with a circle and squares motif.[6] Behind the counter, a square window gives a first tantalising hint of prospects to come.

The view from the information desk might be a Hockney. Framed to exclude both the sky above and the roof tops below, it forms a two-dimensional composition of blue sea with a band of golden sand across the bottom. (Marcus Binney)

With the Information desk on the right, straight ahead the visitor now enters a sequence of gallery spaces: a series of five rooms, each of different scale, proportion and lighting. Between each space is a doorway, without a door. The architects think of these areas as 'small pause spaces' in the visitors' journey of discovery. In fact they are functional, concealing cupboards and services for the building. The entire route is intended to reflect an exploration of St Ives, with its myriad interesting walkways; the sudden opening up of a view; a distant landmark beckoning you on; a hidden garden and places in which to pause and contemplate.

Walking into Gallery One, the immediate impression is of a pleasant coolness, due to the air conditioning system that operates in each of the gallery spaces. The room itself has a low ceiling and relatively low lighting. Eight small square windows, high on the right-hand side, are almost totally covered by white blinds.

The door out of Gallery One brings the visitor into the Upper Terrace of Gallery Two. A stunning vista suddenly opens up. At this point a decision now needs to be taken about the next part of the route. One choice is to turn left and walk around the semi-circular balcony which contains curved glass protecting a collection of ceramics.

The alternative route is to turn right, walk down two flights of slate steps (or take the lift behind on the right) and enter the Lower Terrace of Gallery Two.

Whatever choice is finally taken, no-one can be unaware of the vast curved glass window, without mullions, that reaches up to the ceiling and gives breathtaking panoramic views of an almost barren landscape: Porthmeor Beach ahead, Clodgy and Man's Head on the left and The Island on the right.

[Evans and Shalev's] building provides a contemplative setting for the work, in a deliberate shift from the frivolity of the holiday town outside, and a reminder of the context that drew the artists of the St Ives school here in the first place. But it doesn't shut the world out; as architecture it is open and outgoing. (Deyan Sudjic *The Guardian*)

In order to withstand the force eleven gales that can bear down on the northwest of St Ives, the glass is 12mm thick. It was made in sections, bolted together and strengthened with glass fins. The fins protrude outwards so that they don't create a fussy, internal feature. The glass sheets were individually curved by a Danish firm and Eldred Evans and David Shalev believe it is the biggest bent structural glass window in the world.

6 The counter, along with others in the building, were built at Dudley Coles's joinery works. Similarly designed furniture can be seen in the three courtrooms of the Crown Courts building.

Michael Musitano

1

1 The small landing with its semicircular balcony is an interesting feature of the main staircase at a level just above the shop. This photograph was taken before the wood (beech) was limewashed and varnished.

2 The area beside the Information desk, entered by the glass panelled door on the left. The double set of stairs leads up to the restaurant, while the space under the staircase leads to the doors of Gallery Five.

Roger Harvey ABIPP

2

A slate seat around the entire base of the window allows visitors to regain their breath, look down into the Loggia where, often, a regular flow of people come in and out of the building. It is interesting to watch their faces as they reach the top of the steps from the road, and survey, with surprise, the sight that greets them.

The balcony above, facing the window, consists of seven large, and two smaller openings in the curved gallery wall.[7] These are reminiscent of private boxes at a concert hall or theatre, where viewers can lean over their railed sills and observe the scene below. Above again, high in the ceiling, ten bays, containing glass bricks, allow a soft natural light to permeate down. Two slim circular columns rise from the curved seating area to the ring beam above.

Almost hidden from sight, at one end of the lower gallery, a small alcove leads to the Education Room, whose door is at right-angles to the service lift. The interior of the low-ceilinged room is dominated by the square aperture through which the coloured glass window in the Mall can be viewed from a high vantage point. The colour of the surrounding Mall walls varies throughout the day, as the changing light filters through the different coloured areas of glass. The Education Room differs from all the other spaces in the gallery. Used both as practical work and lecture room, its walls are usually covered with children's paintings and constructions; a video sometimes broadcasts changing shows; and the state of the floor reflects the results of many lively painting sessions. Formality turns here into informality. The visitor has a chance to pause before resuming the journey.

Returning to the Lower Terrace of Gallery Two, the dark grey slate floor continues up the stairs at either end in an unbroken sweep to the Upper Terrace. From the top of both these stairs the visitor can view the specially designed ceramics display, which is protected by a seventeen foot long curved glass 'wall', and lit both artificially and naturally from concealed windows high above.

On the balcony, with the long curving display of St Ives pots behind you, you get the most dramatic view of all and it is particularly moving to see the pots with such a backdrop. To look at that blue-grey shimmering horizon, as [Bernard] Leach did daily from his study window, is to understand something of what his pots were about. (David Whiting *Studio Pottery*)

Immediately to the right of the ceramics display a doorway leads to a small vestibule, the Apse, which in turn, brings the visitor to the last three galleries. These are so designed that, from the Apse, a work of art hanging in the furthermost Gallery Five, many metres away, is framed several times over by ever increasing light and dark rectangles, depending upon whether the eye rests on the light space of a gallery, or the dark space of a double 'door' area in between. So the visitor is beckoned onwards, through three studio-sized, but differently proportioned spaces.

Gallery Three is strangely five sided; its light source coming from one side of the ceiling only. The natural lighting in this and Gallery Four, as in the ceramics display, is diffused. The architects use the term 'clerestory lighting' to describe this method of illumination.[8] A soft, uniform luminance, bouncing evenly onto the walls, is very easy on both the works of art and the eye, they feel. The large rectangle of Gallery Four has its light source down both lengths of the ceiling, making it much lighter and more spacious in feel than Gallery Three.

Gallery Five is different again. Of double height and with a pitched roof, its lighting comes directly from visible windows high above. Here, some people have experienced the sensation of being in a church or chapel. Above the door leading out of the gallery is yet another circular window, through which people appear to be walking in space.

From this last gallery visitors pass through the glass-panelled door and return to the area that contains the Information desk, passing on the left a secluded and unexpected outdoor area. Entered by double doors, the small quadrangle-like

7 The circular wall is reminiscent of the circular gas holder that for many years occupied this particular space, although the gallery's walls do not follow exactly its circumference.

8 Clerestory lighting means a natural light coming from high above, without the viewer being able to see its source. Such lighting was used in public buildings in Renaissance Italy.

1 Looking down from the Upper Terrace of Gallery Two, this view shows Sue Dalton standing on the Lower Terrace; the Loggia filled with scaffolding and the beach and sea beyond Beach Road. The photograph was taken on a Friends' 'Open Day'; the first opportunity a large number of people had to view the new gallery before the works were hung.

2 A morning view of Porthmeor Beach through the curved glass of Gallery Two, looking west towards Man's Head and Clodgy.

3 An evening shot of the same panoramic view. The sun is setting behind the left-hand glass pillar.

space contains a covered semi-circular granite bench at its far end under a circular window. From the left-hand side, two hidden stairways lead directly onto the roof terrace above.

But the usual way to the upper floor is by the pair of curved stairs opposite the Information desk which join near their top, bringing the visitor outside the doors of the restaurant. This popular and bustling amenity consists of two rooms, the first, and largest of which contains a wooden counter occupying about half of the space. Placed around the outside walls are white tables and chairs. Above these, three square windows, each divided into four equal panes look out onto a stunning view over the grey and lichen-covered roofs of the town, with Harbour and bay beyond. The Island, too, can be seen through a narrow window, cut diagonally across the corner of the building. Marcus Binney has called this view:

A sort of country cousin panorama of Paris rooftops from the top of the Pompidou Centre.

On the north side of the room, double doors lead onto a small glass-enclosed structure whose design echoes the many balconies dotted along Porthmeor Beach that lie between the gallery and The Island.

The second smaller and brighter space contains a window with six large square panes of glass reaching from floor to ceiling. Standing on the landing at the top of the stairs, and looking across the curved balcony that runs along one side of this small eating area, the windows provide scenes that resemble abstract paintings. Through the top pair only the sky is framed; from the middle pair the sky and sea make contrasting bands of colour, varying in hue as the lighting changes; and from the lower pair the bands are created by the yellow of the beach and the blue or purple and green of the sea. Thirteen rectangular concealed windows above, five of them curved, give a beautiful white diffused light that is accentuated by the white walls and furniture, and which is sometimes almost blinding in its intensity. The only tiny patches of colour in the restaurant come from the delicate flower arrangements that always decorate the tables.

A quite different and surprising scene is viewed by looking from the smaller room, away from the window, and over the low curved balcony beyond. Visitors can be seen ascending and descending the hidden double staircase, while behind them again the upper half of a large circular window rises up. From close to, the window gives a voyeuristic outlook onto Gallery Five below.

Two sets of doors lead to the rooftop terrace; one from the restaurant itself, the second from the area at the top of the double stairway.

The terrace gives the sensation of being on the deck of a ship, especially on a sunny day, with seagulls perched on the surrounding high white walls, or swooping over the gallery's roofs. On the sea-side, a high glazed screen acts as a wind-break.[9] The roof flooring is made of reconstructed stone paving, the same colour as that used in the Loggia, entrance hall and Mall, and matching the sand on the beach below. Each stone sits on a small cantilevered concrete slab, leaving space between it and the next stone, to allow the rain to run off the flat surface and into pipes below, rather than settling into undesirable puddles.

Further investigation reveals more roof space leading off the terrace. The area between the glass blocks around the top of Gallery Two and those concealed high above the ceramics display, create a curved pathway leading to an area used for showing contemporary sculpture; one more secret space waiting to be discovered by the more adventurous visitor.

The tour of the building over, the visitor is aware of having participated in a total visual experience. The gallery's fascinating individual parts have created a stunning whole. And its unexpectedly comfortable and friendly atmosphere has allowed the visitor to linger and explore at leisure a building that many feel to be a

9 The duckboard projecting beyond the glass overlooking Porthmeor Beach makes for easy window cleaning.

211

Colin Orchard

Two evening shots of Porthmeor taken from inside Gallery Two with remarkable reflections in the curved glass of both the sea, land and sunset, as well as works of art and people inside the gallery.

Colin Orchard

work of art in its own right.

The gallery received much praise from the architectural press at the time it opened. Stephen Greenberg, the Editor of *The Architect's Journal* wrote:

This is a building rooted not only in its context, but also, hauntingly, in the Arts and Crafts tradition. One thinks of Mackintosh, not with any easy literal connection, but in the sensate experience. Like the Glasgow School of Art, this is a large building consisting of a string of marvellous rooms, with more than one hidden delight.

Catherine Slessor in the *Architectural Review*, ended her commentary on the building with :

...the new Tate is a much more complex and considered response to its setting [than Chermayeff and Mendolsohn's De La Warr pavilion at Bexhill]. The orchestration of spaces, routes and views grows out of Evans and Shalev's practical and passionate commitment to placemaking - like architectural shamans they seem able to connect with organic forces and translate them into serenely powerful buildings.

David Jenkins in the *RIBA Journal* pointed out:

...the new Tate is evidence enough that Evans & Shalev have become masters of the art of fitting complex programmes into equally complex but highly legible structures in which richness and clarity work hand in hand...there is always a generous implicit element to complement the explicit functional requirements of both client and programme.

An architectural article in *The Economist* concluded with the words:

The blend of gallery, coast and art is so sensitive it should influence the work of architects everywhere.

The architects themselves wrote of the Truro Crown Courts building several years earlier:

To some it is a 'breathtaking place'; to some 'an elevating experience' or just 'church like', 'theatrical' or 'memorable'. It takes bricks and mortar to make a building. It takes more to make a place.

These words seem to be even more pertinent when applied to Tate Gallery St Ives.

Two aspects of the curved ceramics display case on the Upper Terrace of Gallery Two, before it was filled. This space is lit from above both naturally (glass bricks) and artificially.

A view through the back line of galleries from Gallery Five looking towards Galleries Four, Three and the Apse. Cardboard has been laid to protect the grey rubber flooring. The contrasting areas between the rooms - the 'rest spaces' between the galleries - make this photograph a dramatic study in light and shade.

1

1 Another view of the Information area,
when the balustrades of the twin staircases
leading to the restaurant were still in their
natural state. The glass-panelled doorway
through the arch leads into Gallery Five.

2 The empty restaurant with panoramic
views over St Ives. Far left is a glimpse of
the sea at Porthmeor; moving left can be
seen: The Island and Porthmeor Beach; the
roofs of the town with Godrevy lighthouse
just visible on the far horizon; the Harbour
beach and Smeaton's Pier (with two of its
three arches), and St Ives Bay looking
across to Hayle Towans.

2

Roger Harvey ABIPP

The smaller restaurant area with a fine early summer view of Porthmeor Beach at low tide. Roger Harvey, the photographer, several times talked to the architect, David Shalev, about the building. Shalev told him that he wanted to 'paint the walls with Penwith light'. This particular photograph has been shown in magazines throughout the world, and Roger Harvey believes it epitomises what David Shalev wanted to achieve.

Roger Harvey ABIPP

The window of the small restaurant, photographed from the landing at the top of the stairs.

1

1 This unusual view of five of the windows in the ceiling of the small restaurant.

2 The roof terrace in bright sunlight, looking out onto a calm sea. The high glass screens behind the row of chairs, provide an effective wind break.

3 The Gallery in evening light in September 1993, from about the same position as the photograph on pages 188-189. The lights in gallery Two, behind the curved glass, clearly reveal the paintings and sculpture in the Lower Terrace. Some people have likened the gallery at night to a space rocket just about to lift off. It is worth remembering that when the gasworks was originally built on the same site, in 1835, it was to give light to the town.

2

1

1 A recent photograph of the Tate Gallery at Millbank with its neo-classical facade. Brittania sits at the pinnacle of the roof, the lion and unicorn to her right and left. Originally constructed in 1897, the building has been extended throughout the 20th century. The latest addition, the Clore Gallery, is just visible behind the tree on the far right.

2 Sir Henry Tate, 1st Bart. (1819-1899) from a contemporary engraving. Head of a sugar firm, he was, throughout his life, an important patron of the arts and a philanthropist. He gave to the nation his own private art collection and the 'Tate Gallery' in which to exhibit it.

2

3 A contemporary engraving of the Millbank Penitentiary on which site the Tate Gallery was built. The modern prison stood on marshy land, known as Tothill Fields, between 1821 and 1892.

3

18 Links With Millbank, Liverpool, Kettle's Yard And Orkney

The Tate Gallery notepaper has printed in its top left-hand corner:

The National Collections of British and Modern Art in London, Liverpool and St Ives.

The logo for Millbank has red lettering on a white background. It has a modern feel, replacing, as it does, the white royal coat of arms set against a red oval background, reminiscent of a government department. The logo for Tate Gallery St Ives, on the other hand has white lettering on a black background. These colours reflect the Cornish flag, one of only two black and white flags in the world. Tate Gallery Liverpool has introduced white lettering onto an orange background.

What has Tate Gallery St Ives become a part of? Only time will tell how each 'branch' of the 'empire' relates to each other, and no gallery has a static existence. Already plans are well advanced in London to divide the British Collection from the Modern Collection, and house the latter in the converted Bankside Power Station in Southwark.

A site close to water is appropriate. As the art critic, William Feaver, observed in an article he wrote for *The Observer* on 27 June 1993 on Tate Gallery St Ives:

All three Tates have fine views over water, but this one has the best.

Millbank looks out onto a usually grey River Thames,[1] and Liverpool onto both the River Mersey and the Albert Dock, but St Ives has panoramic views over the Atlantic Ocean.

Both Millbank and Liverpool have interesting histories, a brief account of which places Tate Gallery St Ives into its wider context.

The name of Sir Henry Tate links both cities. Born in Chorley, Lancashire in 1819, Sir Henry had been manager of a successful chain of grocery shops. Then, as a sugar refiner and importer in Liverpool he became very wealthy, apparently patenting a method for cutting sugar into cubes. Sir Henry was an enlightened Victorian businessman and philanthropist who invested his money wisely. Marina Vaizey, in her short essay 'Sir Henry Tate and his gallery' wrote that 'Tate's benefactions were concerned with education, health and art in Liverpool and London'. His efforts were directed 'against a general urban atmosphere of selfish materialism and lack of provision of common enjoyment.' He acquired a great art collection, buying from the annual Royal Academy shows as well as directly from the studios of the most prominent academicians of the day. Sir Henry founded the University Library at Liverpool, and gave the nation a building in London to house his art collection, which opened in 1897, two years before he died.

The building was erected on the site of Millbank Prison, on the north side of the Thames, and on land which was originally marshy and unstable. Its name was taken from a mill once standing on ground that had belonged to the Abbots of Westminster, although the area was known as Tothill Fields. The prison, constructed early in the nineteenth century, was designed to incorporate the very latest philosophies of the prison reformers of the time. When completed in 1821, at a cost of £458,000, it was the largest prison in Europe. An interesting short history of the building was given in *The Tate Gallery Illustrated Biennial Report 1984-86*. Apparently the large imposing hexagonal building containing a chapel, surrounded by six pentagonal wings possessing the cells and circled by a moat, covered an area of about seven acres. The Ordnance Survey map of 1867-1874 shows it lying next

1 Bankside's view over the Thames will be the more distinguished: St Paul's Cathedral versus the new MI6 building opposite Millbank.

223

1

2

3

4

1 Joseph Duveen, 1st Baron Duveen of Millank (1869-1939), an English art dealer, he financed several extensions to the Tate Gallery; the great sculpture hall running most of the length of the building, bears his name.

2 A view of the restored Duveen Sculpture Gallery photographed in January 1990, empty except for Rodin's 'The Kiss'. For many years this space was covered with false walls and ceilings, but Nicholas Serota had these removed soon after he took up his directorship, in the autumn of 1988.

3 An aerial view of the 1979 extension to the Tate Gallery, still under construction. (The front of the building is to the left of the photograph.) Clearly visible are the twenty-one individually top-lit 'pods' which house twenty-one exhibition spaces. However the walls are flexible and much larger spaces can easily be created.

4 The Clore Gallery extension, designed by James Stirling and opened in 1987. It houses most of Turner's paintings and drawings. Stirling has made use of bright colours throughout; here green highlights the main entrance and small windows.

to two gasholders!

The site, however, was so unhealthy that there were constant epidemics inside the prison walls. Its pioneering work with offenders had to be abandoned, and in the middle of the century it was utilised as a point of departure for criminals transported to the Empire's colonies, until that method of punishment was brought to an end in 1871. Gradually the construction of other London prisons made the Millbank building superfluous, and the prison was demolished at the end of 1892.

Sir Henry Tate was not, however, the first person to think of establishing a gallery on the Millbank site. Exactly thirty years earlier, the Victorian art critic and author, John Ruskin, gave a paper to the British Institution entitled 'On the present state of modern art, with reference to the advisable arrangements of a National Gallery'. In his lecture he said:

...knock down the Penitentiary at Pimlico...clear away the gas-ometers [sic] on that site...and build a National Gallery.

The new building that rose beside the Thames, designed by Sidney Smith and opened by the Prince of Wales on 21 July 1897, originally consisted of eight galleries. Two years later Sir Henry Tate provided the necessary funds to construct an extension. The gallery expanded further when the dealer, Sir Joseph Duveen, later to become Baron Duveen of Millbank, financed two major additions: the first in 1910 to house paintings and drawings by J M W Turner, and the second, in 1926, to exhibit modern foreign art.[2] In 1937 the philanthropist funded the great central galleries that still bear his name for the display of sculpture. Opened by King George VI and Queen Elizabeth this fine space was later to be clad in false ceilings and screened walls. However careful restoration returned them to their original glory soon after Nicholas Serota became Director in 1988.

Several further extensions have increased the overall exhibition space in recent years. In 1979 Her Majesty the Queen opened new galleries to house the Tate's collection of twentieth century art, the first time it had been satisfactorily displayed. Built with a contribution from the Calouste Gulbenkian Foundation and designed by Llewelyn-Davies, Weeks, Forestier-Walker and Bor, the extension provided about fifty per cent more display space. Also incorporated into the design were new conservation and photographic studios as well as storage facilities. In order to show as large a part of the modern collection as possible when the new galleries were unveiled, the works were hung very close together - and in places, two deep.

In 1987 Her Majesty returned to Millbank to open the Clore Gallery housing the Turner collection, a project that had been planned for many years. J M W Turner had left his works to the nation in 1856, and they had been displayed at the Tate Gallery since 1910. However, due to severe flooding of the Thames, for safety the works on paper were transferred to the British Museum in 1928, where they remained until the Clore Gallery finally reunited them with the paintings.

This latest extension was made possible by the generosity of the Clore Foundation, and was designed by James Stirling, Michael Wilford and Associates at a cost of £7.8 million. It was James Stirling's first London building. With its own entrance onto a small garden area, the gallery was built on the site of the Queen Alexandra Military Hospital adjoining and linked to the main building. Its rooms were the first at Millbank to have temperature, air conditioning and lighting controlled by computer. As well as nine linked galleries of unequal size, the extension accommodates a two-hundred seat lecture theatre, a public reading room and staff accommodation, a print room and space for storing all of Turner's works on paper, which total approximately 38,000 individual images.

2 Sir Joseph Duveen also founded a gallery at the British Museum to display the Parthenon Sculptures, which although completed in 1938, due to war damage was not opened until as recently as 1962.

The day after Richard Carew Pole convened his first Steering Group meeting at

County Hall in Truro on 24 May 1988, HRH the Prince of Wales opened Tate Gallery Liverpool.[3] During his visit to that city, His Royal Highness declared open the whole of the Albert Dock redevelopment, of which the gallery was a significant part.

Sir Alan Bowness recalls that he had the idea for a Tate in the North as early as the summer of 1979 before he took up his appointment as Director of the Tate Gallery.

Lord Bullock [Chairman of the Tate Trustees] had asked me about my plans; the Millbank extension had just opened, and I said that I thought the Tate should do something outside London before continuing with the development of the hospital site [at Millbank]. There were too many works not on display, and a Tate in the North, preferably in some distinguished Victorian building, seemed to me to be the answer. A native Yorkshireman, Lord Bullock was enthusiastic, and so were the Tate Trustees when I put forward the idea in 1980. Curiously enough, the speech of Lord Hutchinson at the take-over of the Hepworth Museum by the Tate Trustees in October 1980 was the first public mention of the proposal.

The new gallery's genesis was rather different from either Millbank or St Ives. In the early 1980s there had been a particular effort by Michael Heseltine, on behalf of the government, to regenerate part of Liverpool[4]. The Merseyside Development Board was set up particularly for this purpose, and between 1981 and 1988 £170 million from the DoE was spent clearing up 650 acres of derelict riverside land 'to create a still expanding business park with some attractive recreational add-ons,' as Laurence Marks reported in a special supplement of *The Observer* to commemorate the opening of 'Tate Gallery in the North'. The Development Board was very keen for the Tate Gallery to open an outstation in the area.

Alan Bowness first visited the Albert Dock complex in the winter of 1981-82 and he and the Trustees chose part of a warehouse building located between the Dock basin and the River Mersey.[5] Coincidentally, these buildings, part of a complex of five blocks of five-storey fire-resistant warehouses, designed by Jesse Hartley and opened in 1846 by Prince Albert, had been used for storing not only cotton, tobacco, tea and silk, but also sugar imported by the firm of Henry Tate, according to an early Tate Gallery Liverpool promotional leaflet. The docks were closed in 1972 and dereliction soon set in.

The outside of the fine brick building, chosen by the Director and Trustees, was hardly altered, and external refurbishment was paid for by the Merseyside Development Board. This organisation, together with the Office of Arts and Libraries, also contributed half the cost of transforming the interior of the old warehouse into an art gallery containing 12,000 square metres of space.[6] £1.7 million was found from the private sector, the majority of which was raised through the efforts of the Director. However Alan Bowness recalls that 'The Arts Ministers...kept warning me not to be too confident of the revenue funding'.

James Stirling[7] was appointed to redesign the gallery's interior space. He had lived in Liverpool as a child and, after the Second World War, attended its University School of Architecture. Always known as a controversial architect, Stirling won fame abroad before he was accepted in Britain. Lawrence Marks wrote of him:

The drama and playfulness of [the Clore Gallery and Tate Gallery Liverpool] are loved by exhibition-goers. They have horrified purists. Stirling seems to be part of the Classical backlash against the Modern Movement...but an eccentric part.

Certainly the bright contrasting orange and blue revolving entrance doors, and the large letters spelling out the gallery's name above are startling, as are the colours he has used both inside and outside the Clore Gallery at Millbank: green, shocking pink, deep violet and turquoise. Stephen Gardiner, *The Observer's* arch-

3 Tate Gallery Liverpool is not yet complete. Phase II is still (in 1994) to open.

4 Lewis Biggs, Curator of Tate Gallery Liverpool, recalls that the city was chosen for the gallery (a) because of the site (b) because of the welcome accorded to the project by the Merseyside Development Corporation (including cash) and (c) because of the tradition of showing contemporary art in the John Moores shows and the wealth of collections of older art already to be seen on Merseyside.

5 The Albert Dock complex is the largest group of Grade I listed buildings in the UK.

6 At ground level, cast iron columns fifteen feet high with a circumference of twelve and a half feet support the floors above.

7 Sir James Stirling was already designing the Clore Gallery at Millbank when he was asked to convert the waterside warehouse into Tate Gallery Liverpool.

itectural correspondent, felt that Tate Gallery Liverpool was the perfect building for showing modern art. He wrote:

Take the galleries...here the structure of the warehouse takes charge of the aesthetic frame for the works of art - the arched brick ceilings, the order of the cast-iron columns.

Comparing the converted warehouse to the Clore Gallery, he thought that the former's total effect was 'even better - simpler, sharper, creating a peculiar stillness for the pure enjoyment of art.'

Tate Gallery Liverpool was especially created to show works from Millbank's modern collection. It has proved to be very popular; the public only paying to see loan exhibitions (as at Millbank). In 1991 and 1992 there were well over 500,000 visitors a year. In the same period Millbank was visited by over 1,500,000 annually.[8]

When Tate Gallery St Ives opened, the Director made it clear that the coming of this small specialist exhibition space would not preclude the works of the St Ives artists from being seen elsewhere. Millbank has therefore, over the last few years, regularly set aside one or two rooms for showing their works in the annual displays, and Tate Gallery Liverpool too exhibited a number of works there in 1994.[9]

However, for some years, there have been two other venues dedicated to the work of those artists living and working in the farthest south-western peninsula of England, and at both, buildings have been very successfully adapted for this purpose. They are Kettle's Yard in Cambridge and the Pier Arts Centre at Stromness in Orkney.

Kettle's Yard was the creation of H S (Jim) Ede, a Cardiff-born man who had always loved paintings. While an assistant at the Tate Gallery, around 1924 he met Ben and Winifred Nicholson, who introduced him to contemporary art for the first time. With his meagre salary he started to buy Ben Nicholson's work at a time when it received little public interest. From Winifred, apparently, he learnt about combining art and daily life. In about 1928, he heard from Ben Nicholson and Christopher Wood of the work of the elderly primitive painter from St Ives, Alfred Wallis, whom the young artists had met at the time they were visiting Feock in Cornwall that year. Wallis started to send Ede bundles of paintings of ships and houses on strangely shaped pieces of cardboard. From each package Ede selected a few, for which he paid a few shillings, and then returned the remainder.

While Jim Ede was in Europe in 1954, he considered creating a house where he could enjoy his continuously growing collection. He wanted to be able to share it with young people who, he believed, would feel more relaxed than they might in a public art gallery or museum. He found four tiny ruined cottages in Cambridge which he restored and moved into in 1957. He lovingly placed his collection all around the house, alongside 'found' objects such as pebbles, fossils, shells and feathers. Until Tate Gallery St Ives was built, the only place in England to regularly show the works of Alfred Wallis, Christopher Wood and Winifred Nicholson as well as early Ben Nicholson's, was in this unique setting in Cambridge.[10] From an early date Ede encouraged students from the University to visit and enjoy the house, and to borrow some of the works for their own studies.

In 1966 the building and its collection were handed over to Cambridge University who agreed to retain it in its entirety. Funds were raised to build an extension on an adjacent piece of land, the design for which was undertaken by the firm of Sir Leslie Martin and David Owers. Sir Leslie Martin, a great friend of both Ben Nicholson and Jim Ede, was known for a number of university buildings at Leicester, Hull, Royal Holloway college, Balliol and St Anne's colleges, Oxford. [11]

David Owers wrote of the way the two parts of the building were successfully

8 Lewis Biggs has written in a letter to the author that 'Tate Gallery Liverpool has been more heavily used in terms of visitors per day, per square metre, than has Millbank'.

9 In 1994, too, there was a major Barbara Hepworth retrospective.

10 Gradually other works entered the Kettle's Yard collection by, for example, Barbara Hepworth, Naum Gabo, William Scott, Paul Feiler and Bryan Pearce.

11 Leslie Martin collaborated with Ben Nicholson and the Russian Constructivist Naum Gabo in the book *Circle : International Survey of Constructivist Art*, published by Faber and Faber in 1937.

1 A view of Tate Gallery Liverpool taken in the early morning of November 1989. Converted by James Stirling, Michael Wilford and Associates from the 1840s warehouses designed by Jesse Hartley, the fine building, with its bright red revolving doors, is seen reflected in the Albert Dock.

2 Kettle's Yard in Cambridge, the home of Jim Ede, and now a museum that contains Ede's collection of paintings, sculpture and found objects. Ede's original house was created from merging three small derelict cottages. Further extensions have since been added. This interior view shows its domestic feel, despite the fact that it is open to the public every afternoon. Paintings are hung throughout, often at floor level (see to the left of the photograph) and every available surface holds both man-made and natural found objects. For example, over the fireplace a circular shell stands close to a silver goblet.

linked in an article 'Kettle's Yard design intentions: What do we call the Kettle?' in the *Cambridge Review* of 19 May 1970.

The first extension has two main levels, and it is the upper level which links the old and the new. The scale and sequence may be considered as a progression, with movement through the existing cottage as a significant part of the experience. An easy transition from the cottage was important...movement through the new building continues...as a sequence of descending levels and increasing volume. The play of natural light contributes to the sequence.

The extension not only houses many paintings, sculpture, pottery, porcelain, antique glass, books, fine furniture and rugs, but also a Steinway piano, for the space is regularly used for concerts. On the day of the opening, on 5 May 1970, a recital was given by the brilliant young cellist, Jacqueline du Pré and her pianist husband, Daniel Barenboim. H R H The Prince of Wales, who at the time was a Cambridge student, spoke. He admitted to his audience that:

As with some modern music, modern painting is not always easy to appreciate, but I think this gallery will perhaps help to make it easier before people enter the comparative jungle of familiar places like the Tate Gallery.

Despite its growth, the many visitors and students who knock on the front door of Kettles Yard, any afternoon, still enter the same tranquil world that Jim Ede created all those years ago. They find it an easily accessible place to rest or work.

To visit The Pier Gallery, Stromness, however, a lengthy journey is necessary from most points of departure. Margaret Gardiner, for many years a friend and supporter of Barbara Hepworth and Ben Nicholson in particular, had a very wide circle of friends amongst artists, architects, critics, scientists, writers and politicians. She collected works of her friends, although she was reluctant to be known merely as a 'collector'. Like Jim Ede, she supported and encouraged artists when they were struggling for recognition.

In 1988, in an introduction to a booklet entitled *The Pier Gallery : The First Ten Years*, Margaret Gardiner explained how she came to choose remote Orkney as the site for her art collection, which had accumulated in her house in Hampstead over a period of forty years. Her first visit, accompanied by her son, Martin Bernal, was made in 1956. She was so overwhelmed by the island's beauty, light and colour, that she immediately fell in love with it. Together, mother and son bought a cottage to escape from London life. A number of years later she decided to give her art collection to the haven that had given her so much pleasure.

A warehouse on a small pier in Stromness, overlooking Scapa Flow - another waterside site - was vacant, as was an adjoining building. She believed that the complex would make a perfect arts centre. Money needed to be raised, of course, and slowly it arrived from many sources, the largest donation coming from Dr Armand Hammer of Occidental Oil, a company who had been drilling, and was now pumping oil in the area. Other funding came from the Orkney Islands Council, the Highlands and Islands Development Board, the Scottish Tourist Board, the Pilgrim Trust and the Hudson Bay Company.

Margaret Gardiner commissioned the architect Katharine Heron to convert the buildings. She had spent her childhood in St Ives and knew the work of the artists in Margaret Gardiner's collection. Katharine Heron, with Levitt Bernstein Associates, altered the warehouse on the outside as little as possible. Inside, galleries were created with partitions to divide the areas into room-size spaces. The house, facing onto the street, was converted into a reception area, library and spaces for temporary exhibitions.

The items in the collection are small in size, consisting principally of works by Ben Nicholson and Barbara Hepworth. However there are also paintings by Terry

1

2

1 The Pier Arts Centre, Stromness, Orkney. The building in the centre was restored by Katharine Heron to house Margaret Gardiner's permanent collection of paintings and sculpture. A major addition to the original warehouse is the steps leading up to the first floor level. Part of the Centre is housed in the white building to the rear of the photograph, which accommodates temporary exhibitions, a reception area and library.

2 An interior view of the Pier Art Gallery, Stromness. The small building, with its dividing walls, gives the exhibition space a domestic feel, and enhances the small works that Margaret Gardiner acquired throughout her life. Natural light plays an important part in the overall feel of the space.

Frost, Roger Hilton, Patrick Heron, Peter Lanyon, Margaret Mellis, William Scott, Alfred Wallis and Johns Wells, and constructions by Naum Gabo.

The intimate gallery, with its fairly low ceilings, was the perfect place to display these works. Peter Hill, summed up the feel of the conversion in *Artists Newletter* of May 1986:

...I sat transfixed within the space refurbished and redesigned by the architect...But this was no ordinary alteration, it was an artwork in its own right, and in keeping with the paintings and sculptures it houses...In the Pier Arts Centre I saw a new paradigm for gallery design, one that put the spectator and the artwork in a human, intimate setting, and then put them both into harmony with the immediate environment.

Katharine Heron's conversion received a number of awards, one from the Civic Trust. The gallery was chosen to be 'Museum of the Year', 'Scottish Museum of the Year' and the recipient of a 'Come to Britain' trophy.

It may seem strange to have a collection of St Ives art so far away from the place where it had been created. However, Patrick Heron, in his essay 'The Pier Gallery Collection : An artist's view', which was published in the gallery's first catalogue, offers a reason:

Like Orkney, West Penwith...is an extremely ancient land, punctuated by natural outcrops of granite, almost entirely lacking in trees... and riddled from end to end with the stone remains of Bronze Age walls and Stone Age settlements. Those celebrated standing stones, hut circles, quoits and cromlechs...surely have their close cousins in Orkney.

The work of the St Ives artists can now be seen, on a regular basis, the length and breadth of the British Isles.

Colin Orchard

COUNTY COUNCIL GALLERY STEERING GROUP MEMBERS

Mr Richard Carew Pole - Chairman
Mr Toni Carver - STAG; St Ives Printing & Publishing
Mr Patrick Heron - Artist
Lady Holland - President of STAG
Mr David McKenna - Retired businessman
Mr Christopher Petherwick - Christie's representative, Cornwall
Mr Martin Rewcastle - Director, South West Arts
Mr John Southern - Owner, Dobwalls Theme Park

County, District and Town Councillors

Mrs Doris Ansari - County Council
Mr Oakley Eddy - County Council
Mr Alan Harvey - District Council
Mr John Hurst - County Council
Mrs Beryl James - Town Council
Mrs Barbara Spring - County Council
Mr Geoff Venn - District Council

Tate Gallery

Mr Nicholas Serota - Director
Mr Francis Carnwath - Deputy Director
Mr Peter Wilson - Manager, Gallery Services
Mr Michael Tooby - Curator, Tate St Ives

Officers in attendance

Mr John Farmer - Library, Arts & Records Officer
Mr Peter Fazakerley - Chief Quantity Surveyor
Ms Jane Geraghty - Minute Secretary
Mr David Goodley - Director of Property Services
Mr Alan Groves - County Architect
Mr Malcolm Henderson - Deputy County Architect
Mr Des Hosken - Clerk of Penwith District Council
Mr Jo Jacques - Assistant County Treasurer
Mr Peter Kendall - Education Advisor
Mr Richard Lester - Deputy Clerk
Mr Ian Martin - Deputy Planning Officer
Mr Mark Nicholson - Press Officer

ST IVES TATE ACTION GROUP MEMBERS

Lady Holland - President
Gareth Saunders - Treasurer 1990-1991
Danny Wilson - Treasurer 1991-1993
Janet Axten - Secretary
Bill Armstrong
Joan Armstrong
Ann Atkinson
David Beer
Mike Bradbury
Jenny Burn
Toni Carver
John Clark
Alison Clarke
Bill Clarke
Betty Clarke
Dawn Clayton
Stephen Dove
John Emanuel
Lynette Forsdyke Crofts
Naomi Frears
Henry C Gilbert
Theresa Gilder
Bret Guthrie
Mary Henderson
Steve Herbert
Pamela Hunter
Hugh Johns
Ann Kelley Marshall
John Kilby
Geoffrey Knights
Jeremy Knights
Sean Lenihan
Terry Lister
Anthony Mangion
John McWilliams
Sheelagh O'Donnell
Sheila Oliner
Colin Orchard
Stuart Peters
Roy Ray
Valerie Royston
George Scott
Jane Scott
Roger Shuttlewood
Janet Slack
Roger Slack
Leon Suddaby
Judy Symonds
Peggy Walker
Roy Walker
Derek White
Marion Whybrow
Eric Williams
Sara Williams

MAJOR FUNDING

Founding Benefactors

Cornwall County Council
European Regional Development Fund
Department of the Environment
The Foundation for Sport and the Arts
The Henry Moore Foundation
The Sainsbury Family Charitable Trusts
St Ives Tate Action Group and its Supporters

Principal Benefactors

Penwith District Council
Trustees of the Carew Pole Family Trusts

Benefactors

The Baring Foundation
The John S Cohen Foundation
Friends of the Tate Gallery
Rural Development Commission
Western Morning News, *West Briton*, *Cornish Guardian* and *The Cornishman*

Donors

Barclays Bank plc
British Gas South Western
British Telecommunications plc
Cable & Wireless
Christie, Manson & Woods Limited
Crafts Council
English China Clays plc
The Esmée Fairbairn Charitable Trust
Pall Europe Ltd
Pilgrim Trust
St Ives Town Council
Sotheby's
South Western Electricity plc
The Summerfield Charitable Trust
Television South West Limited
TSB Foundation for England and Wales
Nina and Graham Williams

Other Sponsors and Donors (£1,000 and above)

Charities

Armitage Charitable Trust
Viscount Amory Charitable Trust
Barbinder Trust
D'Oyly Carte Charitable Trust
The John Ellerman Foundation
Worshipful Company of Fishmongers
J Paul Getty Jr Charitable Trust
Landmark Trust
Lord Leverhulme's Trust
The Manifold Trust
Worshipful Company of Mercers
Grand Metropolitan Charitable Trust
The Monument Trust
New Moorgate Trust Fund
Ptarmigan Trust
Rayne Foundation
Summerfield Charitable Trust
Tate Gallery Trustees
Weinberg Foundation
Wingate Charitable Trust

Commercial

Barclays de Zoete Wedd
BICC Group
Carlton Communications
Christie's
Cloakworth Ltd.
Dewhurst House
Dixons Group plc
Forte plc
Thomas Gibson Fine Art Ltd.
Gimple Fils
Bernard Jacobson Ltd
Lloyds Bank plc
Marlborough Fine Art
David Messum Fine Paintings Ltd
The Mayor Gallery
Mercury Asset Management
Meyer International plc
National Westminster Bank plc
New Art Centre
Phillips Fine Art Auctioneers
Royal Bank of Scotland
South West Arts
South West Water plc
Sun Alliance Group
Toshiba Corporation Europe Office and Toshiba Consumer Products (UK) Ltd
Unilever plc
Wembley plc
Westlake & Co

In addition to these organisations, numerous individual donations were received.

BIBLIOGRAPHY AND FURTHER READING

BASSETT, Douglas A, *The Making of a National Museum*, an extended version of a lecture given to the Society in London on May 26, 1982 under the title 'The National Museum of Wales 1907-1982', reprinted from 'The Transactions of the Honourable Society of Cymmrodorion', 1982

BEST, R S *The Life and Good Works of John Passmore Edwards*, Dyllansow Truran, Redruth, Cornwall, 1981

BOWNESS, Alan *Barbara Hepworth Museum*, 1976, reprinted 1981 and 1984

BRAY, Lena and Donald *St Ives Heritage*, Dyllansow Truran - Cornish Publications, Redruth, Cornwall, 1981

BUCKLEY, J A *Geevor Mine*, Cornwall County Council, 1993

COCK, Stanley (ed.) *St Ives Museum*, (undated)

CROSS, Tom *Painting the Warmth of the Sun : The St Ives Artists 1939-75*, Alison Hodge, Penzance/Lutterworth Press, Guildford, 1984

CURTIS, Penelope and WILKINSON, Alan G *Barbara Hepworth A Retrospective*, Tate Gallery Publications, 1994

EDE., Jim *A Way of Life - Kettle's Yard*, Press Syndicate of the University of Cambridge, 1984

GEOTECHNICAL-ENVIRONMENTAL CONSULTANTS LTD. *A report on a ground investigation for a proposed gallery at St Ives, Cornwall*, May 1990

GILBERT, Henry C., RAY, Roy and ORCHARD, Colin *Art about St Ives*, Wills Lane Gallery, Cornwall, 1987

HERON, Katharine RIBA with ANDREWS, Peter FRICS FCIArb and RYDING, Norman BSc PhD, *Tate of the West - A Report on Three Sites in St Ives*, October 1988

HERON, Katharine RIBA with ANDREWS, Peter FRICS FCIArb and RYDING, Norman BSc PhD *Tate of the West - A Report on the Old Gas Works at St Ives*, January 1989

HERON, Patrick *St Ives and the Penwith*, June 1977

JOHNSON, Diana and REWCASTLE, Martin *A Survey of the Arts in the South West*, South West Arts, 1984

LAITY, John Curno (Intro.) *The Penzance Art Collection at Penlee House*, Cornwall (undated)

MAY, Roger *The Story of St Ives and its People*, a resource document for the Middle School, Penzance, Local Teachers Centre, Cornwall, 1980

MULLINS, Edward *Alfred Wallis - Cornish Primitive*, Pavilion Books Limited, 1994

MURT, Eddie *Downlong Days - A St Ives Miscellany*, St Ives Printing & Publishing, Cornwall, 1994

NOALL, Cyril and FARR, Graham *Wreck and Rescue round the Cornish Coast - The Story of the Land's End Lifeboats*, D Bradford Barton, Ltd., Truro, 1965

NOALL, Cyril *The Book of St Ives - A Portrait of a Town*, Barracuda Books Limited, Chesham, Buckinghamshire, 1977

NOALL, Cyril *Yesterday's Town - St Ives*, Barracuda Books Limited, Buckingham, 1979

NOALL, Cyril *The St Ives Mining District*, Volume Two, Edited by Philip Payton and Leonard Truran, Dyllansow Truran, Redruth, Cornwall, 1993

O'DONOGHUE, K.J. and APPLEYARD, H.S. *Hain of St Ives*, World Ship Society, Kendal, 1986

PERRY, Ronald, NOBLE, Patricia and HOWIE, Susan *The Economic Influence of the Arts and Crafts in Cornwall*, a Report for South West Arts and Cornwall County Council, 1986

POYNTON, BRADBURY & ASSOCIATES *Feasibility Study to assess the suitability of the Stennack School, St Ives for conversion to a community centre*, commissioned by the Stennack School Preservation Group, 1985

RENAISSANCE, PIEDA, NEWLYN AND ORION GALLERIES LTD. and MWT Consultant Architects *Feasibility Study Proposals, Tate Gallery - Collection*, for Cornwall County Council, September 1987

ROWE, Phyllis M and RABEY Ivan, *When Bombs Fell*, Ivan Rabey, St Columb, Cornwall, 1987

SHEWELL, Loveday *St Ives Gallery - a report on estimated running costs for Cornwall County Council*, 12 July 1990

VAIZEY, Marina *Sir Henry Tate and his Gallery*, (undated)

WHYBROW, Marion *St Ives 1883-1993 - Portrait of an Art Colony*, Antique Collectors' Club, Woodbridge, Suffolk, 1994

Catalogues

First Exhibition, Penwith Society of Arts in Cornwall, Printed by James Lanham Limited, St Ives, in collaboration with Guido Morris, Summer 1949

Tenth Anniversary Exhibition, Penwith Society of Arts, with an Introduction by Sir Herbert Read and 'A note on the history and purpose of the Penwith Society' by Alan Bowness, The Arts Council, 1960

The Penwith Galleries, with essays by Frank Halliday and J P Hodin, Penwith Galleries Ltd., St Ives, Cornwall, 1976

Cornwall 1945-1955, New Arts Centre, London, 9 November - 3 December 1977

The Pier Gallery, Stromness, Orkney, with essays by Patrick Heron and Alan Bowness, 1978

The Collection of Mr and Mrs David Lewis, Gallery D, Museum of Art, Carnegie Institute, Pittsburgh, July 10 - September 7, 1980, with an essay 'Collecting : A Personal Affair' by David Lewis

St Ives 1939-64, Twenty five years of painting, sculpture and pottery, The Tate Gallery, London, 13 February - 14 April 1985

Cornwall 1925-1975 'a sense of place...a sense of light', Michael Parkin Fine Art Ltd., London, 1985

The Pier Gallery - The First Ten Years, Pier Arts Centre, Stromness and tour, April - December 1988

Evans and Shalev, 9H Gallery, London, 29 November - 23 December, 1988

A Century of Art in Cornwall 1889-1989, an exhibition to celebrate the Centenary of Cornwall County Council, County Hall and County Museum and Art Gallery, Truro, September 1989

Tate in the East, Newsletter No. 1 published by the Tate in the East Steering Group, June 1990

Auction of Fine and Applied Art, presented by St Ives Tate Action Group to raise funds to help build Tate Gallery St Ives at The Penzance Auction House, Penzance, Cornwall, with essay by David Brown, MRCVS, 12 October 1991

St Ives Tate News, published by St Ives Tate Action Group, June 1992

Alfred Wallis - Artist and Mariner - a celebration of his life and work on the 50th anniversary of his death, programme prepared by St Ives Tate Action Group, 5-19 September, 1992

Tate Gallery Publications

Illustrated Biennial Report 1978-80, 1980
Illustrated Biennial Report 1980-82, 1982
Illustrated Biennial Report 1984-86, 1986
Illustrated Biennial Report 1986-88, 1988
Tate Gallery Liverpool - The conversion to an art gallery, (undated)
Tate Gallery Liverpool, 1988
Tate Gallery St Ives, fund raising brochure, 1991
Tate St Ives - An Illustrated Companion, Michael Tooby, 1993
Press Package, Erica Bolton and Jane Quinn, 5 April 1993

Cornwall County Council

Cornwall Education Committee *Works of Art for Schools*, introduction by E H H Dorman, Chairman, May 1980

European Regional Development Fund, County of Cornwall *A National Programme of Community Interest for part of the South West Assisted Area of the United Kingdom 1988-1991*, October 1988 version

Planning and Economic Development Committee, *Proposed Gallery, St Ives - Penwith District*, 11 October, 1989

County Planning Office *The St Ives Gallery - A new collection of Cornish Art in association with the Tate Gallery - An opportunity for a high profile corporate investment*, October 1989 - October 1991, plus three updates, and translations into German, French and Japanese. Corporate brochure produced January 1991

County Architects Department, *St Ives Gallery, Cornwall - Competition Conditions*, 17 November 1989

County Architects Department, *St Ives Gallery, Cornwall - Architects' Brief*, 1989

Agenda and Reports, 27 February 1990, including Policy Committee Report dated 8 February 1990

Memorandum and Articles of Association, Cornwall Arts Foundation, (draft), 4 April 1990

Planning and Economic Development Committee, *Art Gallery and Ancillary Facilities, St Ives - Penwith District*, 9 May, 1990

Planning and Economic Development Committee, *Art Gallery and Ancillary Facilities, St Ives - Penwith District*, 22 May 1990

County Planning Office *The Tate at St Ives - an assessment of visitor numbers attracted to a new art gallery at St Ives and their impact on employment in the town*, 1990

Agenda and Reports, 26 February 1991

The Rural Development Programme *Work Programme*, 1993

Journals and national newspapers

'New County Museum and Art Gallery - opened by HRH the Prince of Wales', Supplement to *The Royal Cornwall Gazette and Cornwall County News*, June 11, 1919

'The Charm of the County Town III - St Ives, Cornwall', Frank L Emanuel, illustrated by Captain R Borlase Smart, *The Architectural Review*, July 1920

'Kettle's Yard design intentions: What do we call the Kettle?', David Owers, *Cambridge Review*, 9 May 1970, pp.170 and 174

'Kettle's Yard: Extensions to an art collection at Cambridge', *The Architectural Review*, 887, January 1971, pp.35-39

'Leslie Martin on the bridges between the cultures', *RIBA Journal*, August 1973, pp.381-388

'Crisis at St Ives', [Penwith gallery threatened by Arts Council's decision to stop its tiny grant], Lesley Adamson, *The Guardian*, April 30, 1977

'Art in Flow', Pier Arts Centre, *The Architects' Journal*, 29 August, 1979, pp.416-417

'Writing is on the wall for gallery', [Penwith Gallery], Jean Campbell, *Western Morning News*, February 1 1980

The Porthmeor Studios, Roy Ray (undated)

'Groves faces challenge to demolition scheme', [the Stennack School], Nick Wates, *The Guardian*, July 30, 1984

'Council defies residents' protest with plan to demolish school', Nick Wates, *The Guardian*, July 30, 1984

'The St Ives school', Terence Mullaly, *The Daily Telegraph*, 16 February 1985

'Beside the seaside', *The Times*, 19 February 1985

'Keeping it in the family', Waldemar Januszczak, *The Guardian*, 26 February 1985

'The Pier Arts Centre', Peter Hill, *Artists Newsletter*, May 1986

'A Prophet Honored at Last in His Own Land', [James Stirling and the Clore Gallery], Paul Goldberger, *The New York Times*, April 19, 1987

'The County Museum: Past, Present and Future', John Stengelhofen, *Journal of the Royal Institution of Cornwall*, Part 2, New Series, Volume X, 1988, pp.120-146

'A city of native culture', Laurence Marks and 'A real picture palace', Stephen Gardiner, from 'Tate Gallery in the North', *Observer*, May 22, 1988

'Transforming tedium - Truro's new Law Courts and public garden', Stephen Gardiner, *Observer*, 24 July 1988

'Passion hidden in the dungeons' [art treasures in the vaults of the Tate Gallery], Simon Parker, *Western Morning News*, September 29, 1989

'Curators question Council's "Glitzy" project', *Museums Journal*, February 1990, p.11

'A cliffhanger set in St Ives', Rory Coonan, *Observer*, April 1 1990

'Tate in the West - the pros and cons', *Peninsula Voice*, No. 84, 1990, pp.20-21

'The "Tate of the West" is Launched' Frank Rurhmund, *Cornish Life*, June 1990, pp.54-55

'Funding shortfall will put St Ives' Tate in jeopardy', Sarah Kitchen, *Building*, September 28 1990

'High noon for the Tate's western union', Kenneth Powell, *The Sunday Telegraph*, February 3, 1991

'The Tate at St Ives', Clive Turnbull, *Modern Painters*, Volume 4, Number 1, Spring 1991, pp.50-53

'The Tate at St Ives', [letter], Martin Rewcastle, *Modern Painters*, Volume 4, Number 2, Summer 1991, p.112

'Salerooms - When kindness is not enough', Colin Gleadell, *Art Monthly*, August 1991, p.37

'Tate Gallery St Ives', Frank Ruhrmund, *Art Monthly*, September, 1991, p.2

'Kiss of life', Giles Auty, *The Spectator*, November 2 1991, pp. 55 and 56

'The Tate Gallery at St Ives Sharing a National Art Collection with a Regional Audience', Corinne Bellow, *MPR News*, issued by the International Council of Museums, Volume 2, Number 2, 1992, pp.26-28

'The artist is king in quaint St Ives', Paula Adamick, *The Toronto Star*, February 8 1992

'Art education is key to gallery's success', Alan Williams, *Peninsula Voice*, July/August 1992

'Building on the past', Michael Tooby, *The Independent*, August 11, 1992

'The state of the Tate', Michael Tooby, *What's On*, August 1992

'The Tate Gallery St Ives', Michael Tooby, *Museums & Galleries*, 1993 Edition, pp. x and xi

'Tate Gallery St Ives', *West Cornwall Magazine*, 1993

'Tate Gallery St Ives - meeting the challenge', *Arts Cornwall*, Spring 1993

'The Tate St Ives: Visions for the New Gallery', Iain Gale, *Contemporary Art*, Spring 1993, Volume 1 Number 2, pp. 6-9

'St Ives is divided over "hideous" Tate Gallery', Susanna Herbert, *The Daily Telegraph*, March 22 1993 (An earlier edition of the same newspaper had a slightly amended article over the heading 'Tate rivals shape up in Hepworth country')

'The Heron has landed', [coloured glass window], Ian Mayes, *The Guardian*, March 27 1993

'Cornish Dream', Nicholas Serota and Hugh Pearman, *The Sunday Times*, 2 May 1993

'Modernism has melted at the edges: the gallery grows out of the cliffside', Jan Dalley, *The Independent on Sunday*, 6 June 1993

'St Ives Welcomes the Tate', *The St Ives Times & Echo*, special supplement, June 1993, reprinted

'Great White Hopes', Marcus Binney, *The Times Magazine*, June 19, 1993

'Tate St Ives', *Western Morning News*, special publication, June 21, 1993

'A breathing space for art', Deyan Sudjic, *The Guardian*, June 22, 1993

'Tate St Ives', *The Cornishman*, special publication, June 23, 1993

'Gallery opens in St Ives', Stephen Greenberg, *The Architects* Journal, 23 June 1993, pp.25-39

'A beacon of fresh light on St Ives', Richard Dorment, *The Daily Telegraph*, June 23, 1993

'Cornwall Village gets a Tate Gallery branch', Carol Vogel, *The New York Times*, 24 June 1993

'Welcome to the best view in the west', Richard Cork, *The Times*, 23 June 1993

'A fine headstone for an artist's way of life', Andrew Graham-Dixon, *The Independent*, 29 June 1993

'Tate by the sea', *The Economist*, June 23 - July 2 1993

'Picture Gallery', David Jenkins, *Royal Institute of British Architects Journal*, July 1993, pp.33-39

'Light in the West', Catherine Slessor, *The Architectural Journal*, July 1993, pp.40-47

'Bring your own surfboard', Simon Morley, *Art Monthly*, July - August 1993

'Biff Weekend', *Guardian Weekend*, July 31, August 7, August 14 1993

'The Tate Gallery St Ives - Pots from the Wingfield Digby Collection', David Whiting, *Studio Pottery*, Number 7, Feb/March 1994, pp.19-21

As well as those quoted in the text, numerous articles have appeared in the following local papers since 1989:

The St Ives Times & Echo
Western Morning News
The Cornishman
The West Briton
The Packet

Quotes from early meetings about the gallery were taken from the author's personal contemporary shorthand notes.

ACKNOWLEDGMENTS

This book could not have been written without the assistance of all those who brought the gallery to fruition. For it is their stories I am telling. I am indebted to them all. They gave me many hours of their time and I received copious correspondence from them, as well as being able to talk to them personally.

My initial information came from the extensive files of the County Planning Department with the permission of the County Planning Officer. This was then supplemented by reading through the appropriate Minutes of Meetings of the Tate Trustees, from which I have been allowed to quote with the permission of the Director. I also looked through a number of Tate Gallery files in the Archive Department at Millbank.

Those who contributed to many sections of the book were: Sir Richard Carew Pole, who very graciously agreed to write the Preface; Sir Alan Bowness, who kindly allowed me to quote from a lengthy personal letter; Patrick Heron, who generously let me read through many of his personal files; Eldred Evans and David Shalev, who shared their vision of the gallery with Colin Orchard and myself. At the County Council I had special help from beginning to end from Ian Martin, and his assistant, Tessa Gregg, who both patiently and promptly answered my numerous queries; as well as Richard Lester, Alan Groves, John Farmer and Mark Nicholson. At the Tate Gallery Peter Wilson kindly checked the London end of the story with me, and Jane Ruddell, Curator, Tate Gallery Records helped me with much early Tate material.

The local history was obtained through many months of pouring through the local newspapers, and I am very grateful to Toni and Trisha Carver for their help at *The St Ives Times & Echo*. My interpretation of the historical facts was carefully checked with Bryan Stevens and his wife Margaret. Katharine Heron and Julian Feary filled in a number of important gaps in the story as, in St Ives, did Henry Gilbert, Malcolm Veal and Shirley Beck. Ann Atkinson's collection of news cuttings between 1989 and 1993 were invaluable, and Liz Le Grice and all the staff at the St Ives Library were always supportive. A very special thanks to Des Hannigan who read my text many months ago and gave me guidance on how to put this complex book together.

I must record my appreciation of all the work Celia Orchard put into the book. During the last weeks she patiently proof read and checked my text and index. Finally I wish to thank Mike Tooby for his constant support and advice from the moment the book was suggested, in early 1993; and John Emanuel who, with much humour has lived daily with this ever growing project.

Specific assistance has been received from:

Chapter 1 - Caroline Dudley, Marion Whybrow, Monica Wynter, and Louise Orchard who drew the map.

Chapter 2 - Wilhelmina Barns-Graham, John Crowther, Margot Maekelburghe and Michael Snow.

Chapter 3 - David Brown, Tom Cross, Alison Hodge, David Lewis, Professor Alan Livingston, Beryl Ray and John Wells.

Chapter 4 - John Chalcraft, Wendy Guthrie, Jane Mitchell, Sir Norman Reid, Joseph Plummer, Brian Smith and Barbara Vallely.

Chapter 5 - Doris Ansari, Linden Holman, Dominic Hudson, John Miller, Martin Rewcastle, Gareth Saunders and Dr Alan Williams.

Chapter 6 - Bret Guthrie, Joe Poynton, Dr Ashley Royston, Lu Simmons, Nan Todd, Dr Barry Whyte.

Chapter 7 - Des Hosken, Jo Jacques, David McKenna, Christopher Petherick, Barbara Spring and John Southern.

Chapter 8 - David Goodley.

Chapter 9 - John Cock, Stanley Cock, Kim Cooper and the Cornish Studies Library - Redruth, Paul Graham, Beryl James, Kit Law, Bryan and Mary Pearce, Philip and Elizabeth Perkin, Dan and Mary Quick, Bob Sadler, Ron Smith of the South West Gas Historical Society, John Thomas and Eric Ward.

Chapter 10 - Malcolm Henderson, Loveday Shewell and Joan Vincent.

Chapter 11 - John Cooper and Sir Geoffrey Holland.

Chapter 12 - Geoffrey Burgess, Jim Cooper, Colin Griffin and David Pattison

Chapter 13 - David Beer, Lady Holland, David Lay and Roy Ray.

Chapter 14 - Jonathan Holmes.

Chapter 15 - Peter Fazakerley, Bryan Hammond, Bryan Hardman, Ernest and Marjorie Lugg, Sally Moore, Chris Trevan and Trevor Vance.

Chapter 16 - Ina Cole, Andy Dalton, Kerry Olkes, Norman Pollard and Carolyn Trevivian.

Chapter 17 - Janet Bennette and Anna and Helen Duncan who walked around the gallery to check on my 'tour'.

Chapter 18 - Lewis Biggs, Barbara Duncan, Sarah Glenny, Janet Wallace and Godfrey Worsdale.

Permission from David Brown to quote from his chronology in the exhibition catalogue *St Ives 1939-64*, 1985

Permission from St Ives Printing & Publishing to quote from Eddie Murt's book *Downlong Days*.

PHOTOGRAPHIC ACKNOWLEDGMENTS

Photographs have been generously supplied by the following:

Ann Atkinson; Janet Axten; Peter Barnes; Sam Bennetts; Bob Berry; Andrew Besley; Cornish Studies Library, Redruth; Tom Cross; John Crowther; Caroline Dudley, Royal Cornwall Museum; Dudley Coles Ltd.; Henry Gilbert; Adrian Glew, Tate Gallery Archive; Bryan Hardman; Roger Harvey ABIPP; Katharine Heron; Rohan James, Kettle's Yard, University of Cambridge; Professor Alan Livingston, Falmouth College of Art; Phil Monckton; Richard Murphy; Michael Musitano; Mark Nicholson, Cornwall County Council; Colin Orchard; Barry Ostler; Mary Pearce; Roger Penhallurick, Royal Institution of Cornwall; Roy Ray, St Ives School of Painting; Jenny and Arthur Richards, Union Inn; Colin Ross; Dr Ashley Royston; St Ives Printing & Publishing; Colin Sanger; Dr Roger Slack; Tony Smith; Barry Swaebe; Tate Gallery Liverpool; William Thomas; Martin Val Baker; Kathleen Watkins, Penwith Gallery; Christopher Webster, Tate Gallery Publications; Western Morning News Company Limited and Dr Barry Whyte.